Musical lives

The books in this series each provide an account
of the life of a major composer, considering
both the private and the public figure. The main
thread is biographical, and discussion
of the music is integral to the narrative.
Each book thus presents an organic view of
the composer, the music and the circumstances
in which the music was written.

Published titles

The life of Schumann

MICHAEL MUSGRAVE

CAMBRIDGE
UNIVERSITY PRESS

CAMBRIDGE UNIVERSITY PRESS
Cambridge, New York, Melbourne, Madrid, Cape Town,
Singapore, São Paulo, Delhi, Mexico City

Cambridge University Press
The Edinburgh Building, Cambridge CB2 8RU, UK

Published in the United States of America by Cambridge University Press, New York

www.cambridge.org
Information on this title: www.cambridge.org/9780521802482

First published 2011
3rd printing 2012

Printed at MPG Books Group, UK

A catalogue record for this publication is available from the British Library

Library of Congress Cataloguing in Publication data
Musgrave, Michael, 1942–
   The life of Schumann / Michael Musgrave.
      p.   cm. – (Musical lives)
   Includes bibliographical references and index.
   ISBN 978-0-521-80248-2 (hardback)
   1. Schumann, Robert, 1810–1856.   2. Composers–Germany–Biography.
   I. Title.   II. Series.
   ML 410.S 4M 87 2011
   780.92–dc22
   [B]
   2011002459

ISBN 978-0-521-80248-2 Hardback

To Liza

CONTENTS

ILLUSTRATIONS

ACKNOWLEDGMENTS

I acknowledge with thanks the materials and help provided by the following institutions and individuals:

Arthur Friedheim Library, Peabody Institute of Johns
   Hopkins University, Baltimore
Bobst Library, New York University
British Library
Gesellschaft der Musikfreunde, Vienna (Otto Biba)
Heinrich Heine Institut, Düsseldorf (Christian Liedtke)
Lila Acheson Wallace Library, Juilliard School, New York
New York Public Library Research Division
Ratsschulbibliothek, Zwickau
Robert-Schumann-Haus, Leipzig (Christiane Schwerdtfeger)
Robert-Schumann-Haus, Zwickau (Hrosvith Dahmen)
Royal College of Music Library
Scherman Library, Mannes College, New School University, New
   York
StadtMuseum, Bonn (Ingrid Bodsch)
Stadtsbibliothek, Düsseldorf

I acknowledge with thanks most valuable exchanges with members of the Music Biography Seminar, Graduate Center, City University of New York; and likewise with Dr Kay Redfield Jamison. Special thanks are to Dr Nancy Reich and Dr Michael Struck for sharing their particular expertise on the Schumanns. It was a special privilege to work on Schumann in the Brahmshaus Studio, Lichtental, Baden-Baden, close to Clara Schumann's home: I thank the Brahms-Gesellschaft Baden-Baden for its kind invitation. Last, but certainly not least, I thank my copy-editor Robert Whitelock for his most painstaking work on my text.

Permission to reproduce the following illustrations is gratefully acknowledged:

Figure 6 and cover illustration: Gesellschaft der Musikfreunde, Vienna.

Figures 1 (Archiv-Nr. 6018-B2), 13 (Archiv-Nr. 10463, 284-C3) and 14 (Archiv-Nr. 2713-B2): Robert-Schumann-Haus, Zwickau.

Figure 12: Heinrich-Heine- Institut, Düsseldorf.

Figure 16: Stadtarchiv, Düsseldorf [Sign. 016–109–001].

Figure 7 (copyright Punktum, Peter Franke): Robert-und-Clara -Schumann-Verein-Leipzig, Inselstraße 18 e.V.

Figures 3, 8 and 15: Musgrave Collection, New York.

All letters cited in notes are from and to Schumann unless otherwise indicated. Though standard English translations have been retained and cited throughout, some amendments have been made to these without further comment. These sources vary in adding or omitting some letters.

Introduction: inherited images

Robert Schumann probably exemplifies the popular image of the Romantic composer more fully than any of his remarkable contemporaries. Not only did he completely absorb himself in German Romantic literature in his numerous songs and choral works, but he recreated its musical personalities and intertwined them with his own life in music of extraordinary characterization and spontaneity. Yet equally – in gradually losing the capacity to relate to outward reality – he, like the iconic figures of this literature, succumbed to madness, attempted suicide and died insane. Thus he appears to express the Romantic concept of 'genius' – that it is not simply an extraordinary level of imagination and technique, but essentially supernatural: and that its ultimate price is madness. And nor was this image confined to his life: though completely unconnected with Schumann, the claim of successors to spiritualist revelations urging the release of his unpublished Violin Concerto, upwards of a century after its composition in 1853, has always seemed to fit this picture, recycling the memory of Schumann's own hearing of voices from departed composers in his final decline. Thus Schumann's reputation has always been one of mystery as well as sadness, constantly reinforced by visual images of the pensive man. And his tragic end has inevitably cast a pall over his entire life: everything has been viewed in terms of what we know is to come.[1]

Nor has this image been entirely revised in modern times. The publication of vastly more of Schumann's correspondence, and, from 1971, of the extensive diaries and notebooks, has served to reveal the fuller extent of his physical ailments and personal sufferings, not known publicly until his final breakdown in 1854, and always filtered in the early publications of documentation (see Further reading and sources (pp. 214–6)). And even in 1998 the revelation (through the publication of his doctor's records from his final hospitalization at Endenich between 1854 and 1856) that he had been treated for syphilis as a young man has fuelled further speculation about the source of his physical conditions by adding a completely new dimension to interpretation.[2]

The diaries, which greatly elaborated even the much expanded detail in Berthold Litzmann's extensive study of the life of Clara Schumann published after her death (from 1902) inevitably intensified interest in Schumann's health prior to his final decline. The added evidence of his frequent depressive episodes was quickly connected with the emerging study of depressive illness, and relations were sought between patterns of creative intensity and quiescence and his mental state, first proposed as that of 'manic depression', subsequently better defined as a bi-polar condition: an illness not merely the product of an 'artistic temperament', but of chemical imbalance that today would be treated with medication. Relations were then further drawn with other known depressive artists, for example Byron and Virginia Woolf. This culminated in Peter Ostwald's very influential study of Schumann, whose chapters are titled to chart alternating emotional states, thus presenting Schumann as virtually permanently ill, and his ailments all the result of the psychological conditions that drove his creative life: for example that his dual creative personalities Florestan and Eusebius were not merely creative alter egos, but evidence of a schizophrenic personality. But paradoxically, this interpretation also had the effect of reinforcing the traditional association between creativity and mental instability.[3]

The possibility of syphilitic infection has shifted interest towards the view of Schumann's many physical ailments as a consequence of the disease and that his depressive periods were the rational response to them. The key new point in this argument is that, though Schumann did not manifest the clear symptoms of tertiary syphilis until the 1850s, his many 'routine' illnesses over the years were manifestations of the 'latent' secondary stage. Whilst Ostwald, and before him others, had long hazarded the possibility of syphilis (the timing of the tertiary phase at between 20 and 25 years after the onset of the disease coincides exactly with the observation of a definite change in Schumann's physical and mental condition from 1851), they saw it as only presenting itself at this late stage, and thus as not contradicting depression as Schumann's major health condition throughout his life. The great unknown in this interpretation is Schumann's own knowledge of this condition. Subsequent to his treatment for a sexual infection, noted in his diary in 1831, he makes no further reference to sexual infection until his statement at Endenich, thus consistent with his then stated view that he thought himself cured. This explains why he subsequently married and had a large family: that Clara did not apparently contract the disease is not a challenge to this view: she could have been a carrier, but not infectious.

In this interpretation, it was Schumann's realization at Düsseldorf of the permanence of the disease that caused his jump into the River Rhine on 27 February 1854 and his statements of guilt and wretchedness to Clara before. And thus that this act was a perfectly rational attempt to end what he had come to regard as a hopeless life. It seems clear that at this time he also discarded his wedding ring as a final act, since Clara later found a note: 'I am going to throw my wedding ring into the Rhine, [you] do the same, [both] rings will be united.' The fact that Schumann actually died of self-starvation at Endenich, and that this was possibly the adverse result of the treatment he received there from 1855, does not challenge the priority of this argument. Nor does the fact that Schumann added to the 1831 diary entry the expression 'only guilt brings forth nemesis' ('nur Schuld gebiert die Nemesis') prove his knowledge either: it demonstrates merely that he felt guilt at the consequences of his sexual appetite, which, from his student days until shortly before his attempted suicide, remained very strong, as can be drawn from the earlier diaries and his later diary specifications of occasions of sexual intercourse from April 1846 until 14 February 1854.[4]

Since posthumous diagnosis of Schumann's many symptoms will always be ultimately speculative, the causes of his health problems will always remain open. Either of these two views requires selective presentation: on the side of syphilitic infection, to play down the extremity of some of Schumann's depressive episodes and their frequency even when they measure closely against standard descriptions where no other infection is involved (and the fact that they began in his life before any evidence of infection, in his teens); and on the side of mental illness, to minimize other explanations of depressive states, for example alarmed reaction to bereavements. Indeed, any judgment is complicated by the fact that Schumann's was a complex personality with many eccentricities, and that he had a strongly superstitious streak with attraction to the paranormal and medical quackery, as well as many genuine reasons for depression. He had many fears: first of disease and premature death, of losing his sanity – he was terrified of being near mental institutions – and of heights. Yet most of these can be related to adult as well as childhood circumstances, and were not irrational, albeit that they were extreme. Physical responses to external pressures, for example through alcohol abuse, fed on each other to cause depression. But fears and seemingly irrational obsessions affect many people without their mental and creative capacities being questioned. Another complicating factor has been a temperamental/ psychological inheritance predicated upon interpretations of his family's mental health: that the father worked himself to death and the mother was depressive, and that the sister allegedly committed suicide. But the evidence of the sister's death is extremely unclear (see Chapter 1); and we do not know the depth of the mother's depressions: only that Schumann was constantly encouraging her to overcome her 'melancholy'.[5]

And there is no question as to the obsessive nature of Schumann's compositional drives throughout his life, and his consequent exhaustion. He found each genre the most important at the time, often conceiving plans far beyond reasonable achievement. But is the condition that produced the 'manic' parts of *Carnaval*, the Fantasia in C or *Kreisleriana* properly called illness? Many clinical descriptions of the 'manic' phase of the bi-polar condition imply a diminished sense of creative reality, of self-delusion – not exemplary capacity. And was the other, depressive, side of this one of total, hopeless depression, or rather of relative incapacity? Most of all, was all his intense work 'manic'? Schumann did a vast amount of time-consuming work as editor and correspondent: he had a deeply scholarly and educative side. It seems inconceivable that he could have achieved all this in the mental state often attributed to him.

But however great the challenges of diagnosis, they must never obscure the central issue for musicians. There is no doubt that the traditional assumption of Schumann's mental illness – whether one of incipient madness attached to creativity, or a progressive mental illness leading to attempted suicide – has influenced the evaluation of his music, especially his later music: and viewed the other way, that the often inward, even brooding character of some later music is evidence of a declining mind. In the present writer's view, there is no such evidence until parts of the *Gesang der Frühe* and *Geistervariationen*, written just before the attempted suicide in 1854, which show a weakening of continuity after the wonderful opening and theme respectively. But otherwise, Schumann's later music is of different character and reflects changing preoccupations. And if there is a certain fatigue, this is the result of physical strain and over-production, not of reduced mental capacity.[6]

No biography can ignore Schumann's health. What became known as the 'catastrophe' of his attempted suicide in 1854 – the shock to his family, the world of music and his historical image – cannot be overstated. But until this event there is every evidence of a creative mind constantly engaged and able to communicate with his family and friends. His illness was certainly a major inconvenience, but not a determining factor in his creativity, his increasingly erratic behaviour from 1851 a consequence as much of his frustrating professional circumstances. As well as voluminous correspondence, Schumann kept detailed records: in reading them, negative images of the man are quickly dispelled. The Schumann of the day-to-day detail often comes across in a very positive way: he strikes one by his practicality, even down-to-earth quality, and his openness, which included acknowledgment of his health problems. He emerges as highly organized, as a competent businessman, sensitive all round throughout the differences with Wieck during his courtship of Clara, and a responsible and loving father and husband.

Nor was his death especially premature. Schumann outlived all his four siblings save the second brother Carl (who outlived him by only two years or so). Dying at 46, Schumann also outlived both his most admired immediate contemporaries, Mendelssohn at 37 and Chopin at 38. He was realistic about his talents and status as a young musician and retained his realism in later years as a sage observer of life and art. He certainly had humour, commenting on one difficult occasion to his publisher Hermann Härtel in 1849 'We musicians are touchy folks.' He had a very strong sense of self, and if he had little to say in spoken words, he was highly articulate in his writings. He commanded deep loyalty and affection for his personality as well as his genius, and dedication from musicians far and wide, and the impact on his close circle remained with them for their entire lives.[7]

It is thus from the perspective of a working musician, and drawing largely on his own words, that this book seeks to approach the challenges and achievements of Schumann's life afresh, completed, appropriately, on the 200th anniversary of his birth.

1   A favourable upbringing: Zwickau 1810–28

Robert Schumann's course in life was set by his particular family circumstances to a greater extent than most musical contemporaries. Even in the Romantic era, musicians were still mainly raised in musical families, or with access to early training. Though outwardly, at least, Schumann was provided with a comfortable life, excellent education, and financial security and status through his father's business and literary standing, he was denied what he needed as a composer, and spent years catching up. Nor till later years did he really have to come to terms with the economic reality of a composer's life.

Schumann was born in Zwickau, Lower Saxony, a town of 5,000 inhabitants situated about forty miles south of Leipzig. His birth on 8 June 1810 was duly announced in the *Zwickauer Wochenblatt* and his father was specified as 'notable burgher' as well as bookseller. Robert was the fifth and last child of August and his wife Johanna Christiane. The father was 37 and the mother already into her early forties, exact date of birth unknown. The elder siblings were three brothers, Eduard (born 1797), Carl (born 1801) and Julius (born 1805), and one sister, Emilie (born 1807); another girl, Laura, had been stillborn the previous year. Though he had lived in Zwickau for only two years before Robert's birth – having since 1808 established a joint bookselling and publishing business, Gebrüder Schumann, with his brother Johann Friedrich Schumann, by now run at separate locations – August already had a national reputation in the world of books as author as well as dealer.

1 The teenage Robert Schumann. Zwickau, c. 1826.

On his death sixteen years later, an account of his life would be written in admiring terms, and he would subsequently have his own personal entry in Pierer's *Universal Lexicon der Gegenwart und Vergangenheit*, the most comprehensive German encyclopedia of cultural and scientific knowledge in the nineteenth century.[1]

August was the driving force in the family, the role model for Robert in his artistic sensitivity as well as creative energy and business sense, and his influence is important for understanding his son. But for all his later status, his life had been one of self-improvement from very humble beginnings. Born the eldest son of a poor clergyman, Johann Friedrich Schumann, in Endschütz near Gera (ten miles or so west of Zwickau), he had fought to reconcile his literary passions with economic survival and the family attitudes he had inherited (his own father had been the first of five brothers to leave the land). Though he received a good school education, attending the Latin school at nearby Eisenburg (where he lodged with family), he never had enough resources to further his education as he wished and was largely self-educated. His difficult early years attempting to become a writer were conducted against the background of mundane work in surrounding towns, mainly in the grocery business. His exceptional abilities are clear from the fact that, in order to raise the money to marry his wife Johanna, herself from Gera, he wrote and published several books in the space of only eighteen months, raising 1,000 thalers as a result. Finally able to concentrate on his literary interests after four years of marriage, and jointly running a grocery store at Ronneberg, he opened a bookshop there (against his father-in-law's wishes) and developed his writings with a balance of literary and commercial topics:[2] in 1797, for example, the romance *Solomon the Wise and His Fool Markoph* – a conversion of an old German folk tale about a Pharaoh's desire for Solomon's wife into a horror story of no fewer than 472 sides – and a mercantile handbook (with a second part the following year) with extensive statistics by region, city and town, a vast project that shows the extent of his ambition in its huge list of subscribers throughout Germany, with royal dedication.[3]

Throughout Schumann's childhood the reputation of August's business grew, developing his specialisms whilst adding translations of modern European classics into German, especially in pocket editions, then becoming current, so that the firm could claim pre-eminence in introducing this literature. Not the least were contemporary British writers, again showing August's business acumen in anticipating the welter of editions to follow: the mania for Walter Scott observed in 1820s Germany was partly a result of the Gebrüder Schumann edition of his works, which appeared from 1822 to 1830; August also personally translated some works of Byron (*Beppo* and *Childe Harold*), in a larger edition continued by his sons. But he also devoted much attention to his own geographical region: the history, geography and trade of Saxony. He founded two periodicals on Saxon interests and in 1814 embarked on an encyclopedia of Saxony that was unfinished at his death and subsequently completed in eighteen volumes; several years later, a 'Picture Gallery of the Most Celebrated People of All Time' was a bestseller.[4]

Family circumstances had determined an excellent education for Schumann. He appears to have had his first private tuition at age 4; at 6½ he was sent to a private preparatory school run by a protestant clergyman, Archdeacon Hermann Döhner. Here he learnt Latin at age 7, and Greek and French at 8, and later declared of himself that 'I was a good, well-mannered child and diligent in my studies.' In the spring of 1820, at nearly 10, he entered the Zwickau Lyceum (from 1835 Gymnasium) for the continuation of his education to age 18. This was the finest school in the town, with 195 boys in his year of entry, and provided a classical education of the highest standard, just as the eminence of such schools began to grow in Germany, with great emphasis on Latin and Greek (in the top class Latin lessons were conducted entirely in Latin) compared with History, Geography and German, and very little attention to modern subjects like mathematics and arithmetic. The deputy headmaster, Carl Ernst Richter, who taught Schumann, was a man of radical political views and a prolific author, who edited the weekly periodical *Die Biene* (*The Bee*), banned in 1833; his liberal attitudes, including religious free-thinking, left their influence on the Schumanns, father and son, and Robert grew up with the foundations of an independent outlook as well as a sense of social status.[5]

Zwickau in the earlier nineteenth century was a quiet little town of 900 houses. August Schumann describes the town picturesquely in his encyclopedia of Saxony as being situated in 'one of the most remote corners of Saxony', evoking the character of its position on the left bank of the river Mulde, its gardens, meadows and fields, and wooded hills, observing that one could 'call it a park with vegetation richer than most other parts of Germany'. But the image had been somewhat tarnished in modern times. As a town situated on east–west trade routes (one main road went to Dresden and southern Germany, another to Leipzig and Bohemia), it became, with Germany in the grip of Napoleon's conquest of eastern Europe in 1810, a place of military transit. In 1812, 150,000 French troops marched in and out of Zwickau. Returning defeated the following year, the soldiers brought disease and famine. The sights recorded by the historian Emil Herzog for 1813 are appalling – with corpses in fields and rivers; typhoid, bubonic plague and smallpox; and even piles of severed limbs in the town. Nine per cent of Zwickau's population was wiped out.[6]

Though Zwickau was not a centre of culture, Schumann had the best it could offer. The Lyceum and the two largest churches, especially the *Marienkirche*, provided a focus for the town's music. And in literature, he had a head start through his father's literary preoccupations. From childhood he had the run of his extensive library, one that inevitably contained far more than the boy could have found at school and in town, and his artistic sensitivity certainly received its greatest early stimulus through literature. His literary sense found various outlets at home and at school – in writing poetry and stories, and participating in plays on themes local, historical and contemporary. 'Robber plays' (reflecting current literary fashion for an earlier genre) were amongst the earliest. 'I, my brother [Julius] and some other school friends had a really charming theatre that made us well known all around Zwickau, and even famous (sometimes we collected 2 to 3 thalers). We performed completely extemporaneously, cracked horrible jokes and made outrageously silly puns.' His father, present at these events, lavished praise and encouragement on him.[7]

At 13, Schumann began to collect his own literary efforts – poems; dramatic fragments, including a scene from a five-act tragedy *Der Geist*; biographical sketches of famous composers; and album verses under the pseudonym Skuländer – in an anthology book entitled *Blätter und Blümchen aus der goldene Aue* (*Leaves and Little Flowers from the Golden Meadow*). At 14, along with his brothers, he was temporarily engaged in the publishing business, helping his father to collect and translate essays for his *Bildergallerie der berühmter Menschen*. Age 15, in autumn 1825, he – apparently chief organizer – and ten fellow students founded a society for the study of German literature, where they would learnedly discuss classical and Romantic authors, as well as members' original creations. Before disbanding in February 1828, this society provided Schumann with a forum for the systematic study of Schiller's dramas, and the essays of Johann Gottfried Herder and Friedrich Schlegel. Also, from age 15 to 18, beginning in November– December 1825, Schumann tried a variety of literary genres, including his own verses based on metrical German versions of Latin poems, and a volume of selected odes of Horace in translation, obviously inspired by school study. Most notable was *Allerley aus der Feder Roberts der Mulde* (*A Miscellany from the Pen of Robert of the River Mulde*). This had lyric poetry – more than thirty poems, dramatic fragments, also some dramatic essays, including one on *Coriolan*; and criticism and essays on aesthetic topics, including extracts from [C. F.] Daniel Schubart's theory of musical aesthetics, *Ideen zur ein Ästhetik der Tonkunst*.[8]

Shortly before leaving school he took an active part as proofreader in his brothers' preparing of an edition of Forcellini's *Totius latinatis lexicon* of 1771, issued in a four-volume German version by Gebrüder Schumann from 1831 to 1835, with the participation of leading literary scholars. By age 18, thanks to both school and home, he had an exceptional literary knowledge. He knew the Latin and Greek classics well and was able to offer opinions on Sophocles, Horace, Plato and others in the writings that he committed to his diaries and commonplace books. Though he was already attracted to the dramas of Schiller (but not as yet as much to Goethe, although he knew *Faust* thoroughly, and was called 'Faust' and 'Fust' by his friends), his chief attraction was now to Romantic literature, especially Ernst Schultze, Franz von Sonnenberg and Byron (knowing some of the latter's works through his father's translations). But he was especially overwhelmed from 1827 by the writings of Jean Paul Richter, reading *Flegeljahre*, (*Winged Years*, or *Carefree Years*), *Titan*, *Hesperus* and *Siebenkäs*; Robert's early letters to his mother are full of references to Richter's works and are often couched in his flowery literary style (though it was already becoming outmoded by the 1820s).[9]

Schumann's musical instincts seem not to have received the same early stimulus in the home. He was not apparently introduced to the piano as a matter of course, but rather comments 'it was probably the great deal of singing I did that made my parents aware of my gifts', most likely at age 6 to 7. Though music had its place, it was a minor part of home life: Schumann's mother sang, describing herself as 'the living book of arias' on account of her knowledge, though there are no records of any performance; and she claimed that it was at her instigation that Schumann had his first piano lessons at age 7 with Johann Gottfried Kuntsch (1777–1855) who, at 40, was organist and choirmaster of the *Marienkirche*. Kuntsch also taught at the Lyceum and was a key figure in the town as an organizer and conductor of concerts, one who made strenuous efforts to raise the town's musical standards. But Schumann must have played the piano earlier, as he was already improvising. Though doubtless inspired by the character of his later piano music, Wasielewski's unattributed statement that from childhood Schumann 'possessed rare taste and feeling for portraying feelings and characteristic traits in melody [and] could sketch the different dispositions of his intimate friends by certain figures and passages on the piano so exactly and comically that everyone burst into loud laughter at the similitude of the portrait' was probably true. And Schumann certainly claimed to confide his deepest feelings to the piano. Early in his musical tuition he also learnt the flute and cello with Herr Meissner, the municipal music director.[10]

His first great musical experience occurred at age 9 in 1819. He was taken to hear the pianist and composer Ignaz Moscheles play in Karlsbad, and thereafter retained a lifelong admiration for him and his works. On his return, Robert demanded and was given a Streicher Viennese grand piano, and now gave home concerts. At around the same age, he was taken to his first opera, *Die Zauberflöte*, in Leipzig. On entering the Gymnasium at Easter 1820 he had a much broader stage. He made various appearances in evening entertainments at the school, showing growing fluency as a pianist, and also appearing as a reciter. The first appearance was in 1821 or 1822, as a pianist in four-handed works – mainly variations by Pleyel, Cramer, Ries, Moscheles and Weber – and also duets with a boy of his own age, the son of the leader of a regimental band stationed in Zwickau named Piltzing and another pupil of Kuntsch. On 6 November 1821, Schumann took the piano part in Kuntsch's performance of Friedrich Schneider's then very popular oratorio *Die Weltgericht* at the *Marienkirche*, standing up to do it.[11] In 1808, within a year of beginning lessons with Kuntsch, Schumann had composed several dances for piano (now lost), doubtless based on the models he knew, some possibly from the music his father obtained through the trade and brought home. Schumann formed a small orchestra of school fellows, and composed, in January 1822 at the age of 11, the work he designated his 'op. 1': a setting of Psalm 150 – of twenty-six pages of thirteen-line score ruled by himself, other pupils and friends – for soprano, alto, and an orchestra of two violins, viola, two flutes, two oboes, bassoon, horn, two trumpets, timpani and piano. In the same year or the one after he followed this up with an 'Ouverture' and 'Chor von Landleuten', numbered op. 1, no. 3 – a nine-page overture followed by a chorus beginning 'Wie reizend ist der schöne Morgen', apparently inspired by Paer's *Achille* – augmenting his orchestral forces with as many of his friends as could sing. The audience consisted of members of the Schumann family. Schumann later recalled his infantile technique: 'I'm almost ashamed when I look at it now. I had no knowledge ... and even wrote like a child.' His *Project Book* for these years also suggests the start of an opera. Informal concerts at his home included the overture to Vincinco Righini's *Tigrane* (the score obtained by his father) with a pair of violins, two flutes, a clarinet and two horns, Schumann filling in the rest on the piano.[12]

In 1823, at around age 13, occurred the most forward-looking musical influence of Schumann's youth when he met the family Carus. Carl Erdmann Carus was a Zwickau merchant, a keen friend of music and musicians. His nephew Ernst August Carus was a surgeon and superintendent at the mental hospital housed in the castle of the nearby town of Colditz. His attractive wife Agnes, a gifted and discerning amateur singer, used to come to Zwickau to visit her brother, who held regular soirées to which he invited Schumann. She was looking for a piano accompanist as well as for artistic stimulus. Eight years his senior, she now provided a focus for Schumann's musical creativity, and her home as a performance venue. In the summer of 1827 she resided in Zwickau, where he not only accompanied her but also composed songs for her. Later Schumann described the atmosphere in C. E. Carus's house:

> it was in his house where the names of Mozart, Haydn and Beethoven were spoken daily and enthusiastically – in his house that I first saw these masters' works, especially their quartets, but seldom heard in that little town, often playing the piano parts [sic] myself, – in Carus's house, so well known to almost every native artist, where artists were always hospitably welcomed, where all was joy, serenity, and music.

Moreover, here he also became subject to the new influence of Schubert, at this point only little known, and heard only in the most progressive circles. Schubert became the closest companion of Schumann's musical imagination. When Schumann heard of Schubert's death on 19 November 1828, he wept all night.[13]

But whilst Schumann's creative imagination was coming under new and vital stimuli, the technical development of his piano playing as such came to a sudden end at age nearly 15 around 1825. Having already reached the level of playing Weber's *Invitation to the Dance* publicly in 1824, he now played Moscheles' *Alexander Variations* at a home concert, and Kuntsch declined to give him any more lessons. Kuntsch would later write to Schumann to congratulate him when he decided to make the commitment to music as a career in 1830. Kuntsch was not a great musician, with limited pianistic skills: Clara later dismissed him as unworthy of her husband's talent. But he was clearly enlightened, opened many musical doors, and gave Schumann crucial support and sympathy. Schumann later dedicated the *Studies for Pedal Piano*, op. 56 to him in 1845, and in 1852 sent him a laurel wreath to honour his fifty years as a teacher, echoing his earlier comment that 'you were the only one to recognize the musical gift that dominated my nature and to set me at an early age on the path on which my guardian angel was sooner or later bound to lead me'.[14]

This was a key moment in Schumann's musical development, with new friends and new musical experiences constantly enriching his imagination, and with his father's sympathetic, supportive eye, surely keen to offer Robert the opportunities he himself had lacked. But its promise was to be thwarted. According to Robert's record, shortly before his death in 1826 August had applied to no less an eminence than Weber himself to teach Schumann – that is, shortly after the lessons with Kuntsch ended. But Weber had left for London, was in fact mortally ill, and soon died there: August's own death followed shortly after. If August Schumann had made this contact successfully, subsequent history might have been very different. As it was Robert was left without a guide. Therefore he had to continue by himself with his compositions, though without clear goal.[15]

In 1827 he notes the beginnings of a piano concerto in E minor, and other attempts would follow in 1828–31. Schumann claimed to have already completed many songs and piano pieces, though none of the solo keyboard compositions survive. In the years 1827–8, he wrote thirteen songs to texts by Justinus Kerner (a medical doctor interested in the supernatural, who had just published a book based on his parapsychological studies), Byron, Ernst Schultze, Jacobi, Goethe and himself. They already reflect experience and show a natural mastery of both simple strophic to through-composed form, and of vocal expression and the relationship of voice and piano; in three Schumann appears as both poet and composer. Some of these, his first truly original compositions, he sent on 15 July 1828 to the Brunswick Kapellmeister and song composer Gottlob Wiedebein, with the appeal 'Be indulgent to a youth who, uninitiated in the mysteries of sound, yet inspired to try his untrained hand at original composition, now lays his first efforts before you for your kindly but strict impartial opinion.' Wiedebein replied quickly that 'your songs have many defects, a great many, and I would like to call them the sins of youth', urging Schumann to discipline himself and look for 'truth in melody and harmony and in expression – in short poetic truth'. Facing his reality Schumann responded in August 1828 'I had probably forgotten to tell you in my last letter that

I know nothing of harmony, thoroughbass, nor counterpoint, but am nature's pupil pure and simple and have merely followed a vague and insubstantial impulse.' Schumann promised he would take a knife to them: 'reason shall mercilessly cut away anything that an unbridled imagination wants to introduce into her domain'.[16]

Though August's business achieved great returns, it was at a cost. He did not enjoy good health and apparently long endured a weak constitution. Frau Schumann spoke of her husband's many years of suffering with a lower abdominal complaint, and, like his wife, he was regularly at the Karlsbad spa. Nor did he apparently know how to help himself. Robert's school friend Emil Flechsig said that he never saw August do anything but work. He left 60,000 thalers to the family. Added to this there must have existed a great tension between his creative literary imagination and the effort required for the more mundane commercial lexicographic works, which were doubtless driven more by economic factors.[17]

Much less is known of Schumann's mother. She was the eldest daughter of Abraham Gottlieb Schnabel, the chief surgeon to the municipality of Zeitz. She was described by Joseph von Wasielewski as 'endowed with innate intelligence, but educated under the influence of provincial, narrowing circumstances. [She] showed special culture … although she was attractive in appearance and gifted with a certain talent for presenting herself well.' Her own comments in letters with Robert certainly suggest an accepting Christian outlook, characterized with such expressions of advice as 'God knows best' and 'Store up treasure in your heart and it will bring interest later on.' But many other factors were to complicate her later relationship with Robert, including her health, which was already fragile: she was prone to depression. As her last child, born at the very end of her child-bearing years, and just after the loss of a previous child, Robert was both treasured and spoilt, as she later pointed out to him on his twenty-fifth birthday. Robert was always very close to her, but also played on her affection to his advantage, as he later admitted in letters after he had left home for university. She appears to have had a happy marriage, commenting in letters to Robert over the years following August's death how much she missed him, and to have enjoyed the affection of her children.

Robert was born into a spacious home, a corner property on the market place: 15 Am Markt; in 1817, when Robert was 7, August moved the family to a larger house at 2 Amstgasse – from which he also ran the business – which Schumann remembered fondly as the home of his childhood and youthful development.[18]

More than his literary and dramatic interests, Schumann's growing love of the piano as a means of self-communication was a major feature in his developing personality and relationships, though not at first. In his early years he seems to have been on excellent terms with his companions and of unbounded vitality and boisterous good feeling, the moving spirit of many games and escapades. He did what was required of him academically and was clearly socialized through his family position and role at school. In fact, he long retained a capacity to lose himself in friendly, even animated, company, which could override his natural reticence, especially when convivial drinking played a part, and he developed a taste for champagne whilst still at school that continued long into maturity. Letters to Flechsig show lively excursions into the countryside around Zwickau in the company of his friends before he left school.[19]

But he was already sensitive to pressure. His first mention of this is at around age 10, apparently through the greater requirements made of him when he entered the Lyceum.

> My life began to become more restless. Overburdened with school work, I wasn't zealous enough, although I wasn't lacking in talent in any way. The anxiety when one hasn't prepared oneself – this all made a bad impression, and the supremely happy years of my childhood began to become irksome ... I liked best of all to go for walks by myself and pour out my heart to nature.

Wasielewski notes that at age 14 he began to become more inward and withdrawn: 'Everything henceforth indicated a more reserved and inward life. The maturing youth was more reflective, more silent, and showed that love for reverie which hinders communion with men rather than with spirits.' The death of Schumann's sister and father in 1825 and 1826 provided the first major test of his temperamental disposition. The blow to him of both these events was immense and manifested itself in a greater turn to introspection, though it was over a year later before he started to communicate his feelings, when he began his diary (the diary was doubtless facilitated by his experience in writing down thoughts about literature and music). He always noted the date of his father's death, like many anniversaries, and associated it with mourning. His reaction was fierce: 'Why must one be thrown about in the storms like this ... My wonderful father ... is it not terrible to be deprived of such a man, so delightful a writer, so keen a judge of human nature, so hardworking in his business?' But he also showed more ominous feelings, such as a fear of madness every time he visited the Carus family at Colditz and passed the mental institution housed in the castle.[20]

Finding the right companions now became especially important. Of various school friends – including August Vollert, an older boy who was a regular visitor to Schumann's home for two years to play duets, and was one of his first musical relationships – Emil Flechsig was by far the most important, and we owe much information on Schumann to him. In the first place he had been selected by Robert's mother to be 'a fitting companion for her precious darling', as the older boy later put it, perhaps because of his artistic inclinations. Schumann wanted to get close to him. But Flechsig was more hard-boiled, observing with candour his companion whilst still at school as

a reasonable fellow ... rather dreamy and inattentive ... and ruled by the absolute certainty that in the future he would be a famous man. Famous at what was undecided. First he let loose on philology for a while, just about his weakest side. Soon he changed to heraldry, following that just as eagerly. Later he wandered into Germanic poetry and got stuck there. He would write love poems to former and non-existent favourites, then began working on tragedies. He was so fond of reciting poetic works that he almost killed me and [Eduard] Röller [another student] with his zeal.[21]

Schumann's strong attraction to the girls in his social circle from early on is recalled in his diaries: at age 8 to Emilie Lorenz, who eventually married his brother Julius; at age 9 to Ida Stölzel. Teenage sexual feelings are attached to Nanni Petsch, who was his 'first fiery love' at 16, and he wrote in Jean Paulian style to Flechsig about her, but soon transferred his affection to Liddy Hempel, although finding her spiritually barren on acquaintance. But at around 13 or 14 he found in the much older and beautiful Agnes Carus a much more powerful attraction, and she introduced him to more literature as well as to more music. She was to continue to be important in his life: the Carus couple moved to Leipzig during Schumann's student years, when Carus became professor of medicine at the university and, coincidentally, became Schumann's first psychiatrist. It was at the Caruses' in Leipzig that Schumann met Friedrich and Clara Wieck at a party on 12 March 1828, when Clara, not yet 9 years old, was invited to play: the most prescient meeting of his life.[22]

The death of Schumann's sister and father brought the stability of his family setting to a sudden end when he was between the ages of 15 and 16. The facts of the sister's death were never clearly revealed. According to the primary source, Schumann's headmaster and family friend, the Zwickau historian C. E. Richter, she apparently suffered a chronic skin disease, which 'threw its poisons into every part of her body', and which resulted in what was described as a 'quiet madness'. Wasielewski appears to draw on this source in observing that she died 'in consequence of an incurable melancholy, which gave unmistakable signs of quiet madness', although only one writer – also of the next generation, F. Gustav Jansen – actually suggests that she committed suicide, stating that 'she threw herself into the water during a fever paroxysm'. The account of Eugenie, Schumann's youngest daughter, published in 1921, appears to contradict this by stating that she died at home, though primarily emphasizing the impact of Emilie's death on her mother: 'twelve sleepless nights, weeping constantly in my suffering, I spent quite alone in the chamber where my dear Emilie passed away. The loneliness made her loss a double agony … A daughter is such a source of happiness for a mother, and her loss is irreplaceable.' However, Eugenie can only have known this through family tradition as it is in no other source. August died of a sudden heart attack while Johanna was away at Karlsbad, having left home without any reason to expect it, so that Robert had, initially, to cope alone. It is likely that Emilie's death had some effect on that of the father on 10 August 1826 aged 53, because she had looked after him and he had observed her deterioration day by day.[23]

In retrospect, these events were the turning point in Schumann's early life. Johanna was left with four sons, no daughters and a large business, yet was physically and emotionally fragile. She later admitted that she simply could not cope – 'to have four sons is really too much for a mother'. What she wanted above all for her sons was economic and social security. All of Robert's surviving siblings were now well into adult life, the brothers having followed their father into the publishing business. Eduard, now head of the family, aged 29 at his father's death, and Julius, now 21, were both running the family firm; the second son, Karl, aged 25, was now running an independent book business in the old silver-mining town of Schneeburg, ten miles from Zwickau. Two were married: Eduard to Therese (née Semmel) and Carl to Rosalie (née Illing); Julius would soon marry Emilie Lorenz. It was assumed that Robert would follow a similar pattern in trade, or do even better in a profession.[24]

Though Schumann was very well educated by age 18, and graduated 'omnino dignus' – 'satisfactory all round', seemingly having improved upon his earlier middling academic standards – his artistic skills were insufficiently developed or focused to pursue a career in literature or music. For all his devotion to literature, and creative impulse, the evidence of the poems is that they were imitative and of insufficient originality – his brothers had even refused to publish them – and as public speaker of his verse he became nervous and incoherent. As a musician he lacked the systematic training and skills associated with the profession: traditionally one studied as an apprentice from early years. One has only to compare him with his contemporary master-composers-to-be for the piano to see how far he was behind. Liszt and Chopin had been playing as virtuosi to the most privileged audiences since their early teens, and Mendelssohn had all-round skills, executant and theoretical, and was a publishable composer used to rehearsing and performing his own works from the same age. Schumann was not equipped to teach, perform or compose in any public setting. His gifts as an improviser at the keyboard were not of use in the current market place and he had no sponsor. For years his piano music would be regarded as too strange. Schumann was also difficult as a man. His reserve of speech, dislike of explaining himself and sometimes autocratic manner reflecting a privileged upbringing emerged from different sources.[25]

Schumann was more than aware of his shortcomings and had to carry the charge of dilettante for some time. Nor, at the time, could he access music through a more theoretical or institutional route, since university or conservatoire study was not then available in Germany. Ironically, it was to be in Leipzig, where he first attended university, that Germany's first modern conservatoire would be established under Mendelssohn himself, with Schumann as an invited teacher, only fifteen years or so after he might have used this opportunity himself. Of all his skills, he was probably best equipped at age 18 to be a literary critic or a private tutor through his knowledge of German literature, breadth of education, creative instincts and disciplined mind.

The arts aside, Schumann also had no motive for the choice of university study other than pleasing the expectations of his family and guardian – J. F. Rudel, a friend of his father – and the requirements of his inheritance. It was a stipulation of receipt of his allowance in his father's will that Schumann study at university for at least two years in an unspecified field, additional allowance for the examination fees being available if he did so. Financial security kept Schumann from the need to face the consequences of a decision regarding a profession. He had never had to work to help to support his family – to have a craft skill as did the sons of working musicians who often left their school education at 14 or so. Such middle-class tradespeople as the Schumanns kept music for a hobby. Schumann's creative destiny as an artist was thus entirely unclear at 18. It now fell to the mother and the guardian to take the initiatives. Johanna wanted a *Brotstudium*; without her husband she could not generate more income by herself. She probably did 'bend him to her will'; but she did it according to her lights. Indeed, Schumann still accepted the economic argument up until the point beyond which he could conform no longer.

In fact, law was a natural choice. Its study was in many ways close to literature, bound to tradition and society, as Schumann later acknowledged. Theology was traditionally for the lower class, offering a means of advancement through the priesthood, and Schumann did not have the temperament or skills for medicine. As he put it him himself at the time, 'I will not study medicine and cannot study theology'. It also represented a step up in the family for the youngest child to go to university rather than into business like his elder brothers. It seems from a later comment that the decision for law had already been made earlier between his mother and guardian. One can only guess at how the father might have modified his requirement had the contact with Weber come about. As it is, he probably felt he needed strong independent evidence of the level of his son's gifts to override his class-based expectations: doubtless this was the real purpose of the contact with Weber. Schumann was not really docile in accepting this decision, as has sometimes been suggested: that is to judge him by subsequent events. He followed convention, the line of least resistance. In this he reflected his father's model and family background: he had been schooled to a certain degree of fiscal responsibility – awareness of the need for hard work and justification, even if he enjoyed his privileges to the full. He was, as a young blood, probably less worldly-wise at 18 than the sons of working musicians and, despite his security, clearly insufficiently guided or focused. There was no precedent for a different decision about a profession in his family.[26]

In deference to the wishes of his mother and guardian, Schumann agreed to matriculate as a student of law at Leipzig University – his nearest big city and the capital of Saxony – which he did on 28 March 1828, after graduating from the Lyceum in Zwickau, having taken his final examination there on 15 March 1828. His letter to Flechsig in Leipzig, written after the final exams, shows in poetic expression the dawning reality on contemplating his new life in Leipzig, and his candour and honesty, yet innocence:

> My school days are over, and the world lies before me. I could hardly keep back the tears the last time I came out of school; but yet the pleasure was greater than the pain. Now my better self must take the lead and show what it is made of. Thrown into life, flung into the night of the world, without guide, teacher or father – thus do I stand; and yet, the world never lay before me in a brighter light than it does at this moment as I stand before it, smiling serenely and quietly at its storms.[27]

2 Undirected student: Leipzig and Heidelberg 1828–30

Schumann's two years at university from 1828 to 1830 would show a constant outward vacillation between the requirements of law and the desire for literature and music, before a final and resolute decision for music. But he never allowed his artistic interests to take second place, and started off as he intended to continue, eager to make the most of his new freedoms. Before taking up residence, and following his final examination in Zwickau, Schumann decided to make a holiday tour (funded as a graduation present) of southern Germany with Gisbert Rosen, a fellow law student he had met in Leipzig in March. In April and early May 1828 he visited Bayreuth, among memories of Jean Paul, who had lived there for twenty-one years till his recent death in 1825, meeting his widow and obtaining his portrait as a keepsake. Schumann was by now intimately acquainted with Jean Paul's major works, the novels *Titan* and *Flegeljahre* being the most important to him and destined to play a role in his forthcoming music. As a result of his next stop at Augsburg, where he stayed with friends of his father, the family of Heinrich Wilhelm von Kurrer, he received a letter of introduction to Heinrich Heine, whom he met during four days in May in the Bavarian capital Munich. Schumann was greatly impressed and thrilled: 'I had imagined Heine to be sullen and misanthropic, but he was completely different from what I thought. He greeted me in a friendly manner and escorted me around Munich for several hours [with a] bitter ironical smile – but a lofty smile at the trivialities of life.' Rosen then went back to Heidelberg to continue his studies. Schumann arrived back at Zwickau on 14 May, but left after only hours to get back to Leipzig, to the great dismay of his family. This was only to be the start of their disappointments with him during his university years.[1]

Schumann did not settle well into Leipzig. Above all he seems to have been lonely and homesick. He missed his mother and his new friend Rosen in this 'ultra Catholic region' as he put it, and not least his home town and its surroundings. 'I long with all my heart to return to where I was born and have spent happy days in nature. Where can I find it here? Only in locked room for the noise outside.' He had a piano, but missed his 'beloved old grand … it contained the sweetest recollections of my childhood and has taken part in all that I endured, all my sighs and youthful tears, but all my joys too'. He commented to his mother as late as 24 October 1828 after visiting home that 'hours in Zwickau made up days in Leipzig'.[2]

Secure living arrangements had been made well before Schumann left Zwickau. Before leaving school he had already decided to lodge with Emil Flechsig, now a divinity student at Leipzig, and additionally with a relative, Moritz Semmel, a law student, the brother of Therese, Eduard Schumann's wife. Even as late as 22 August 1828, he wrote to his mother that he only associated with three friends in Leipzig – Flechsig and Semmel, and Wilhelm Götte – a student from Brunswick, that apart from the Carus family 'I do not visit any families', and that he was unhappy with people who did not 'understand' him. But relations were soon strained with Flechsig, doubtless because Schumann was a demanding flatmate: 'Flechsig told me I'm a little pest', Schumann says in his diary, 'He's a fussy little pedant.'[3] Of student life he was very reserved. He wrote to Rosen that 'student life is too low to tempt me to plunge into it'. He avoided the *Burschenschaften* that many students attended (militant, highly nationalistic fraternities given to duelling, martial arts and other aggressive pursuits, which the sensitive Schumann abhorred). With Semmel, he 'laughed at their cloudy and undecided notions of nationality', though he requested fencing lessons with others at a fencing school in apparent fear of duels: 'one has to be very careful'.[4]

Schumann expected a comfortable student life and had an excellent room in the lodgings with Flechsig and Semmel, telling his mother 'But I pay for them 90 thalers', and adding, as if to assure her of his good behaviour, 'I am much tidier than you used to think.' He also rented a piano, commenting 'if I had 400 Th. to spare, and you and my guardian allowed it, I would buy an instrument here'. His allowance came through his guardian, Johann Gottlob Rudel, and was 25 thalers per month. Schumann was businesslike and knew what he wanted, telling Rudel when he wanted his allowance paid. His letters show his desire to indicate that he was responsible with money, even frugal: thus his comment to his mother that he had to 'write as small as possible' because 'postage is expensive now'. However, he invariably overspent, and went to his eldest brother Eduard for advances against his inheritance. But just as he acknowledged the virtue of financial restraint, he also bridled at it. His brother Julius was seemingly the least patient, eventually lecturing him on the poor economics of a proposed short visit to Zwickau from Heidelberg in 1830.[5]

He was clearly overwhelmed by Leipzig, so that, rather than celebrate its musical riches, which he obviously explored – notably the great churches such as St Thomas's and St Nicolas's, the Gewandhaus, the opera and theatre, as well as the predominantly High Baroque architecture, gardens and palaces, to say nothing of bookshops – he rather complained in his letters that everything in Leipzig was 'ornamented by art' and that he was worn out by the city, with no one to talk to. He describes to his mother that he preferred to take long walks in the park in Zweynaudorf, a suburb east of Leipzig, and that he went there all alone for entire days to work, and write poetry.[6]

Though Flechsig claimed that Schumann 'never set foot in a lecture hall', this cannot have been entirely true, since he later compared the lectures at Heidelberg to those at Leipzig, and specified the subjects of study. But it is likely that the retiring and restless Schumann attended as little as he could and studied much from books. Certainly he commented to Rosen that he was making 'more progress in the art of spending money than in the lecture rooms', and his replies to his mother are often formulaic: 'I go to lectures as regular as clockwork', or 'working away at Jurisprudence', suggesting that he was creating the picture that he wanted her to accept. But he did not disguise his reserve towards the law from early on either. By 21 May 1828 he was writing that 'the dry study of the law, which crushes one at the very beginning by its cut-and-dried definitions, does not suit me at all'. But he also claimed 'I must attack Jurisprudence. I will overcome myself', while dropping her hints about his broader interests and needs: 'but philosophy and history shall also be among my most important studies'.[7]

Insecurity and ambivalence drove Schumann's decision, against the assumptions of his mother, to continue his law studies in Heidelberg. He first mentioned it as early as August 1828, and by 7 November he had written to Rosen that he planned to go at Easter 1829 for the following academic year, 1829–30. He listed his three reasons in the August letter: for his own sake – he was 'getting rusty', for the sake of meeting more people of the world and because the greatest jurists of the day taught there. True as all this was, it was also a way of staying a longer-term decision, and had personal motivations. Of the two famous Heidelberg jurists, Anton F. J. Thibaut and Karl Josef Mittermaier, Thibaut was also a music scholar and enthusiast who had published a book, *On Purity in Music*, in 1825 – advanced for its time in lauding the music of the Renaissance and Baroque, soon to be an interest of Schumann's – and who, as well as his theoretical knowledge, also held performances of Handel's choral works in his home. Additionally, Schumann certainly wanted to be near Rosen, still the friend to whom he felt closest. He perceived, partly through Rosen, that the student life in this citadel of German Romanticism and one of Europe's oldest universities would be superior to that in the much larger and commercial Leipzig, and would elevate his spirits. To influence his mother more, Schumann co-opted a legal emphasis – that it would help his success in the difficult Saxon bar exams: 'Being a native of Saxony, I must go up for my examinations at Leipzig and study there for 2 years ... Then in [sic] Easter, 1830, I can come back to Leipzig and get into the way of [classes] again.' His mother, persuaded by the prospect of greater success at the law, happily agreed, though Schumann's brothers were much more resistant. Schumann arrived at Heidelberg on 21 May 1829 via Frankfurt, to spend the three terms from summer 1829 to autumn 1830 in the city.[8]

Prior to the commencement of the academic year, Schumann took the opportunity, as he had done the previous year, for a preliminary holiday. Students at Heidelberg were given two months off in late summer to travel and enrich their education. Italy was a favourite destination. But Rosen, whom Schumann wanted to accompany him there, refused to go. This time, after the experience of Schumann's ineffectual first year, family resistance was aroused. After matriculating on 13 July 1829, Schumann set off for a journey to Switzerland and Italy that would last from 28 August to 25 October, again with literary – and especially now musical – purpose. But the extent to which he felt he had to justify the decision and the expense shows the pressure he was under at home. Though well provided for, his allowance did not permit such expense. Having no additional funds of his own, he needed an advance from his inheritance. On 3 August 1829 he wrote a challenging letter to his mother to approve his plans, again bridling against the restrictions. 'The vacation is not, as you seem to think, arranged by me, but is the regular Michaelmas vacation [of the university]', he wrote, following this with detailed justifications and the claim that he would not miss lectures, that Eduard had only to write a cheque, and that above all he needed to experience Italy. He wrote in turn to all the members of his family during the trip to keep them interested, angling the information to suit them, and always stressing that he was being economical.[9]

But once returned to Heidelberg, Schumann was faced with the same issues as in Leipzig and right through the rest of the academic year, with the plans needed to finalize his studies and take law exams effectively to be quickly decided. His certificate of study in September 1829 confirms enrolment in courses of Roman, ecclesiastical and international law. But whether, in this second year, he ever seriously intended to complete his law studies is not really clear. Claiming regular attendance, he seems to have been attempting to persuade himself of their value – 'I am only now beginning to appreciate its true worth and the way in which it assists all the highest interests of humanity' – and he praises Heidelberg students as different: quiet and engaging. But this was passing: he continued to broaden his cultural interests and skills. He took private lessons in French, Italian, English and Spanish, all incurring additional expenses, and ran up debts. Money was more of a problem in Heidelberg because the town was much more expensive, well-off students setting the rates, as he stressed to his guardian and again to Eduard, and he had to shift from his first 'aristocratic' lodgings to a cosier 'den'.[10]

Behind the front he presented to his mother and family, the main result of Schumann's student life was to be closer contact with his true concerns, literature and music. Leipzig initiated a new burst of literary activity: from the first he continued to study Jean Paul – 'where might I be if I had not come to know Jean Paul; yet he seems on the one hand to be interwoven with my inner being; it is as if I had an earlier premonition of him' – and now even noting that Jean Paul drove him to 'the verge of madness'. He began literary projects in the Jean Paulian manner: *Hottentotianna*, a diary of literary character begun on 2 May 1828, shows the absorbing of ideas to flower later, in autobiographical analyses, sketches for poetic projects, aesthetic speculations and musical composition as poetic activity. Schumann's analysis of creative genius appears in *Über Genial-, Knill-, Original- und andre -itäten (On Geniality, Getting High, Originality and Other Items)*, which treats the Jean Paulian idea of the *hoher Mensch* ('higher person'): the individual with Promethean energy and Olympian restraint. In Jean Paul's *Flegeljahre* he continued to observe (in *Vult und Walt Harnisch*) the opposing character types soon to be basic concerns in his thinking and evidenced in his Jean Paul-inspired *Bildungsroman* fragment, *Selene*, and he also planned a poetic biography of E. T. A. Hoffmann.[11]

But the greatest focus of his artistic life and greatest consolation in letters home was clearly his piano playing, the biggest constant in all this change. With a rented piano, he spent much time improvising – 'fantasizing', as he called it. This soon found a focus in a new friendship with the piano pedagogue Friedrich Wieck, further to his meeting him at the Caruses'. Through them he had been able to hear and meet local and visiting performers, and to gain more perspective on and take more pride in his own talents. Wieck now opened the door much wider, and by 28 August 1828 Schumann was his piano student. The Wieck connection involved not just lessons and contacts, but the serious discussion of musical issues, fulfilling Schumann's dedicated pursuit of like minds in the exploration of his special world of musical ideas; the outstanding circle that met at Wieck's home embodied what he wanted. For example, he soon met Heinrich Marschner, director of the Leipzig Opera, then performing his opera *Der Vampyr*. But Schumann was not a good piano pupil. His attendance was erratic from the start and he didn't like the basic exercises Wieck demanded; rather he tried difficult works, such as Hummel's Concerto in A minor. As with everything, his questing imagination overran his technique.[12]

As well as the songs of the preceding March, playing piano duets with Wieck's pupil, Emilie Reichold, stimulated his first known piano compositions: polonaises for four hands. In addition to the songs and the polonaises, he also wrote variations on a theme by Prince Louis Ferdinand of Prussia. By late summer 1828 he had intensified his passionate attachment to the music of Schubert from his first contact in 1827:

> Schubert is still 'my only Schubert', especially as he has so much in
> common with 'my only Jean Paul', and when I am playing his music
> I feel as if I were reading one of Jean Paul's novels ... altogether I
> think nobody's compositions are such a psychological puzzle in
> the course and connection of their ideas as Schubert's, with their
> apparently logical progressions. Very few composers have succeeded
> in stamping their individuality upon a mass of tone pictures in the
> way he has done, and still fewer have written so much for themselves
> and their own hearts.

Clearly, Schumann had now found a soul mate and model in his emerging musical world.[13]

By November 1828 Schumann had also organized weekly piano quartet evenings with friends in his rooms for reading, sometimes attended by Carus and Wieck: the other players were a cellist, Christian Glock (also later his doctor); a violinist, Johann Taglichsbeck; and a viola-playing student, Christoph Sorgel. They played not only Schumann's own works, but also difficult works by Beethoven, Schubert and other established figures. Lively discussion followed. The most ambitious Schumann work to emerge was a quartet in C minor (EI) for piano and strings, apparently inspired by the several quartets that the players had studied. According to his diary, Schumann sweated over the quartet, which he completed on 21 March 1829, and which he passionately rehearsed up to January 1830. It was a work of great structural interest, if limited craftsmanship; he intended to 'cobble it into a symphony', though never did so. Schumann was now increasingly seeing himself as a composer. Flechsig describes his foolish posture: 'he always puffed on cigars, would squint when the smoke bothered his eyes', yet also 'liked to whistle his melodies' the while, creating an impossible contortion. Schumann was now seeking much wider influences and stimuli. The prime motivation for the Italian trip in 1829 was, as well as the cultural experience, largely musical, especially to experience opera and singing. To Wieck he declared 'how enchanted I was with Rossini, or rather with [Giuditta] Pasta, of whom I will say nothing at all, from pure veneration – nay, almost adoration ... You have no idea of Italian music, for it must be heard under the sky which inspired it.'[14]

In the relatively small and select artistic circle of Heidelberg Schumann soon became known as a notable pianist. According to Theodor Töpken, a law student with whom he played duets, 'the whole time he was in Heidelberg, piano playing was his main occupation'. Early in 1830 Schumann played Moscheles' variations on La Marche d'Alexandre (which he had previously played in Zwickau on 29 April 1829) at a student-sponsored musical society concert, and became 'the darling of the Heidelberg public'. Töpken also describes his improvisation: 'Ideas poured out of him in an inexhaustible abundance. From only a single thought, which he would allow to take shape in every possible way, there welled up and gushed forth everything.' Töpken observed that Schumann wanted to reach his goal of technical command as a pianist quicker than was possible, and thought about ways of shortening the time. Though Schumann had partly rationalized to himself his move to Heidelberg through musical reasons, he knew all along that his musical roots were now in Leipzig – and this put him under pressure. He wrote to Wieck in Leipzig quite differently than to his mother at the same time. Now critical of Thibaut for his 'narrow-minded and truly pedantic approach in music', he inclined towards Wieck, commenting 'why did I leave Leipzig, where the Olympus of music was being so delightfully opened to me', and ending his letter by lauding Wieck as 'honoured master of my mind'. Schumann now wanted to progress seriously as a pianist. He requested Wieck to send him all of Schubert's waltzes, Moscheles' G minor and Hummel's B minor concertos, new works by Herz and Czerny, and also anything interesting that had appeared since.[15]

As an emerging composer, Schumann's problem was to make the shift from improvisation to notation. He was pressured from inside with an imagination 'so overflowing with sounds that it is impossible to write anything down'. The first published music, for piano, grew out of his early experiments with conventional dances and virtuoso technical devices, especially associated with variation idioms. The twelve Papillons completed in 1832 grew from dances dating from 1829. He explained the title to his mother in a letter of 17 April 1832 as being prompted by the last scenes of Jean Paul's Flegeljahre, a masquerade, 'because the Papillons are intended as a musical representation of that masquerade'. He added more fully in a letter to Rellstab soon after this the various events and personalities of the masquerade – including the twins Walt and Vult Harnisch – and the Larventanz had so preoccupied him that he 'found [himself] at the piano and thus one "Papillon" after another came into existence'. The title

Papillons arises from the pun on the German word for 'mask', *Larve*, and doubtless from the capricious nature of the movements (the six bells rung out for the approach of dawn was Schumann's own idea). The Toccata, later published as op. 7 in 1834, appears to date from 1830 as a wild study (*Etude fantastique en double-sons*). And Moscheles' variation style is evident in the official op. 1, the *Abegg* Variations, issued in November 1831, which also show the emergence of the verbal and personal fantasy behind the notes: the theme spells out the name 'Abegg' in musical notation, and though Schumann knew a family named Abegg, and their daughter Meta, the 'Mademoiselle Pauline Comtesse d'Abegg' of the dedication was the product of his imagination, just as he had earlier penned poems to imaginary lovers, as Flechsig recalled.[16]

As the tensions between the need for a professional decision and the development of his creative imagination grew, so the physical and mental symptoms of Schumann's vulnerability became more apparent. The pattern of withdrawal from the outside world continued from school. One notes his early comment in Leipzig to his mother: 'that I often require little excitement I know very well'. His closest friends observed the reticence too: Eduard Röller observed that 'he was not sufficiently clear and open to disclose himself, or make himself understood'. He also showed the tendency to become alienated from people: 'it sickens me to see idiotic people ... what my fellow creatures cannot give me is given me by music'. In seeking a superior world of artistic feelings, he expressed to Götte the overwhelming desire that arises in those of 'lyric natures ... when the sweet realms of sound are opened, or in the dim twilight, or during a storm, or when the sun is rising'.[17]

The tension was beginning to become difficult to contain. He experienced his first serious mental disorder on 27 May 1828, just before his eighteenth birthday, of which he describes an anxiety attack: 'I was agitated but I don't know by what. It seems to me that I'll go mad one day. I don't know whether I am still alive. I might be dead ... I was frightened by Jean Paul's *Siebenkäs*, but wanted to read it a thousand times again.' Fortunately Schumann had medical help to hand through the continuing contact with Dr Carus, 'though when I went to Dr Carus my heart pounded and I turned pale.' In Heidelberg he also suffered a kind of stage fright, as he had done at school when he was unable to speak his lines publicly without breaking down. He had accepted an invitation from an English family to play at a soirée, but didn't turn up, causing considerable offence.[18]

Schumann had little interest in communicating all this to his mother for several reasons. First, he was concerned to offset her own depression and not to worry her; his letters from university are full of support and encouragement to cheer up – imagining her brooding and going for lonely walks. He felt it necessary to reply to her 'dreary conclusions about [her] mental state and physical condition' by promising to be a model student, behave well, attend college 'like a machine', and treasure the ring she had sent him 'like a talisman against every vice'. Second, he knew that if he imparted too much about his real attitudes to law and music this would produce a crisis he couldn't handle. He was obviously telling himself as well as his mother that the law might work. One is struck by Schumann's dependent, almost childish tone. He wrote to his mother more than to anyone else – warm expressions of affection, in which he imagined looking into her eyes, receiving her 'intellectual response'. And she inevitably leant on him and sought to control him with sympathy.[19]

Schumann's attraction towards girls became the more notable in his new freedom at university. He continued to long for Agnes Carus as his unattainable romantic ideal, perhaps also as a substitute mother/ sister figure. But at the practical level, he took his opportunities. The diary shows how much he was attracted by Wieck's pupil Emilie Reichold: with her he went to parties, danced, and made eyes and pleasant conversation, as well as playing duets. His holiday trips, especially the long one to Italy, gave him many more opportunities, though he seems to portray himself as observer rather than participant in the diary, noting his 'escapes' from awkward situations: he kept a record of every encounter. When finally back in Leipzig, he definitely embarked on his first fully fledged sexual relation with a woman he refers to in the diary simply as 'Charitas', identified by some writers as probably a student or servant in the Wieck household. There are many references in the diaries to sexual relations, to his symptoms from over-activity and to the advice to refrain that he received from Dr Glock, and also to Schumann's anxiety about the relationship, seemingly posing him a moral dilemma between experience and restraint.[20]

If never by nature a 'bohemian', Schumann had an irregular life in student years, with poor sleep and too much alcohol. His sleep problems have been traced back to childhood as he anxiously awaited the return of his mother when he was 2 or 3. In Leipzig he had difficulty falling asleep and kept himself awake by reading ... and floated in and out of consciousness with vivid dreams, for example of his sister-in-law Therese calling him home to Zwickau. The stories he read late were often disturbing – Byron's *Manfred* and *Childe Harold*, and Jean Paul's *Siebenkäs*. Many nineteenth-century artists were interested in darkness, and Schumann would later explore such moods in his *Nachtstücke* (his father had been similarly affected by the writings of Edward Young). As in Leipzig he had to keep the light on to avoid terror. He would wake in the night bathed in sweat and terrified. Two evenings in a row he fell asleep with a burning cigar in his mouth.[21]

Schumann drank to excess, not only socially, but also alone, as a way of escape, and his Heidelberg diaries are full of over-indulgence and hangovers. On 18 March 1829 he came for the first time to what may have been the brink of suicide, recording 'I am terrified and disgusting – drunk because of boredom – very high – my longing to throw myself into the Rhine'. Any suggestion of past unhappiness upset him. During his Italian travels in 1829 a young man, speaking of a similar bereavement, brought back Schumann's memories of his father's death, memories of which he was afraid: 'the spectre of dead people seems to be pursuing me'. He was already a poor traveller, suffering from stress through worry, and from homesickness. Money worries also stimulated fear and anxiety. It was with great relief in mid October 1829 to be 'back on German soil', when he stopped briefly at Augsburg where his family friends, the Kurrers welcomed him and saw to his finances.[22]

Despite the upsets, Schumann survived the challenges and pressures of student life because of self-identity and self-esteem, as well as the ever-present financial support of family and friends. This emerges unmistakably in an autobiographical essay appended to his diary. Writing of himself in the third person he declares 'I would not wish to count Schumann among the ordinary people. He is distinguished from the masses by his talent for many things, and his unique individuality ... He is born "to be the first".' Schumann had always known this. Now, finally, the direction of that talent was to become clear.[23]

For three months after the impact of hearing Paganini play in Frankfurt on Easter Saturday in 1830 before leaving Heidelberg, Schumann debated his future with himself and his mother. The emerging revelations throw light on the complex relationships preceding: of Johanna's ignorance and pressure on him, supported by his brothers, and of Robert's musical insecurities and loyalty to his family. Only after the accumulation of factors – growing experience as a player, belief in himself, success with the public, the sense that he had ideas that were worth something – was Schumann ready to move forward. The contradictions finally played out in a brief and decisive drama in which Schumann came of age and finally revealed his real person. He told his mother on 1 July 1830 that, whilst he really wanted to be a great lawyer, he did not have the heart to go further, and that Thibaut had asserted 'heaven never meant me for an official'. Then – at five in the morning on 30 July 1830 – asserting his potential as a pianist and composer even more strongly: that his whole life had 'been a 20 year struggle between poetry and prose, or if you like to call it so, Music and Law'.[24]

Now he knew that music was the only way forward: and that he was at the crossroads. If it was to be law, he told her, 'I must undoubtedly stay here for another Winter to hear Thibaut lecture on the Pandects'; if music, 'I must leave this at once and go to Leipzig, where Wieck, whom I could thoroughly trust, and who can tell me what I am worth, would then carry on my education', adding with a foresight that suggests long consideration, 'afterwards I ought to go to Vienna for a year, and if possible study under Moscheles'. Now he charged her with taking his life forward as his agent, both a recognition of her authority in his life, yet also of her responsibility towards him: 'Write yourself to Wieck and ask him point blank what he thinks of me and my career. Please let me have a SPEEDY answer.' He would add, on 22 August, 'remember ... father's penetrating mind, who saw through me very early and always destined me either for art or music'. Much later Schumann would reiterate this now powerful realization in application for his degree: 'my father intended me for music'.[25]

Under this duress, his mother, greatly upset, agreed to solicit Wieck's opinion, though she had never met him nor corresponded with him. She praised her son for his talent 'not given to others', and as a good, young, inexperienced person, 'who only lives in the higher spheres and does not want to go into practical life', observing 'when the time comes to show what he can do he will have spent his entire modest fortune and still be dependent on other people'. Wieck replied in early August, promising to make Schumann a greater artist than Moscheles or Hummel, but insisting on daily lessons, music theory with a teacher of Wieck's choice, and a review of his progress after a six-month trial. This was, of course, unrealistic. Such comparisons did not have to be made for Schumann to be trained to a successful career as a pianist and teacher, and suggest that Wieck either wished to train him as a champion of his method for public display, or that he was more interested in his 'modest fortune'. He clearly realized already that the problem Schumann would face most was that of the self-discipline to study subjects he did not find congenial. Thus Wieck also observed to Johanna that Schumann's 'greatest problem lay in the cool, quiet, thoughtful mastering of piano technique', and that 'every day he will work, at the blackboard, three to four part exercises'.[26]

Johanna now unloaded her emotions and wrote in very distressed tones to Schumann in giving grudging approval. 'I do not reproach you, since that would lead to nothing. But I cannot approve your views or ways of dealing with things at all. Look at your life since your good father's death and you must admit that you have only lived for yourself. Where will it end?'. She reiterated, 'When you do everything that Wieck demands, you will still not have attained a secure future. Think of your age.' Schumann was now determined, however. He wrote to Wieck on 21 August 1830:

> I confide entirely in you, and give myself to you altogether: take me just as I am and be patient with me in everything. No blame shall crush me, no praise make me any lazier. A few [buckets] of very, very cold theory will not hurt me either, and I will bear them without flinching ... I will deserve to be called your scholar.

To his guardian, Rudel, he hedged his bets. 'If after six months Wieck should have the very smallest doubts, I shall have lost nothing as regards Jurisprudence, and will gladly go up for my examinations within a year, and even then I shall not have studied more than four years.'[27]

So, in September 1830, Schumann returned to Leipzig, on a circuitous route via the Rhine steamer and over land with a clear realization of the hard grind before him. But surely Schumann and Wieck had different visions: Wieck (perhaps) to create a star; Schumann to explore his inner world and everything necessary to realize it.

3 A career in music: Leipzig 1830–5

Schumann arrived in Leipzig early in October 1830 and had settled into two rooms that Wieck made available to his students in his house in the Grimmaische Gasse by 20 October. This new connection with Wieck was now to be beneficial to Schumann in many ways. But it also confronted him head-on with his biggest artistic challenge so far: to submit entirely to the demands of a really tough teacher. Wieck's approach to musical training was entirely commendable, an integrated method that approached harmony and counterpoint through keyboard improvisation, composition and ear training, which had provided Clara with the excellent background from which she became an accomplished composer, and that he later outlines in published writings. The virtual suspension of his diary during the period suggests that Schumann probably did submit to Wieck's requirements for practice seven hours a day and nothing else. But Schumann had always done things his own way – and Wieck was an autocrat: there was bound to be a clash. By the end of the year Schumann wrote to his mother that he was disenchanted with his teacher, whom he found to be only interested in Clara's career. He had by now decided he wanted to study with Hummel in Weimar.[1]

Johann Nepomuk Hummel (1788–1837), pupil of Mozart, friend of Beethoven and the greatest piano pedagogue of his day, was surely the biggest name Schumann could imagine, and shows the level of his ambition – indeed he told his mother explicitly in December 1830 that he wanted 'to call myself a pupil of his'. He eventually wrote to Hummel

2   Robert Schumann with moustache. Anonymous portrait, c. 1834.

on 31 August 1831 for lessons, echoing his remarks to Wiedebein of six years earlier, but now with the added anxiety of the pressing need for a finite decision:

> I went my way without guidance, a blind follower of Nature. I could have no examples in our small town, where probably I myself was held up as one. I came to this university [Leipzig] without much thought of what I was destined for, or of my future career. I have attended a few lectures, but have also studied piano and composition with enthusiasm under a good master. You may imagine how much he found to correct and check, when I tell you that though I could play any concerto at sight, I had actually to begin with the C major scale.[2]

Schumann's quotes to his mother on 26 May 1832 from a recent letter from Hummel (of 20 May) indicate that a correspondence had ensued: 'Hummel's former letters will no doubt interest you, so I will look them out and send them.' In this letter Hummel acknowledged Schumann's

> evident talent. The only thing I might say about [your compositions] is that occasionally there is too sudden a change of harmony. You also seem to me to give way rather too much to your own peculiar originality, and I should not want this habit to grow upon you, because it would detract from the beauty, freedom and clearness of your compositions, even when well written ... If you continue to be so industrious and steady, I have no doubt, but that you will entirely accomplish all you are aiming at.

As a result of his plans, Schumann's ambitions had already created tensions with Wieck, whom he had anyway found volatile and inconsistent (and even cruel to his son, Alwin). He had first 'aired them' to Wieck in December 1830 to a strong rebuke, as he recalled to his mother. And the situation became even more problematic when, on 21 September 1831 Wieck took Clara on tour through Saxony and the Rhineland and then Paris till May 1832. This meant that Schumann now had to leave the house, find new lodgings and direct his own playing.[3]

He had also already sought another theory teacher – just as urgent given his accelerating compositional ambition, for which he desperately wanted technical advice. Wieck had wanted the Cantor of St Thomas's, Christian Weinlig (who had taught Clara, and also numbered Wagner among his pupils). But Schumann chose the new director of the Leipzig Opera, Heinrich Dorn, whom he may have thought more aligned to his compositional needs and interests. Lessons began by mid July 1831 and lasted till Easter 1832. Dorn shows what a novice Schumann still was when he came to him: '[He] played his variations on Abegg for me. At that time he had never had any theoretical instruction, at least not on a regular basis. Because I had to start him on the ABC of figured bass. His first 4- part exercise showed most unruly part writing.' But Dorn shows that Schumann's motivation was very high:

He was an indefatigable worker throughout this apprenticeship. Whenever I gave him one assignment he would deliver me many more. The first lessons in double counterpoint took up so much time that he sent me a letter saying that that he 'couldn't tear himself away' [and that] I would come to his house; he normally came to mine. I went and found him drinking champagne with which we then moistened our dry studies.

Schumann worked at figured bass to chorale harmonization, canon and double counterpoint, subjects to which he would repeatedly return.[4]

Dorn also had other important recollections of their nine months' exchange. 'Schumann was already neglecting his piano playing – he lacked the courage to play in public – and always gave the impression of a shy young man; with me in private he was in better humour and became more talkative.' But there were by now good reasons for Schumann's pianistic reticence: that he had chronically over-practised, perhaps over-inspired by Clara's skills. Already in January 1830 in Heidelberg he had complained of a 'numbed finger', apparently the middle finger. This condition came and went, but by May 1832 the finger was 'completely stiff'. It appears that he and Töpken may even have experimented in Heidelberg in 1829 with restraining mechanisms in the desire to increase independence of the fingers; both his friend Semmel and Clara recall his use of a dummy keyboard for quiet practice, or while travelling, where dull repetition would create strain. Wieck had claimed (though insincerely) to oppose artificial aids, insisting to Schumann on natural exercise.[5]

Schumann had wanted to perform for Clara's return on 22 May 1832 but cancelled through anxiety, as well as finger problems, and on 13 June he quarrelled with Wieck about his condition. Wieck provides further confirmation of the cause in recalling, albeit with posthumous animus, a 'finger torturer thought up by a famous pupil of mine to the just outrage of his third and fourth fingers, which he fashioned against my wishes and used behind my back'. And it is not entirely clear that it was of Schumann's own devising, as such devices were widely available: his diary only refers to 'a cigar mechanism'. Further evidence comes from his friend and doctor Moritz Reuter, who used the hand injury as part of a successful defence to keep Schumann out of the army in 1840 (shortsightedness was the other reason – he regularly wore glasses in later years): but as well as mentioning a 'machine', he also states that Schumann could not use his middle finger at all, and the index finger only partially, confirming this further diminishment of control by stating that Schumann was completely unable to grip with this hand.[6]

With Wieck, Schumann now visited doctors (one in Dresden) for herbal bandages and even a six-month treatment of animal baths (*Thierbäder*): this involved the immersion of the hand in the entrails of an ox, an example of the quackery commonplace in the medicine of the period. Schumann told his mother in a letter of 9 August 1832 that his house had turned into a chemist's shop. He began to make plans to return to law studies and by November wrote to his mother of being resigned to his injury as being incurable. So, a little more than two years after his crisis decision for music, his career as a pianist ended. He told Töpken on 5 April 1833 'I play the piano but little now ... I am quite resigned and consider it providential – having injured and crippled the fingers of my right hand. The injury began by being very slight but through carelessness it has got so much worse that I can hardly play at all now.' He made two more attempts at a cure, with a homoeopathic doctor in June 1833, and then with electrical treatment, but to no avail.[7]

He never recovered. His subsequent attitude to this huge shock to his plans varied according to mood. On 3 December 1838 he told Clara 'I sometimes feel unhappy that I have an ailing hand ... I can tell you it's getting worse and worse. I've often complained to heaven and asked:

> God. Why did you do this of all things to me? It [the ability to play] would be of great advantage to me here [Vienna]; the music is ready and alive within me, and playing it should be as natural as breathing. But I can barely play at all now, and one finger stumbles over the other. It is quite dreadful and has already caused me a lot of pain.

But in March 1839 his comment to his supporter Simonin de Sire was of rational acceptance:

> by an untoward fate I am myself deprived of the use of my right hand, and cannot play my things as I feel them. There is nothing the matter with my hand except that several fingers have become quite weak, probably from too much playing and writing in former days, so that I can hardly use them. This has often made me sad – well, Heaven sends me a powerful thought now and then to make up for it, and so I think no more about it.

And he admitted in similar vein to Clara that year that one hand was useless for playing, but that otherwise 'everything would be quite different'– that it was a good thing in retrospect, because he had been able to concentrate on composing.[8]

Schumann's theoretical studies were also to be of limited duration. At first all went well, though he soon observed critically that he would 'never come close' to Dorn, who had 'no feeling' and a 'Prussian temperament', and (to Wieck) that Dorn 'conceived everything as a fugue'. But Schumann was clearly really put out when Dorn dropped him in around April 1832 (though probably because of Dorn's impending departure to a post in Hamburg). He obviously wanted to continue:

> What can have induced you to break with me so suddenly? I suppose that I begged so often for indulgence and forgiveness that you got sick of it. But I could not have believed that my guide would have deserted me so close to the goal; and only now, having assisted two of my friends as far as syncopations, I do appreciate your thorough and certain method of teaching.

Schumann now indicated his desire to continue with counterpoint on his own, 'going quietly on where we left off (after Marpurg)' and still hoping to study the theory of canon. As for Wieck, Schumann must have been an infuriating student, desperately wanting technical instruction and support yet also artistic freedom, all at once.[9]

But the experience had been positive. He worked at what he affectionately referred to as 'noble figured bass', chorale harmonization, canon and double counterpoint: preoccupations to which he would repeatedly return. Indeed, in writing to his Zwickau teacher Kuntsch, he mentions that, in addition to Marpurg, 'who is a capital theorist ... the Well Tempered Clavier is my grammar, and is certainly the best. I have taken the fugues and dissected them down to their minutest parts.' He also sought from him 'oldish scores, say of the Italian church music'. In applying contrapuntal skills, Schumann missed Dorn's help in arranging the Paganini Caprices for the piano 'as the basses were often doubtful; but I managed to get on by keeping everything very simple', however, he also proclaims that 'Otherwise I have finished six Intermezzi with "Alternativos" and a Prelude, concluding with a fugue on 3 subjects (think of that) in the old style.'[10]

Schumann's studies had again failed to live up to his hopes. He would play the piano little publicly thereafter: only as duo partner with Clara or as vocal accompanist in private, though he claimed that his problems did not stop him improvising or composing. Nonetheless, his creative work would reflect his continuing interest in piano technique, which he advanced in most original ways and which must reflect many aspects of his own playing. In the theoretical sphere, his experience was more obviously positive, anticipating his lifelong interest in traditional compositional technique and strict working. Nonetheless, when he parted from Dorn around the beginning of June 1832, Schumann had great plans for the future orchestral chamber and piano works he hoped one day to complete. By November of that year he had approached C. G. Müller, director of the Musikgesellschaft 'Euterpe' in Leipzig from 1831, with the request for lessons in instrumentation – and to assist him 'in revising a symphony movement of my own [the Symphony in G minor], shortly to be performed in Altenburg. I have been working on my own without any sort of guidance, and am also not at all confident of my abilities.'[11]

Though the termination of Schumann's pianistic ambitions by late 1832 or early 1833 was traumatic, it also removed an illusion and provided a focus. He was thrown back on his real gifts and interests: his improvisation at the piano; his knowledge of German and foreign literature; his curiosity for the current state of music, its history, theory and aesthetics. His talents and energies quickly coalesced into imaginative critical writing as well as his ongoing musical composition. Piano playing had never dimmed Schumann's literary interests. Shortly before beginning lessons with Dorn in September 1831 they had taken another form: he had become newly enthralled by the imaginative literary world opened by E. T. A. Hoffmann. Hoffmann's style shared much with Jean Paul in presenting a weird blend of reality and fantasy, in which a community of different characters related to the artist was central, but whose chief focus was now on music, and the imaginative creation of musically gifted eccentrics that captured the Romantic spirit, most famously his Kapellmeister Johannes Kreisler. The attraction was that Hoffmann was expressing what Schumann already felt in his need to know himself and understand his inner drives.[12]

Schumann's characters began to appear in his diary in June 1831, when he decided to give 'more beautiful, appropriate names' to his family circle: most notably 'Meister Raro' to Wieck, 'Cilia' to Clara, 'Charitas' to Christel and 'Musikdirector' to Dorn, with further names for Semmel, Glock, Renz, Rascher, Probst and Flechsig. Shortly after 'entirely new persons entered...my two best friends: Florestan and Eusebius.' He regarded these as counterparts to the twins Vult and Walt in Die Flegeljahre, and later clarified to Dorn himself, by which time he had created the Davidsbündler (League of David):

> Florestan and Eusebius represent my dual nature, which, like Raro,
> I should like to melt down into a man ... The Davidsbund is a purely
> abstract and romantic society, as I dare say you found out long ago.
> Mozart was just as great a member as Berlioz and you are, without
> having been exactly nominated by a diploma ... All the rest is in the
> paper. The other veiled characters are partly people, and much in the
> life of the Davidites is taken from reality. I could fill whole pages. Let
> this suffice.

Other refinements and the characterization of Florestan and Eusebius emerge in retrospective comments in the Gesammelte Schriften as well as through their musical criticisms in the Neue Zeitschrift, and above all in musical characterizations in the contemporary piano works. Florestan, fiery and impetuous, and the dreamy Eusebius, apparently drawn from the figure of St Eusebius the Confessor. That Florestan derives from Beethoven's Fidelio is clear from Schumann's comparing himself in this role to Clara's Leonore in a letter of November 1837, and he often acknowledged St Eusebius' day when it occurred, in his letters.[13]

If Schumann could not speak publicly with sufficient confidence or, as soon emerged, play to the level he wanted, he could write. And given his special interest in the piano, not least the reigning cult of empty virtuosity that typified its prominence as the now central instrument of the rapidly growing middle class, a life as critic was predictable, and its focus significantly preordained. Promptly on 27 September 1831, Schumann first offered his services to G. W. Fink, editor of Germany's most prestigious music journal, the Allgemeine musikalische Zeitung (AMZ), published by its most prestigious house, Breitkopf & Härtel in Leipzig. Since Schumann's acquisition in May 1831 of Chopin's newly published variations on the 'Là ci darem la mano' duet from Mozart's Don Giovanni, Chopin had became his new idol, a revelation of new musical possibilities, as Schubert has been earlier. Linking each variation with a character and scene of the opera, he spoke through the two personas of Florestan and Eusebius, and in the spirit of E. T. A. Hoffmann's writings, to produce an entirely new kind of autobiographical and poetic criticism:

> Eusebius entered not long ago. You know his pale face, and the ironical smile with which he awakens expectation. I sat with Florestan at the piano. Florestan is, as you know, one of those rare musical minds that foresee, as it were, coming, novel, or extraordinary things. But he encountered a surprise today. With the words 'Off with your hats, gentleman, a genius!' Eusebius laid down a piece of music. We were not allowed to see the title page ...

But though this heralded his new approach, it also cut him off from that source of reviewing, since Fink never asked him again: indeed Fink accompanied Schumann's review not only with a conventional one of his own with music examples, but an introduction explaining why he had accepted his piece 'as an example of the new modern criticism' (even misattributing the review to 'K. Schumann') and laying the basis for recurrent tensions between them regarding Schumann's own music, even though they were members of the same circles in Leipzig.[14]

In surrounding himself with like-minded thinkers, Wieck was key. His large circle of contacts became increasingly useful to Schumann and a group coalesced around him, first at J. Hofmeister's music shop, and later very regularly at the *Kaffeebaum* in the Fleischergasse, operated by Andreas Poppe. By June 1833 it was firmly established, Schumann now beginning to establish himself as well by presiding over this group of musicians and writers, also writing to his mother on 28 June 1833 that 'now ... I have made the acquaintanceship of the most celebrated artists, [excepting Hummel]'. He had just met the pianist Friedrich Kalkbrenner (1785–1849). On 4 January 1834 he writes 'my daily companions are Herlossohn, Wieck, Stegmayer, Schuncke, Stelle, Ortlepp, Lyser, Berger, Bürck and Pohlenz. I see a good deal of Fink too. The other day he invited me to a big musical matinée. You see I don't lack plenty of intellectual intercourse, and am made welcome in the most select circles.'[15]

Karl Borromäus Sebastian Herlossohn (1804–49) had founded the newspaper *Der Komet* in 1830; Ferdinand Stegmayer (1803–63) was a composer and music director; Ernst Ortlepp (1800–64) was a writer and translator of Shakespeare, and music critic; Johann Peter Lyser (1803–70) was a writer on music, painter and composer; Ludwig Berger (1777–1839) was a composer and pianist; August Bürck (1805–62) was a writer on music and a contributor to the *Neue Zeitschrift für Musik*; Christian August Pohlenz (1790–1843) was director of the Gewandhaus concerts at this time. Others were Julius Knorr (1807–61), pianist and piano teacher; Amadeus Wendt (1783–1836), philosopher and writer on music; and Eduard Moritz Rascher (1807–49), a boyhood friend from Zwickau, now a Leipzig law student. As Schumann later recalled, they wanted not only to erect a barrier against empty convention

3   The Leipzig *Kaffeebaum* in Kleine Fleischergasse today. Author's photograph.

and virtuosity, but to reject the ignoring of great figures of the past –
Beethoven, Weber and Mozart – as well as of the present, 'with Chopin,
Berlioz unappreciated'. But in purely musical terms, the biggest influence on Schumann's personal path was the most gifted musician of the
group, the pianist and composer Louis (Ludwig) Schuncke, (1810–34),
whom Schumann met in December 1833; by the spring of 1834 they

were sharing lodgings. Schuncke had undertaken his first concert tour at the age of 11, and studied from 1828 to 1830 in Paris with Kalkbrenner and Anton Reicha.

Schumann now took a further step in creating his artistic world and making his artistic goals tangible through the *Davidsbündler*. Headed by Florestan who, as King David would rout the Philistines – alluding to the Old Testament Hebrew poet-king and his battle with the pagan Philistine giant Goliath – their mission was to destroy the 'Philistines' of music, identified not only through empty display in the concert hall but in the opera house. From August 1833 Schumann had begun to draw together various writings of his own – autobiographical, poetry, novels, plays, essays – into the concept of a publication. The *Davidsbündler* made their debut between December 1833 and January 1834 in two essays jointly titled *Die Davidsbündler*, a mixture of fanciful prose, critique and aphorism that was first published in Herlossohn's *Der Komet*. Now quickly, in turn, the concept of the *Davidsbündler* became a contributing force behind the idea of a new musical newspaper to further these goals; he later recalled the *Davidsbündler* as a 'red thread running through the journal'.[16]

Several phases mark the origins of what was to become the *Neue Zeitschrift für Musik*. The retrospective picture given by Schumann of the plans of these 'idealistic young hotheads' in his *Gesammelte Schriften* completely obscures the struggles involved in establishing the paper. There were major problems: varying interest by central participants; changing personnel, with illness, even death; changing publishers; and difficulty in recruiting contributors. But events also served to show, like much else in his early life, that Schumann had considerable business acumen, great organizing ability and the capacity for sustained hard work when motivated and not unwell.

Discussions had begun 'in Hofmeister's garden' in the summer of 1833, with plans for a paper directed by Schumann, Ortlepp, Wieck, and apparently Knorr and others, and prospectuses put forward by Ortlepp and Schumann, who was clearly the motivator. Hofmeister, Schumann's closest Leipzig publishing contact, had been his first approach, but he was met with lack of interest. Schumann now turned to his brothers, mentioning to Carl as the four joint editors Wieck, Knorr, Ortlepp and himself. But by August no agreed prospectus was in existence. Worrying also, his mentor Wieck showed lack of interest: Schumann had to write to him on 6 August 1833 for a firm clarification of his commitment. And he still wanted a commitment from Hofmeister, writing bitterly to him around the same time that he should not let this opportunity pass him by:

A few weeks ago I sent you half a sheet of paper all about our newspaper arrangements. May I ask you to return it to me? I doubt whether my brother will undertake it now as he is too busy with his more important publications. You are not going to neglect the right moment for an enterprise that can only bring you honour and glory? ... Do you want more money? I shall be glad to let you have 1400 Thalers in Saxon four per cent bonds. You can give me cheques and after they have become due, send me back all the papers *in natura*. They are more likely to rise than fall; but in either case the risk is yours.[17]

The project was dropped through the winter. New plans suddenly emerged in March 1834, first with Wieck, his new friend Schuncke, Knorr, Stegmayer and Schumann himself; then with a founding contract for the *Neue Leipziger Zeitschrift für Musik* to appear twice weekly, published by Christian Hartmann, a local Leipzig book dealer, the editorial board comprising Wieck, Schuncke, Knorr and Schumann, though with Knorr as editor-in-chief. The first issue of 3 April 1834 promised theoretical articles, belletrist pieces of criticism on the spirit of the time and numerous concert reports. It was credited to 'a *Verein* of artists and friends of art'. But Schumann continued to carry most real responsibility: from 1 March till 23 September 1834 he wrote to thirty-nine prospective contributors, commissioning reviews and articles, though he only listed himself in a minor role 'for artistic, aesthetic matters' in the first issues.[18]

By the end of 1834 these promises had been more than fulfilled, with concert notes from about fifty cities. Schumann's letter to Pastor

Gustav Keferstein of 8 July 1834, also signed by Wieck, Schuncke and Knorr, describes the circumstances:

> [We] do not know how much you know of our paper, otherwise you could have no doubts as to its tendency. We admire the olden time, condemn the recent past as inartistic, and are endeavoring to prepare for and hasten the future, which is to be altogether fresh and poetical. You will already admit that all this cannot be accomplished in twenty numbers. We would gladly refrain from restricting you in any way as to the form and length of your works.[19]

Though Schumann had been the guiding light in the establishment of the journal from the first, he was still only one member of the board. Events would soon change this. With the prospect of serious commitment to an expanding project, problems and dissension loomed. Knorr was now ill; Schuncke was inexperienced in writing and anyway increasingly ill as well; Wieck was travelling and professionally preoccupied; Stegmayer dropped out. The publisher Hartmann was naturally unhappy. A dispute between Knorr and Wieck prompted Hartmann to try to seize legal control. This infuriated Schumann, and, together with the death of Schuncke in December 1834, seems to have motivated him on his return from Zwickau and Asch to act to take sole charge for promotion of what he regarded as his own idea. With Knorr's incapacitation he now bought the *Zeitschrift* outright from Hartmann for 350 thalers (though Knorr tried to sue him unsuccessfully for disputed expenses, resolved only in July without the expected court appearance). Schumann was now free to start the new journal with a new publisher. He negotiated a new contract with J. Ambrosius Barth of Leipzig with himself as sole editor and owner. On 18 December 1834, the publication of what was now renamed the *Neue Zeitschrift für Musik* was announced, and the first issue under Schumann's editorship appeared on 2 January 1835. Thus, in claiming 1834 at the end of his life as its most important year, he recognized the beginning of his professional life in music.[20]

Schumann's belated attempt to catch up in music and follow his creative star in Leipzig from October 1830 did not sever him from home ties in his early years there; he was too vulnerable for that, and home was still only a few hours south by regular coach. Behind the excitement, as he was increasingly drawn into Leipzig's musical and intellectual life, he easily became lonely and depressed: he did not settle easily. Zwickau was still his emotional base, and as soon as things went badly with his piano ambitions, he took the opportunity of four months there and in Schneeburg from mid November till early March. He maintained a regular and full correspondence with his mother, to whom the vast bulk of his surviving early family letters are addressed, and in which he seems to have shared almost every aspect of his thoughts and concerns, whether his health worries, his enthusiasm or plans. He always remembered the anniversary of his father's death, and wanted to be remembered to family and friends. He tried to share his artistic plans with them and kept them informed, though various comments suggest he knew his music was difficult for them: as early as autumn 1831 he wrote to the whole family on his new music, asking 'if to some of you it is unintelligible', and was put out when they did not reply.[21]

However, one definite reason for his eldest brother's reserve was Schumann's regular asking for money. In addition to requiring a comfortable lifestyle, his prodigious musical activities required much more than his allowance. The 60,000 thalers of August Schumann's estate were left as equity in his business, equally divided between his widow and four sons, obviously in order to keep the business intact rather than be dissipated in bequests: that is 12,000 thalers each. Consequently, the fate of the business was left chiefly in the hands of Eduard as eldest son: the question of its eventual destiny was thus deferred. Carl had already used his inheritance to found his own book business in Schneeburg, as the earlier reference to joint publication by Gebrüder Schumann at Schneeburg indicates: at some point in the early 1830s Schumann had invested a substantial sum in it. It seems that, as fourth son, Robert was never expected to play any part in the business; indeed, the special allowance to him if he undertook university study – unlike the brothers who were all involved in the family and the book business – indicates the father's wish to encourage this, and thus the recognition of his special talents and inclinations. But Schumann's ultimate inheritance depended on how the business prospered.[22]

Thus he always had mixed feelings between interested concern in its fortunes and eager entitlement to his eventual share. Robert clarified his claims to the business when he later discussed family financial matters with Clara in May 1838. Regarding Carl:

> [E]verything has been arranged *legally* so that my mortgage (terrible word) [that is, investment] has precedence over everything else; I don't have that with Eduard since, in his case, the under-aged children of my late brother Julius have precedence. I am, however, familiar enough with his business so that, at worst, if he were to have an accident or make bad speculative investments, etc., *at least* half of the debt would be paid anyway. Besides, Eduard is honest and meticulous, and at the [Leipzig] trade fair he'll pay me more than I'm asking.[23]

Meanwhile Robert received interest. His largest asset was investment in Gebrüder Schumann in Zwickau, from which he drew 500 thalers annually; and additionally he possessed his own Saxon state bonds, though these – doubtless because he had purchased them himself – he was very reluctant to liquidate. Though Schumann had long claimed to his mother that he did not know anything about money, he really meant that he could not plan or control his spending: he was, as emerges later, very aware of what he was owed by his brothers all the time his share remained held in investment. Since he was significantly short each month, he continued to be a persuasive writer of the begging letter. His allowance was inadequate. He claims to his mother in 1832 that he cannot live on the 500 thalers but needs 200 thalers more for five years. And still in 1834: 'You ask me whether I can make my money last. Honestly no. My income, including my earnings, does not amount to more than four or five hundred Thalers at present, and unfortunately, I have never spent less than six hundred.'[24]

But he had to be careful in going to his family, because he had to give account of his reasons. He knew that they were suspicious of his

reliability with money and apparently of his lack of a conventional profession and his ambitious plans. He did much better with friends, who
recognized his talents, and admired his ambitions and the measure
of what he was putting into the *Neue Zeitschrift*, often literally from his
own pocket, as to Töpken on 18 August 1834:

> You don't as yet know, good Theodor Töpken, what one feels like
> when one has to crave the landlord's indulgence from fortnight to
> fortnight, and can then only beg for still more time, for you were
> always in funds. In consequence of our secretary's long illness
> [Knorr] all the work has been thrown on me, so that today again I can
> only pay off a small amount of my debt to you.[25]

Having decided for music, Schumann's domestic security in
Leipzig lay in Wieck's house and family; he always regarded this as
his only real home in Leipzig, and was obviously happy there (and still
asked for his mail to be sent care of Wieck after he left). As a student,
he worked with Wieck in the mornings if he was not away touring
with Clara. Afternoon was for walking; the best time was in the evening: then Robert took the children – Clara and her two brothers, Alwin
and Gustav – to his room and became a child with them again. He told
fables he invented himself, made up charades for them, and created
stories for Clara.[26]

After Schumann left Wieck's house, the unsettled nature of his existence is suggested in his frequent changes of lodgings and their location.
Though Wieck lived right in the middle of town, at 36 Grimmaische
Gasse, and Schumann moved early close by into 21 Burgstrasse, he preferred the quieter parts of the city. At Rotes Kolleg (where he was soon
sharing with friends, Schuncke and Günther); Rudolfs Garten; 1246
Querstrasse; 462 Hallische Gasse (after Schuncke's death in December
1834); and again, after he returned from Vienna, Rotes Kolleg.[27]

He kept a regular day. In a letter to his mother of May 1833, he recalls
of the house with Günther:

> About 5 a.m. I jump out of bed like a deer, and keep my account
> book, diary, and correspondence in capital order; then I alternately

study, compose, and read a little till 11 o'clock when Luhe appears
and always sets me a splendid example of order and regularity.
Then comes dinner and I read either a French book or newspaper. I
regularly go for a walk from 3–6, generally alone. When I get home at
about 6 o'clock I improvise till nearly 8, then usually go to supper with
Kompe and Wolf, then come home.

With the social intensification created by the planning of the *Neue
Zeitschrift*, in the evenings he would spend several hours socializing
with friends, smoking cigars and with beer constantly replenished
without order, though even in this setting he could often appear
self-absorbed, or even leave without comment under the inspiration
of an idea. Other than the company of his companions, and Wieck's
social and musical entertaining, the most important social setting for
his personal and his musical development was the home of Carl and
Henriette Voigt. Though young (Henriette was only 25), they were
socially prominent Leipzig music lovers who were well known for the
protection and shelter they gave young artists. They invited Schumann
to their house. Schumann was very fond of Henriette – 'a model housewife and mother' – her generosity, tenderness and modesty. And they
were very supportive of Schumann's friendships.[28]

Much of Schumann's emotional fragility in Leipzig was associated
with his health. The existing signs of his emotional and physical instability at school and as a student began now to become steadily more
marked. Of old fears and insecurities, Schumann was already hyper-
sensitive to infection. His fear of cholera went back to childhood and
re-emerged when it broke out in Berlin in September 1831. At this time
he genuinely feared death and decided to go to Italy to avoid the out-
break (he told his mother 'the cholera will be here in four days'), making his will. Although by mid October he was feeling better, a series
of sad family events now broke into his new life in Leipzig and had a
profound effect on him. They began in June 1832 with the death of his
nephew Robert, Karl and Rosalie's child, named after him. In this
event he saw a premonition, arising from the shock of the deaths of
his father and sister. By summer 1833 three family members were ill,

including himself: Rosalie and he with malaria, and his elder brother Julius with tuberculosis.[29]

The deaths of Julius on 2 August and Rosalie around 17–18 October left him distraught and in deep depression. The fear of tubercular infection had already returned, and after visiting Julius he could not face going to see his body after death, partly for this fear. These deaths had a rapid cumulative effect on his sanity and triggered Schumann's first major mental disturbance. He recalled (though not until 1838, to Clara) the night of 17–18 October 1833 as the 'most frightful night of my life':

> [During the night], the most terrifying thought a person can ever have suddenly occurred to me, the most with which heaven can punish you, that of 'losing my mind'. It overwhelmed me so violently that all consolation and every prayer became as ineffective as scorn and mockery. The anxiety drove me from place to place: my breathing was disrupted by the idea 'what would happen if you could no longer think?' In my endlessly terrible excitement I ran to a doctor, told him everything, that I often seemed to lose my senses, that I didn't know where to turn because of the anxiety, yes, that in such a condition I could not guarantee that I might not raise my hand against my own life.

Recalling witnesses, Wasielewski states that 'from one source I learn that Schumann tried to throw himself out of the window on that night; but this story is contradicted by other parties'. He moved from his fifth-floor apartment at 21 Burgstrasse to the ground floor. He recalled to his mother at the end of November that '[only] excessive work brought back life by degrees', much of it obviously devoted to the establishment of the journal.[30]

In the face of these trials he increasingly revealed a self-protective response to suffering and death. He also came to know that Schuncke, as well as Julius, was tubercular, and even though Schuncke was rapidly declining in later 1834 he left Leipzig for Zwickau and was there when Schuncke died on 7 December. Nor could he face the funeral. Rather, he spoke eloquently in a letter to his Viennese friend, the piano pedagogue Joseph Fischhof (1804–57), and wanted to memorialize Schuncke in the *Zeitschrift* (he would also lose Henriette Voigt to the disease in 1839). Schumann's rational response was to look for a more stable life. When he was not dragged down emotionally, the gradual establishment of a social framework in Leipzig created a lifeline and the plans for the *Neue Zeitschrift* gave him a new lease on life. By early 1834, with the prospect of growing professional status, he changed his physical appearance by growing a moustache, and began to think about establishing himself through marriage. On 2 July 1834 he informed his mother that 'two glorious beings of the fair sex have lately appeared in our [circle]': Emilie List and Ernestine von Fricken. Both had influential fathers. Emilie was the 15–16-year-old daughter of the economist Friedrich List, who had returned to Germany as an America consul and settled in Leipzig in 1833 to promote the German railway network. Emilie would become a family friend – particularly close to Clara.[31]

But the relationship with Ernestine was altogether different. She was introduced to Schumann as the 17-year-old daughter of a Bohemian noble, Captain Ignaz F. von Fricken, who had heard Clara play in Plauen, near their home town of Asch on the Bohemian border, and had approached Wieck for lessons for his daughter. She had come on 21 April 1834, to live in Wieck's house as a pupil. Schumann was quickly physically attracted to her, the relationship escalating through the summer of 1834. They often met at the Voigts, and he gave her a ring. Schumann appears to have liked the father, who left him his compositions, and on whose theme Schumann composed his *Etudes symphoniques*, but he was certainly also impressed by Fricken's position and wealth, telling his mother that he was rich. Though there was a difference in class – Schumann was in trade and Fricken an aristocrat – it seemed like a good match and Wieck was strongly in favour of it. Social conventions towards eventual marriage proceeded. Ernestine and her father returned to Asch in September 1834, breaking their journey at Zwickau on the 5th of the month. Schumann went to Asch to be vetted by the family.[32]

But there was a hidden dimension to the unfolding relationship, and another reason for marriage from Fricken's point of view. Ernestine was not in fact his child, but the illegitimate daughter of his sister, Countess Caroline Ernestine Louise von Zedlitz, and had been raised as his own. It was only with the prospect of marriage that he now adopted her in December 1834, yet would not provide a dowry, giving his permission on the condition that a future husband would make no claims to his money or property. It is not clear whether Schumann's ardour was in any case beginning to cool by the summer of 1835, but after Fricken asked to meet Schumann, in anticipation of the marriage, in August 1835, it rapidly did so through the autumn. Schumann's embarrassment has naturally restricted the evidence. He later claimed that Ernestine's illegitimacy was the reason – plausible in view of his later, somewhat formal attitude to marriage. However, more powerful is his later comment to Clara in 1838 reflecting on his past life and pressures, and stating his fear that with a penniless spouse he might have to 'work for my daily bread like a craftsman'. But Schumann kept in touch with Ernestine after the break-up, and she remained a loyal friend to the couple, denying for Clara's benefit that she had been engaged. In 1838 Ernestine married Count Wilhelm von Zedtwitz-Schönbach, but was widowed within eight months and penniless. She returned to Asch and the Frickens, and died there in 1844 of typhus.[33]

However, the resolution of this relationshiop coincided with the development of his real marital future. Clara Wieck was now waiting for Robert. She was already notably protective towards him. They had been musical contemporaries and friends over the four years of Schumann's association with Wieck, providing ideas and stimulus to each other. She played his music. So when Clara came to Leipzig at the end of September 1834 after a recital tour, she was devastated to find that the godparents of her father's latest child were Robert and Ernestine, and had the impression they were engaged. Robert later claimed to Clara that he had to go through the relation with Ernestine in order to realize his true feelings for her. But by the end of 1835 he really had to come to terms with his commitment.[34]

Schumann's compositions between 1830 and 1835 continue to mirror deeply his literary as well as musical inclinations, but are increasingly inseparable from his life and ambitions as a whole. The literary and autobiographical dimensions of *Papillons* and the *Abegg* Variations continued to provide the vehicle for Schumann's gifts. To Töpken he described the six *Intermezzi*, op. 4 – composed in 1832 using earlier material, and full of allusion to his own work and that of others (originally conceived under the title *Pièces phantastiques*) – as 'extended *Papillons*'. Of the *Impromptus*, op. 5, on a theme of Clara Wieck (the *Romance variée*, op. 3 (1831, published 1833)), he stated that they 'may be viewed as a new kind of variation'. To these he planned a sequel, telling Härtel of '12 *Burlesken* something like the *Papillons* that appeared at Kistner's, and they are at your service on the same conditions for some future occasion'. As well as the virtuoso ambitions already clear when he had been a student in the *Etudes sur double sons*, which he now completed in 1832 as the Toccata in C and revised in 1833 as op. 7 – a fiercely demanding *moto perpetuo* in semiquavers, transforming technical exercise into extended composition – he responded to hearing Paganini in Frankfurt in 1829 with two books of etudes after the Paganini Caprices, his op. 3 and op. 10, of 1832 and 1833. Schumann adds new figures, counterpoints and harmonies, as well as several pages of extensive technical analysis and advice to players for op. 3, paralleled for op. 10 in an article in the *Neue Zeitschrift*, effectively not only presenting himself as virtuoso, but as teacher.[35]

Schumann's aspirations were already also towards larger forms, though the formal challenge would prove too great in the short term. In 1831 he began a Sonata in B minor, of which only one movement survives as the Allegro, op. 8. Of the three sonatas he mentions in March 1834, one in F minor (apparently quite different from the later work published as op. 14) does not survive. The Sonata in F sharp minor, op. 11, draws its first movement from a 'Fandango', previously a *Fantasie rhapsodique pour le pianoforte*, 'op. 4', of 1832, and its second movement reworks the song 'An Anna' of 1828. The pioneering op. 14 Romantic Sonata in F minor, op. 14 (with a scherzo with inserted intermezzo and a monumental last movement) did not itself see completion until 1835 because of the time taken up with the *Neue Zeitschrift*. The much more concentrated G minor Sonata (though with an expansive coda to the finale) was written at various times between 1833 and 1838 and only published in the final year as op. 22.

The many diverse stylistic sources of these works are more closely fused in *Carnaval* and the *Etudes symphoniques*, the culminatory works to 1835. The collection of fourteen pieces named *Carnaval* dates from December 1834 to early 1835. It draws not from a pre-existent literary scene, as does the end of *Papillons*, but from Schumann's own imagining of the characters of the *Davidsbündler* and others of his circle, mingling with those of the *commedia dell'arte* at carnival time. But like the *Abegg* work, it is based on musical notes spelling names (the original title was *Fasching, Schwänke über vier Noten für P[iano]f[or]te von Florestan*, and the published subtitle 'Scènes mignonnes sur quatre notes'), which he presents in three statements in block notation titled 'Sphinxes' (between the unnumbered eighth and ninth pieces) as E flat–C–B–A, manipulating the notes A, E flat (*Es* in German), C and B natural (*H* in German) = ASCH. Schumann's retrospective explanation skips over the profound emotional background to the intertwining of musical anagrams at the height of his passion for Ernestine von Fricken:

> The name of a city, in which a musical friend of mine lived, consisted of letters belonging to the scale which are also contained in my name; and this suggested one of those tricks that are no longer new, since Bach gave the example. One piece after another was completed during the carnival season of 1835, in a serious frame of mind, and under peculiar circumstances. I gave the names of the pieces later on and called the whole collection *Carnaval* including interludes and culminating in a 'Marche des *Davidsbündler* contra Philistines'.[36]

Exactly coincident in time and place was a more conventional variation work emphasizing and displaying the technical stylistic sources as well as a new symphonic pianism, in which technical exercises alternate with the variations: the twelve *Etudes symphoniques* were first called *Etuden in Orchestercharakter von Florestan und Eusebius*. Schumann had already written three sets of more traditional variations on themes of Beethoven, Chopin and Schubert (*Verzeichnis* F.25, 26, 24).

Obscure as was Schumann's position in the musical world, publication was not a major problem: all the completed piano works were published, and generally within a year or so. One reason was the huge emerging market for piano music, much of which was of convivial character and subsidized more difficult works. But there was also the circumstance that Schumann now lived in the publishing capital of Germany for music as well as books. In Leipzig he cultivated direct contacts with publishers, made easier through the access given by his paper, for which he requested all new music for review, not just that sent gratis. He first wanted to be published by the leading house of Breitkopf & Härtel: on 2 November 1832 he had written to them 'the protection of your firm is so tempting for a young composer, that I venture to send the enclosed *Fantasieübung* [later the Toccata in C], as well as twelve Burlesques.' In addition to *Papillons*, Kistner also took the *Abegg* Variations. Schumann was similarly successful with Hofmeister, who published the Paganini Studies, *Intermezzi* and *Impromptus*, as opp. 3, 4 and 5 respectively.[37]

Without public promotion Schumann's published works generated hardly any income. But at this stage, unknown to the larger public, he was seemingly more interested in attention and reaction than money, giving large numbers of copies of *Papillons* to his family (the dedicatees) and friends, and requesting of Breitkopf regarding the *Fantasieübung*, 'as to payment I have always had 5 Thalers per sheet. In this respect, I will accept any offer you like to make.' Above all he wanted reviews in established journals. Since reviews would be of the published music rather than of public performance, he lobbied and sent copies. From the first they were taken notice of in the musical press, though further to his initial brush with Fink, only opp. 3 and 5 were considered by AMZ, and other early works (opp. 8, 9, 15, 17, 22, 23) only reviewed in a collective review as late as 1844 – to his obvious annoyance. Schumann had sent the *Impromptus*, op. 5 to Fink in August 1833: 'I am rather surprised and hurt at your silence respecting several of my compositions which I sent you some years ago.' And Schumann's mother wanted to know why he was not in the Leipzig paper.[38] Rather, serious note was first taken of him in Vienna and Berlin. Most frequent were the reviews in the *Musikalische Anzeiger* of Vienna, edited by Ignaz Seyfried (1788–1841; a very senior figure – a pupil, amongst other teachers, of Mozart), which reviewed all of opp. 1–8, 14 and 16, beginning on 28 June 1832 with the *Abegg* Variations. Schumann wrote to Töpken on 5 April 1833, 'I will enclose a review from a Vienna paper which pleased me very much' (of *Papillons*), and added 'you will also find some nice things about me in the Berlin *Iris*'. The Berlin *Iris im Gebiete der Tonkunst*, edited by Ludwig Rellstab (1799–1860), took great early interest, reviewing opp. 1–4. Schumann first felt more able to respond positively to the criticism of Rellstab. Though initially irritated by his criticism of *Abegg* and *Papillons*, he soon warmed to the attention: 'Kindly accept my most sincere thanks for the friendly, kind-hearted criticism of the *Abegg* Variations, which hardly deserve higher praise. Not so much for the sake of the Editor of the *Iris*, as because I consider you a poet and kindred spirit with Jean Paul.' He added his explanation of the origin of *Papillons*: 'the thread which connects them is a very tender one indeed', and ended 'hoping that the *Iris* may never lose its pithiness and freshness which runs through every page, and that you may continue to suppress everything unwholesome and sickly. I will now close this letter, which is my first approach to a great and honored person.' Emboldened by the subsequent review of *Papillons*, he wrote of this review on 7 December 1832 that 'I recollect that Leipzig was at first very surprised at your criticisms of the *Papillons*, because nobody understood them, whilst I sat quiet and unobserved in a corner, knowing perfectly well the hidden meaning of your remarks. What a debt of gratitude I owe you for them!' He then countered some of the criticisms and offered his next opus, 'Paganiniana' (the *Paganini Etudes*, op. 3) – 'Please give my work your kind consideration and grant me your powerful help ... I should be extremely obliged to you, if you would allow a critical notice of my work to appear in your *Iris*. I will not wince if it should fall like a thunderbolt' – looking forward to a personal meeting. At the same time Schumann commented to Wieck of one of the Iris's favourable reviews that 'that sort of thing gives one a fresh impetus and makes one love one's work'. However, he seems subsequently to have regarded Gottfried Weber, editor of the Caecilia, as 'our greatest critic', and acknowleged his favourable reviews also.[39]

But such exposure was never matched in public performance. Virtually all performances were private, at soirées with sympathetic listeners. The performance context was Wieck and his circle, especially. From the first, Clara was the only pianist with both the interest and capacity to play it initially, and she was already a musical stimulus for Robert. But she was constrained in what she could do by audience (let alone public) taste. She gave Papillons in May and June of 1832 at a small gathering of friends, location unspecified, and of two of the Paganini studies op. 3 at Wieck's private evening on 13 January 1833. But since private performance is less easily systematically recorded, it is not possible to know who else in the circle played. Schuncke, to whom the Toccata is dedicated, played it vividly to Schumann, but apparently privately. In the 1830s the only other recorded performances were of the op. 12 Fantasiestücke, by Adolf Henselt (No. 1) and Robena Laidlaw (Nos. 1, 4, 5) – both personal acquaintances of Robert and Clara – also in 1838, and of Kinderszenen, op. 15, again in 1838, by Ferdinand David (in the unusual role of pianist), all privately. Public performances were rare, especially of complete works. Clara played the Toccata, op. 7 at her Leipzig concert in the Saal of the Hotel Pologne on 11 September 1834, and the G minor Sonata, op. 22 in the Saal of the Berlin Singakademie on 1 February 1840. It was only after Schumann's death that these slowly became more common; for example, the first public performance of the Fantasie in C, op. 17 was by Hans von Bülow in 1858.

While the piano was Schumann's primary means of expression, he soon hankered after wider genres, though doubtless some of the motivation reflects the dashing of his hopes as a pianist. Following the ambitious Piano Quartet in C minor, he now worked seriously in Leipzig, Zwickau and Schneeburg, home of his sister-in-law Rosalie, towards the G minor Symphony later in 1832. He told Töpken in

April 1833 'the whole of last winter my time was taken up by a great symphony for orchestra. It is finished now, and without being vain, I expect the most from it in the future.' But the work gave him much trouble. The first movement was performed on 18 November 1832 at Clara's concert, but to mixed reception. Schumann quotes to Wieck that the Zwickau conductor Thierfelder had written that 'I was to remodel the first movement entirely, revise all the individual parts and the score, and to polish the other movements. I am up to my eyes in work.' He then worked on a revised version at Schneeburg, in mid February 1833. Meanwhile he had sketched a second and third movement as well as a finale. The first movement was performed at Clara's Leipzig Gewandhaus concert on 29 April 1833. But its limited success still showed him that he had a long way to go.[40]

4   The *Neue Zeitschrift für Musik*, Clara and new horizons: Leipzig 1835–40

Schumann's control of the *Neue Zeitschrift für Musik*, while still at age 24, was the key moment in the establishment of a professional life in music, not least in Leipzig. For the ten years of his editorship, this connection would be infinitely more important in promoting his name than his compositions, and would consume an increasingly resented amount of his time. Yet his real creative ambitions cannot be separated from the paper: it was a way forward – and on the masthead he describes himself as 'composer'. He was realistic about the balance forced on him between journalism and composition – 'to give up the *Zeitschrift* would mean sacrificing the entire support which every artist must have if he wants to get on easily and well' – though adding reluctantly '[but] I can compose small things at all events'. Yet it was not just a necessary digression. It was for a time a mirror of his creative development in revealing his musical passions, values and capacity for interpretation of the emerging scene, and gives the observer insight into the extraordinary degree of his energy. The newspaper's rapid rise in importance can be gauged by the fact that the major Parisian publisher Schlesinger planned to buy it as early as 1837 to represent his interests in Germany, as emerges from Breitkopf & Härtel's Paris representative, Heinrich Probst.[1]

The thirty-four names listed in his first issue included not only contributors but founding supporters. The emphasis was all on practical musicians, not professional critics: on music directors and organists,

4 The first issue of the *Neue Zeitschrift für Musik* under Schumann's editorship, 2 January 1835.

teachers, composers, and only some theorists and other writers. The core was still members of his original Leipzig circle. But even though many were sympathetic or were prepared to provide contacts, he could not rely on their contributions; Schumann's exchanges show the rather nebulous position he was often in, battling away between idealism and reality. Thus, in 1836, to Dorn (now cathedral organist in Riga): 'Many thanks for the sympathy you have so often shown with our efforts. Much still remains to be done but we are young yet and the best comes with maturer years. I must also thank you for speaking about the paper and obtaining patrons for it.' And in 1839, of C. F. Becker, one of his most reliable contributors who had helped to found the paper, he requested kindly support in the form of a major review, since Schumann himself was unable to give the attention from Vienna: 'Are you not inclined to write a *detailed* review of Marx's "Theory of Composition"? It is well worth your best attention.'[2]

But his major problem was obtaining foreign correspondents. Ignaz Moscheles had first helped Schumann to get music critic and composer George Hogarth (1783–1870) as London correspondent, but they fell out and Hogarth was replaced by a lesser-known writer, John Thomson. But getting a Vienna correspondent was a persistent problem for several years, and Schumann eventually had to lean on Joseph Fischhof 'for news of the most important novelties – new operas, fresh rising talents, extraordinary musical performances etc.'. Nonetheless, Schumann managed to set up and maintain contributors throughout Germany and Austria and as far afield as Moscow, St Petersburg and later even New York, as well as London, though his mainstays were soon largely new names: [Abbé] Joseph Mainzer (1801–51), writer on music, pedagogue and priest, reporting from Paris, had soon become his most frequent correspondent, followed by Anton Wilhelm [Florentine] von Zuccalmaglio (1803–69), best known later as a collector of folk songs. Other new names were Julius Becker (1811–59), music teacher and writer; Hermann Hirshbach (1812–88), writer on music and composer; the music theorist Adolf Bernhard Marx himself (1795–1866); and the music writer and philosopher August Kahlert (1807–64). Of many occasional contributors, Schumann gave Wagner one of his earliest journalistic openings in a contribution of 1836.[3]

But the most important contributor was Schumann himself. Though he described himself to Keferstein as only the instrumental reviewer (and stressed that he never reviewed vocal music) he actually did most of the work, often under other names (as did other contributors) as well as his *Davidsbündler* names, and with names coded by numbers. But more than this was the energy he put into shaping the paper: his enthusiasm, criticism, perspective, his sense of the importance of the present yet equally the past, as well as the help he gave to his contributors, such as to Hirschbach. '[W]hat are your ideas about musical festivals, prize competitions, [the] Beethoven monument?', he wrote to Hirschbach, 'You have only to look round you; there is plenty to be uprooted and put in order ... I have altered a few words in your letter to Otten.' (G. D. Otten, the conductor of the Hamburg Philharmonic Orchestra, had just expressed his ideas on the performance of Beethoven's Ninth Symphony.) And Schumann was not slow to encourage comparison with other journals. To Dorn in September 1836 (changing his tack slightly from his first reaction to a favourable review in 1832): 'the Iris [im Gebiete der Tonkunst] supplement is just like the Iris. Very dry and artificial ... A comparison between Breitkopf & Härtel's paper [Allgemeine musikalische Zeitung] and our own would by no means be uninteresting either. But it would have to appear in a third paper – the Elegante Zeitung, Komet, or Abendzeitung.'[4]

The editorial would remain in Leipzig through his editorship. But from March 1838, following Clara's great success in Vienna, the couple planned to relocate there: it was Clara's suggestion, and Schumann eventually planned to settle no later than Easter 1840. He made an exploratory visit from September 1838 till April 1839, to flesh out the plans, already anticipating success and a new start, as to Zuccalmaglio in August 1838: 'After January 1, 1839, the Zeitschrift will be published in Vienna ... promise not to desert me here [Vienna]. Above all I would ask you to flood me with manuscripts.' Through Fischhof, he contacted the leading Viennese publishers Tobias Haslinger and Anton Diabelli. But he failed with them and others, and ultimately because of the Austrian court censor, whose approval was necessary if the paper was to be issued from Vienna: only Austro-Hungarians were allowed to publish newspapers in Vienna, and Schumann did not want to give up his Saxon citizenship. Clara, using the new status provided by her success, had written to the head of the Austrian bureau of censors to argue that the paper was musical, not political. Robert was frustrated by her absence and imagined that self-interested local politics also had an influence, telling Clara that Haslinger wanted to take over the paper 'as absolute proprietor', and – worse – noting Haslinger's comment 'you will regret ever having come here'.[5]

Following the final rebuff in March 1839, Schumann temporarily abandoned the idea of Vienna, though reluctantly, as he always wished to return. But he had enjoyed its rich cultural life, and regular visits to the opera rekindled his interest in dramatic music; he met numerous musicians and deepened his knowledge, adding to his letter to Becker that 'you [really] ought to come. How much you would find to interest you in the Imperial Library and the Society of Musicians ...' Moreover, his absence from Leipzig was giving the outward impression that he was losing interest in the *Zeitschrift*; and he was now concerned about the loss of early supporters and contributions: he commented somewhat equivocally to Clara, 'If people in Leipzig and north Germany berate me for having changed and for being cowardly and weak, I don't know what I'll do ... if it were not for you, my Clara ... I wouldn't ever leave Leipzig ...'[6]

Of the expanded and comprehensive format, the most striking feature of the *Neue Zeitschrift* was the extraordinary attention Schumann gave to many young composers and their works: in his ten years he reviewed hundreds of works large and small (indeed, he created a free supplement early on to promote them). For example, he writes to Hermann Hirschbach (a composer as well as contributor to the *Zeitschrift*): 'your efforts are the most tremendous I have met with in modern art ... but I have got some doubts about individual passages, principally as a musician. I will tell you what they are ... I have read [the overture to *Hamlet*] through, and must admire the extraordinary invention and imagination. But I cannot possibly approve of certain octaves, and the same of the quartets. More of this when we meet ... If you wish it, my frank opinion of your quartet shall appear in one of the 'quartet mornings' of the *Zeitschrift*.' Schumann was a major channel of communication regarding works now of world importance, though unknown at the time. He gave an extensive analysis of

Berlioz's *Symphonie fanstastique* in the piano transcription by Liszt, since chances of hearing a live performance were so limited, and the piano version was the only means of access; likewise an analysis of Schubert's Symphony no. 9 in C after he found it in the possession of Ferdinand Schubert and sent it to Mendelssohn for performance by the Gewandhaus, as well as the *Grosses duo* for piano, four hands. Late Beethoven was also considered new because so little known. Schumann wrote to Hirschbach regarding a review of the last quartets: 'the one in A minor is heavenly and the Adagio is beautifully clear'; and a little later, 'I am now living through some of Beethoven's quartets in the truest sense, and feel even the love and hate in them', adding, in the apparent absence of a review copy, 'would not Marx have the score of the B flat quartet [op. 130]?'.[7]

An essential part of the ethos of new music was the emerging interest in what, relative to the 'classical' repertory of Mozart, Haydn and Beethoven, was first known as 'early music' – especially that of J. S. Bach and Handel, for mastery of keyboard writing and choral effect respectively. Despite Schumann's interest in and enthusiasm for Thibaut's singing class of Renaissance and Baroque music in Heidelberg, his interest in Bach's choral music was as yet limited: it was his keyboard music that fired both Schumann's developing compositional taste and his sense of a specifically German tradition. Early in 1837, he undertook the study of Bach's *The Art of Fugue* and the organ chorale preludes, commenting to Keferstein that 'the thoughtful combinations, the poetry and humour of modern music, originates chiefly in Bach ... In fact, all the so called romantic school (of course I am speaking of Germans) approach Bach far nearer in their music than Mozart ever did ... Mozart and Haydn only had an imperfect knowledge of Bach.' Wider dissemination of Bach's keyboard music had begun with editions of *The Well Tempered Klavier* in 1800–1, greatly increased with Czerny's performing edition in 1836; Czerny's edition of *The Art of Fugue* appeared in 1839.[8]

Through the *Zeitschrift* and his residence in Leipzig Schumann met an increasing stream of important musicians, though one of the first, Chopin, was primarily drawn by Clara's reputation. Chopin called on her in mid September 1835, when she played him one of his concerto movements and two of his etudes, as well as Robert's F sharp minor Sonata. Chopin 'overpowered her with praise', and played his own music, including a Nocturne. Both Robert and Clara were overwhelmed by the meeting, and met him again the following year when Schumann stated his view of the Ballade, op. 23 as his best composition to date.[9]

It was only shortly after that Schumann met the star destined to illuminate Leipzig musical life for upwards of a decade: Felix Mendelssohn, whom he met at a party at Wieck's on the eve of Mendelssohn's first concert on 4 October 1835 as new director of the Gewandhaus in succession to Pohlenz. Schumann gave him the *Davidsbündler* name Felix Meritis. To his sister-in-law Therese, Schumann wrote 'Mendelssohn is the man to whom I look up as to a high mountain. He is a perfect god and you ought to know him'; and to Clara, 'He is certainly the most eminent man I have met.' Mendelssohn was destined to become Schumann's musical model, and source of more contacts. They became close and lunched together for a time. The relationship was founded on mutual veneration for the German classical tradition and interest in painting, as well, less obviously, as shared admiration for Jean Paul, and shared recreations in their passion for chess and billiards.[10]

However, such a relationship could never have been problem-free. First there was the gap in their respective musical positions and musical maturity. In particular, Mendelssohn initially only knew Schumann as a writer: since he had little time for writing about music, he naturally approached him as an amateur of music, lacking all the deep practical experience Mendelssohn himself had gained as a child. Thus Schumann never rested entirely assured of Mendelssohn's professional esteem in the early years of their relationship, commenting to Clara 'people say that he is not sincere with me'. But this also steeled his own identity:

> I know exactly what he is to me in music, and could go on learning from him for years. But he can also learn something from me. If I had grown up in the same circumstances as he did, and been destined for

music from childhood, I should now beat every one of you; I can feel that in the energy of my ideas. Well, everyone's life has something peculiar about it, and I will not complain of mine.[11]

Mendelssohn's tenure at the Gewandhaus attracted every important solo performer in Europe. So Schumann both met and was able to review performances by an unrivalled sequence of musicians. 'A lot of young geniuses have arrived, who often come to see me. I certainly enjoy being among younger men than myself, although, curiously enough, I have all my life chosen older men for my friends.' Of the numerous performers passing through Leipzig, his letters mention the singers Clara Novello and Pauline Viardot; the violinists Henri Vieuxtemps, Ole Bull and Karel Lipinski; and the pianists Adolf Henselt and Stephen Heller, though Franz Liszt not until 1840.[12]

Schumann's new professional responsibilities with the Neue Zeitschrift coincided with a vital change in his personal life: his rapidly changing feelings for Clara Wieck. From now on it is impossible to separate her from his innermost drives, artistic as well as personal. Certain basic realities had now become clear to him: he was an increasingly ambitious composer, yet his works were difficult, both to perform and appreciate, and he could not play them or promote them adequately himself. Clara – not just Wieck's pianistic creation, but deeply musical and already composing fluently – understood the measure of his genius, had the ability and will to respond as a player, and was clearly very fond of him. Falling in love with an already world-class musician and pianist as well as a very attractive and highly motivated young woman was essentially falling in love with his future. And his instinct was right. Although their talents were inherently competitive, what mattered most – deeper fulfilment – was more powerful. She would be a tireless supporter for the rest of his life. He trusted her to advance his cause and protect him.

When she returned from a tour of North Germany on 8 April 1836, she made a different impression on him. He later recalled to her (in 1838): 'you looked taller, different – you were no longer a child I could have played and laughed with'. For his part, Robert, as well as his extraordinary talent, had an attractive appearance, with long, brown hair; deep, expressive, dreamy blue eyes; an elegant and noble bearing; a fetching dimple; and a light tenor voice. They grew rapidly closer through 1835, with mutual declarations of love and nocturnal trysts in Leipzig at Christmas 1835; but it was to be a very difficult transition: he had to grow up as fast as she. Neither anticipated the consequence that would now unfold.[13]

As soon as Wieck realized that friendship had gone beyond companionship he reacted sharply to intervene. Not only was his control over Clara and her future, in which he had invested years of effort, being threatened, but he must have observed Schumann's obviously immature, if not unstable, temperament; his fondness for drink; and his fondness for girls – and certainly his selfish treatment of Ernestine von Fricken. This was the beginning of four years of Wieck's intensifying opposition, which would dominate their lives and test their commitment to one another to the very limit. Wieck's first strategy was to keep them apart by increasing Clara's concert tours, and immediately fixed one from mid January 1836 until April, to Dresden, then Görlitz and Breslau. At the same time he showed, when challenged, implacable opposition to Robert, and sought to plant suspicions in Clara's mind. Robert had reacted to Clara's sudden disappearance with desperation and anger: for several days he did not know where she was until she got a message to him and he tracked her down in Dresden, where they spent three 'unforgettable days' from 7 to 11 February in Wieck's absence. Wieck's reaction on discovering this was violent: in a reputedly insulting letter to Robert he threatened to shoot him if he should ever try to see Clara again. He further demanded that Clara return of all Robert's letters, which Clara, being above all dutiful at this early stage – and for long after – did. He instructed her to tell Robert that she no longer wanted to marry him, and appointed his pupil Carl Banck as teacher/escort.[14]

Wieck had the initiative. Clara and Robert were confused and Clara had no choice but to submit to his control for the next year and a half. From 10 February 1836 to August 1837 not a spoken word passed between the couple, and for the vital written word they had to use friends as messengers, increasingly – especially in 1838–9 – resorting to myriad subterfuges in the addressing of letters for safe receipt to avoid Wieck's spies, and becoming increasingly paranoid about whom they could trust. Clara's return to Leipzig in April 1836 led to awkward social situations when their friends took sides. This was a time of immense stress: neither could really be sure of the other's loyalty and they were forced to analyse their feelings. As well as throwing himself into Leipzig's musical life and the company of his new contacts – Mendelssohn, Ferdinand David, William Sterndale Bennett (an English pupil of Mendelssohn's), the Voigts and others – Schumann also fell back into his old dissolute habits of escape. Clara now either doubted his moral character, or was prompted to do so by the father. Indeed, Schumann later admitted to Clara in January 1838 that 'the darkest time was when ... I forcefully loved a woman who had me half ensnared' (widely concluded to be a return to Christel). Finally, however, in mid August 1837, Clara broke the silence. Acting through their mutual lawyer friend E. A. Becker, she invited Schumann to a forthcoming performance at the Börsensaal in Leipzig on 13 August 1837, in which she would include three of his Symphonic Etudes. He took this as a hopeful sign and attended, though he was still suspicious of her relation with Banck. He wrote on 13 August asking a simple 'yes' as token of her willingness to present her father with a letter in which Wieck was requested to bless Schumann's 'spiritual bond' with Clara: 'Are you still faithful and steadfast? [You are] the dearest [to me] in all the world', and insisting on confidentiality. Her joyful acceptance on 15 August sealed the 'dawn of a second alliance'. Aided by Clara's maid Nanni the pair began a correspondence of 275 letters by 1839; both later regarded 14 August as their real engagement day.[15]

The impending period of separation through Clara's seven-month tour to Dresden, Vienna and Prague, from 15 October 1837 till May 1838, was to pose a profound challenge. On Robert's part this was the need to overcome his denial concerning the actual implacable opposition of his erstwhile teacher and friend, to maintain a civilized balance in his own feelings, and to cope with the profound threat to his emotional equilibrium posed by separation. On Clara's, she must consider as well her musical and filial needs from Wieck. Robert was, at first, in complete denial about Wieck. He now intended writing to him to obtain Clara's hand on her eighteenth birthday, 13 September 1837. But Clara, already more attuned to reality, was horrified at the possible outcome and insisted first on a prior meeting face to face with Robert: their first private meeting since February of the previous year, to take place on 9 September 1837; she was later to recall of it 'you were so stiff, so cold'. Schumann's letter to Wieck on 13 September 1837 began with an apology and ended with a plea for Wieck's friendship. But Wieck replied completely negatively, and Robert subsequently recalled a 'terrible' conversation with him: 'such coldness, such maliciousness, such confusion and contradictions'. Wieck again demanded no contact, at least only in public – 'a real spectacle for everyone', as Robert commented, and pressed on with plans for Clara's concert tours. Robert continued to her on 18 September that Wieck insisted that marriage was to be out of the question: Clara was too young, would lose out as an artist; and they needed more money than they thought, as she was accustomed to a certain standard of living. Robert was crushed and now entered a period of intense emotional turmoil.[16]

The separation now induced further tensions, misunderstandings and recriminations. Personal loyalty was the first issue: they taunted each other. Schumann was naturally very sensitive to Clara's attractiveness to rich suitors, which was very great and which Wieck did nothing to discourage. Her artistic success in Vienna depressed Schumann, and he was sarcastic about her social fêting; and on his side, he did nothing to discourage her jealousy either. Clara was well aware that he was still attracted by the new performers that came to his attention through the Neue Zeitschrift, notably the soprano Clara Novello, whose gifts and success he reported to her, and the pianist Robena Laidlaw (1819–1901), who, as he lets drop, 'has a crush on me, I think ... she gave me a lock of hair, just so you know'. Then for Robert there was a growing

5 Königliche und Kaiserliche Österreichische Kammervirtuosin Clara Wieck. Lithograph by L. Staub, Vienna, 1838.

issue of status. To spare his feelings Clara did not first tell him of her receiving the great court honour of Royal Austrian Chamber Virtuoso (Königliche und Kaiserliche Kammervirtuosin) and of her rapturous triumph at the Musikverein, fêted by aristocracy and crowned heads; when subsequently in Vienna in 1838–9, Schumann himself became particularly conscious of his comparatively lesser professional position and felt the need of distinction of his own: 'I certainly have received an honorary title also [he had been made an honorary member of the Gesellschaft der Musikfreunde] but it is not the same thing.' Using both his sister-in-law's and Keferstein's connections, Schumann sought to get a doctorate from the University of Jena on the basis of his status as a prominent editor, and as a composer.[17]

Clara was certainly buoyed by her huge success in Vienna, where she had now become regarded as a leading player, noted for her musical maturity (her programmes, becoming more serious, now included Beethoven and Bach), musical dedication and directness of execution, with striking absence of fashionable affectation: she was even celebrated in verse by the national poet, Franz Grillparzer. But she was also realistic about public success, and notably was taking more charge of her own life. On their exhausted return from the Vienna tour on 14 May 1838, Wieck was now growing tired of coping with her growing independence. From now on she increasingly organized everything herself – including transport and the booking of halls. But he still had plans to keep her touring, now to France, for which she would embark for Paris on 8 January, arriving 6 February and travelling until 14 August, with a French woman as travel companion. Wieck hoped it would be an organizational failure. But no: Paris built her network of influential friends, as had Vienna.[18]

Schumann's own unsuccessful return to Leipzig from Vienna on 8 April 1839 coincided with bad news from Clara. She had learnt through Emilie List, to whom Wieck had written, that he was threatening to disinherit her, to keep her money from concerts, and to initiate a legal process that would last between three and five years 'unless I let go of you'. Now she was really frightened of the future: would she have to abandon music, acquire her own fortune to live, or even become a housewife? By the end of May 1839, Wieck had renewed earlier demands insisting that the couple were not to live in Saxony during his lifetime. Although there was no question of Wieck's preventing the marriage – Clara would be 21 in little over a year – the real point was the framing of future family relationships: Clara's continuing anguish, torn between her judgment of, yet need of, her father as continuing teacher, and the strain this would put on her relationship with

Robert. Wieck's draconian vengefulness and her own professional independence had also now made her much more aware of the need for money.[19]

Though Schumann first sought to negotiate through his lawyer, Wieck's negative reply determined him finally to go to court. To Becker he wrote 'my grief is terrible. I hardly think I shall live to hear the decision of the court. A friendly compromise is not to be thought of.' Equally disillusioned, Clara signed the affidavit on 15 June,1839. Wieck was furious at this presumed disloyalty and refused to have her live in the family house or receive any support. Clara left in September to live with her mother Marianne Bargiel – who sided with her and Robert – in Berlin, whence she would set off on concert tours until close to the wedding. Schumann filed his complaint on 16 July 1839 with the Leipzig court. In response, Wieck now began to temporize with increasingly extreme demands and queries, mainly concerning Schumann's income. By now even Clara no longer believed in his protective stance. These demands were refused by the court and a new date of 18 December set in Dresden. But on 14 December 1839, Wieck again filed lengthy papers to stall the proceedings: he questioned their capacity for happy union, charging that Schumann was lazy, unreliable and conceited; unable to support himself; had squandered his inheritance; had paralysed one of his fingers; was a mediocre composer whose music was too difficult to perform; was an alcoholic; and didn't love Clara, but wanted to exploit her. Although Wieck appeared on 18 December, his erratic behaviour damaged his credentials. The way forward was becoming clear. Though Clara was ambivalent in court (she would not now see her father again till well after the marriage), the judge was moved by her loyalty to him and ruled that permission would be withheld if proof of financial irresponsibility and alcoholism could be found. Wieck was given until 14 January. His appeal arrived at the court at the last minute on 13 January 1840. On 26 January he handed in another long disputation about money.[20]

Schumann's rebuttal was presented to the court on 13–14 February. He tried to persuade the court he would have no problem in earning the minimum amount of money Wieck demanded: an annual income of 1,500 thalers – 500 from interest from invested securities and the rest from his newspaper, compositions and so on – quoting assets of 12,688 thalers. But these were inflated figures: he did not earn 1,000 thalers from compositions per year. However, they were accepted, and the remaining charge of alcoholism soon dismissed after supporting letters as to Schumann's quiet character were easily obtained through friends. Wieck had to admit that he could not corroborate the charge of drunkenness: no one would testify, and his supporters were now embarrassed by his behaviour, which included saying that Clara was not worth the sacrifice he would have to make to protect her from an unhappy marriage. By now Schumann had also obtained his doctorate from Jena.[21]

But Schumann had still desperately to engage in damage limitation after Wieck's vicious professional defamation of both Clara and himself, since Wieck had begun to and continued to circulate printed copies of his Declaration against them amongst concert managers in every city in which Clara was to play. Schumann now sought redress by suing Wieck: in June 1840 he successfully charged Wieck with defamation of character with the upper court in Dresden. It is not clear whether Wieck served the eighteen-day prison term that Schumann refers to; nor could he provide the necessary redress. Schumann wrote on 31 August 1840 to the censor of German periodical journals asking him whether he had no influence

> to stop the mention of a personal matter in the society papers (as happened only last week in the *Planet*), and to do so in such a manner as not to make matters still worse. How very grateful those concerned would be to you! If private affairs in general are not intended for the public, how much less such a very delicate subject, the discussion of which must necessarily deeply wound the lady whom it concerns and myself. Lines . . . only dictated by my intense longing for peace.[22]

One factor that cannot be ignored in Schumann's growing attachment to Clara is the death of his mother. She died suddenly on 4 February 1836 aged about 70. Schumann had heard that she was ill only shortly before her death, but had no immediate cause for alarm and was, rather, consumed with anxiety over Clara's sudden disappearance to Dresden and his visit there: he did not know that his mother had already died when he left Leipzig on 7 February. He also missed her funeral, only arriving at Zwickau for the reading of the will. Her death inevitably weakened his relation to Zwickau and shifted the emphasis quickly towards Leipzig (after Eduard's death on 10 April 1839, he would say that Zwickau too was 'now dead' to him). The role of female confidante and link to the family was taken by Eduard's wife, Therese, to whom, since the death of Carl's wife Rosalie in 1833, he had become increasingly close. He clearly regarded her as especially sympathetic to him and she certainly gave him a supportive female voice through the coming traumas of the struggle for Clara; he already acknowledged his dependence on her in November 1836.[23]

Robert's liaison with Clara was inherently difficult for the family. By the time they knew that Robert was really serious about her, she had become a world-renowned pianist. Though Schumann's mother had thought them ideally suited, she had little concept of Clara's rapidly ascending artistic status, nor likely the family either: she still thought of Clara as a musically matched fellow student. Nor was it easy for Clara to maintain contact in her circumstances. And he was defensive about the fact that she had little contact with them: 'Clara has long been wanting to write to you herself'; and 'she has not yet found time to write, she can hardly manage to write to me, so don't be angry with her'. Robert continued to be on the defensive with his family. He already knew – as well as being conscious of their limited understanding of his music – that they were suspicious of his plans about moving to Vienna and lack of economic realism.[24]

Robert also needed Therese in lieu of his mother, for intercession with Eduard for continued advances against his inheritance, which his lifestyle now increasingly required. Thus, in his November 1836 letter to her, he wanted 50 thalers by the end of the month and another 50 in December for short-term expenses: 'I could still borrow of anyone, from David, for instance, who has placed his purse at my disposal; but, as you may imagine, one only does that sort of thing as a last resource.' In fact, he did lean on them, having written a little earlier to Dorn 'I have sat down with the firm resolve of working off my old debt.' But this was obviously professionally embarrassing.[25]

But the prospect of marriage, however premature it turned out to be in 1838, focused Robert's mind on finances even more. He now needed not just small advances but larger sums. He had to project an image of respectability to Wieck, writing to Eduard and Carl on 19 March 1838 'I must not appear before Wieck empty-handed', and to Therese on 17 December 1838 'though anything but extravagant, still I must look respectable', adding that 'at first, before I knew the cheap places, that cost me a great deal of money'. He reasoned to Clara in January 1838 'I want to get to the point where I have *at least* twice what I need for myself, normally 600 to 700 Thalers' (Wieck had wanted around 2,000).[26]

Schumann now forcefully proposed to his brothers the provision of a large lump sum from his part of the family investments, though paid in instalments:

> You are to henceforth to pay me 600 Thalers every Easter, besides the interest, or if possible, rather more – but I will be contented with that. In this way you will, without feeling it very much, pay off your debt in six or seven years' time and I shall not receive it in driblets, which are apt to burn holes in one's pockets. Then, when we first get to Vienna (1840) I shall have a capital in hand of 2,400 Thalers, which I need not touch until then, as the income I make from the *Zeitschrift* and my own compositions is steadily increasing, and will amply suffice for my personal wants. Just consider what depends on it.

He then wrote, precipitously, to Clara in April 1838: 'I'll receive 1,200 from my brothers at Easter, and more, too'; and again, in May 1838, 'as I mentioned in my long letter [of 13 April] they will pay off 1,200 a year. It's totally secured by Carl's house and business which is worth six times the 4,000 he owes me.'[27]

The emphasis had changed by 1839 with Eduard's illness, which frightened Schumann for their future economic security (and had precipitated his return from Vienna). It prompted his comment to Clara that Eduard's death could be '[an economic] misfortune for us, too. If I were to become a very poor man and told you to leave me because I brought you nothing but trouble – wouldn't you leave me then?'. He meant that if the business was not sold – and he did not want to take it on himself at this stage – its future would be unclear and equity in the stock would diminish or disappear. Wieck had already claimed that Schumann's figures were wrong, and that the business was in the red: and Schumann's (wavering) estimates of its value may suggest that it had not generated good profits over the years. Nor did Schumann wish to realize the other investments with Carl.[28]

However, Schumann's financial situation improved significantly after Eduard's death, and he noted to Clara that he was 'almost guilty' at their wealth. He quotes in May 1839: 'Bonds 1,000 [thalers]; Eduard's business 3,540; Carl's business 4,000; from Eduard's estate 1,500'. By 26 July 1839 the documents presented for the legal process showed lower numbers: 'Bonds 1,600; Gebrüder Schumann in Zwickau 2,900; Carl Schumann in Schneeburg 3,777; part of Eduard's estate 3,330'. But most important, his share in Gebrüder Schumann did not diminish: the family business was successfully sold to Therese's new husband, Friedrich Fleischer, thus preserving her part as well as his (about which Robert had been very concerned on her behalf as a widow). But the depth of Schumann's economic concerns at the time is clear from the fact that he seriously considered himself buying the business jointly with the Leipzig publisher Robert Friese and making his business entirely musical. But though Schumann was now infinitely better off in cash terms, that would all change with marriage and a family because of the need for higher income from limited equity. Above all, the legal process had served to reveal just how little Schumann actually earned from his own financial efforts: most income and assets were from other sources.[29]

Though by 1839 Schumann's longer-term financial security seemed clearer, and marriage a growing possibility, the years from 1835 had imposed severe emotional and physical pressure upon him. The death of his mother in February 1836 could not have come at a more difficult time: that so little reaction is recorded by him seems indicative of its importance, even allowing all the current pressures: he did not record the anniversary till two years later. By this time, Schumann's vulnerability to pressure had become a factor in his life that could not be ignored. Though nothing again as terrifying as the event of 1833 (he had now passed a marker with the trauma of the deaths of Julius and Rosalie), each of the developing personal and professional pressures served to bring on worry and often periodic bouts of depression. The death of his new friend Schuncke in December 1834, that of his mother, the sudden separation from Clara, and the equally sudden and continuing attack by Wieck and the ensuing loneliness of separation affected him deeply through 1836–8. From July 1839 he also told Clara of regular headaches, alarming her: 'your headaches really scare me – aren't you taking anything for them? What does Dr. Reuter say?'. It was just before her Vienna debut, in a letter of 29 November 1837, that Schumann had also first mentioned to her his proneness to brooding and depression, though this was probably no surprise to her by then: 'I'd like to reveal to you someday a deep secret about a *serious, psychological affliction* which befell me some time ago; but it requires a lot of time and involves the years from … 1833 on. You shall hear of it some day, and then you will have the key to all my actions and to my odd personality' (Schumann's emphasis). All Robert's fears – of the uncertainties of their relationship and plans, of the chance that Clara might believe her father right about him and whether he was in fact unstable – all created over-excitement followed by exhaustion. In April 1839 Robert again warned Clara about his health – though also in June 1839 about hers as well. In January 1840, she writes to him alarmed: '*Take care of your health* – do you hear, Robert? Write *at once* and tell me how you are' (Clara's emphasis).[30]

His initial response to the pressures had been to fall back on bouts of heavy drinking around Christmas 1836 with an old companion: a music teacher, Wilhelm Ulex. Schumann's lifestyle, which included a need to play music in his apartments, naturally caused problems. In 1836 he had to negotiate with his landlady, Frau Devrient, to stay, since his behaviour disturbed the rest of the house; so when he wanted to come back to her lodgings in 1839, he had to use his charms all over again. But he fought back against negative impacts on his well-being: the challenge of the *Neue Zeitschrift*, the thrill of composition, and his hopes for a new life of creative and personal fulfilment with Clara drove him forward. On 31 May 1840 he wrote to her, overcome with the fluency of his inspiration: 'Oh, it's so painfully clear to me that music should have been the only thing in my life. Everything else is really unworthy by contrast.'[31]

Schumann's horror of losing his fortune confirms how much he had been able to take for granted financially in pursuing his creative ambitions: nothing was now stopping his onward development. He was indeed now composing with greater ease and assurance (though all pieces to 1840 would still be for piano) and becoming by 1839 aware of his maturing compositional technique. Again, in the revealing letter to Clara of 11 March 1839, of the *Humoresque*: 'look how quickly things are going for me. Conceived, written and printed. That's how I like it. I finished 12 sheets in a week.' And around the same time to Simonin de Serre: 'formerly I used to ponder a long time; now I hardly correct a single note. Everything comes to me spontaneously.'[32]

And not only the outward stimulus of musical ideas. Schumann defended the individuality, even strangeness of his music – which brings together increasingly diverse tendencies – in broader terms, as to the scholar and composer Eduard Krüger in June 1839: 'literature, surroundings, mental and physical experiences, also [influence] me', having given a fuller sense of this to Clara earlier:

everything that goes on in the world affects me, politics, literature, people – I think about everything in my own way, and have to express my feelings, and then I find an outlet in music. That's why so many of my compositions are so difficult to understand; they relate to distant, often significant concerns because all the strange things in this age touch me, and I must then express them musically. That's also why so few [modern] compositions satisfy me because, aside from all their technical faults, they indulge in musical sentiments of the lowest order, in ordinary lyrical effusions, etc.; the best that can be achieved that way does not even approach the beginning of my musical world. The former may be a flower, but the latter is a more inspired poem; the former is a lyric impulse, but the latter is a work of poetic consciousness.[33]

The stimulus for all this was Clara; indeed, she dominates almost all compositions of the period, either as emotional prompt – their joys and sorrows alike motive for musical expression, often communicated by musical themes, many her own – or, and often, as a practical advisor on performance. Indeed, the dramas of their personal lives had now begun to provide more than enough impetus to the autobiographical character of his music: he composed to keep his emotional equilibrium as well as to realize his imaginative world. Looking back in 1839 he put it plainly to Dorn:

> Besides, there is someone on my side who encourages and elevates me – Clara ... I dare say the struggles I have endured about Clara are to a certain extent reflected in my music, and I am sure you understand it. The concerto [*Concerto sans Orchester*, op. 14], sonata [Fantasia in C, as first titled (op. 17)], the *Davidsbündlertänze*, *Kreisleriana* and *Novelletten* were almost entirely inspired by her.

He had already written to Clara at Easter of the previous year: 'It's strange, but if I write to you as much as I am now, I can't compose. You receive the music then, may it be music to you.' And however one interprets the roots of creative stimulus, Schumann certainly attached them in his conscious mind to Clara almost exclusively.[34]

The Fantasia in C, op. 17, Schumann's supreme achievement in the piano sonata genre (in three continuous movements) followed the completion of the Sonata in F sharp minor, op. 11, and the huge new F minor Sonata, op. 14, with its slow movement as variations on the 'Andantino de Clara Wieck', a new piece of hers. The Fantasia in C was occasioned by Schumann's decision to write a major work inspired by Beethoven for the funds towards a Beethoven statue in Bonn (destined, ironically, to be one of Schumann's last places of contact with the outside world). It was first conceived in September 1836 as 'Sonata for Beethoven', then noted to the publisher Kistner as a contribution 'by Florestan and Eusebius for Beethoven's monument' titled *Ruine. Trophaeen. Palmen*. By March 1838, Schumann speaks to Clara of a Fantasia in three movements (now called *Ruine, Siegerbogen und Sternbild*, and *Dichtungen*, to distinguish it from the *Fantasiestücke*, op. 12), and called 'a profound lament for you'. Subsequently, in 1839, he explained to her that it was she who had actually driven its creation. '[Y]ou can understand the Fantasie only if you remember the unfortunate summer of 1836 when I gave you up'; and 'the "tone" in the motto is *you*, isn't it? I almost believe it', alluding to the poetic quotation from Friedrich Schlegel on the first page: 'through all the tones in earth's many coloured dream, there sounds for the secret listener, one soft, long-drawn note'. The first movement is further punctuated by allusions to the final song of Beethoven's song cycle to a distant beloved, *An die ferne Geliebte*, op. 98, beginning 'Nimm sie hin, denn, diese Lieder' ('So take them, these songs ...'), poignantly reiterated at the movement's close.[35]

Kreisleriana expresses Schumann's identification with E. T. A. Hoffmann's reckless and eccentric Kapellmeister Johannes Kreisler, in *Fantasiestücke in Callot's Manier*', all brilliantly captured in eight contrasted movements, whose first movement takes the listener straight into his mad obsessions and modulating moods. Schumann had Clara's playing in the forefront of his mind: 'You and one of your ideas play the main role in it, and I want to dedicate it to you – yes, to you and nobody else.'[36]

In complete contrast to both these works, it was hope, not hopelessness, that drove the *Davidsbündlertänze*, on which he worked feverishly in October 1837 to be ready for Clara's mid-October departure in 1837 to Dresden and Vienna, while still planning a wedding and about to plan a move to Vienna. Later he told her that there were 'many wedding motifs in the *Tänze*. I wrote them in the most wonderful state of excitation that I can ever remember. I'll explain them to you sometime'; and soon after, 'they are my property ... the story is a complete *Polterabend* [stag party], and you can imagine the beginning and the end'. He signed many of the eighteen short pieces 'F' and 'E'. Some have verbal comments, and there are several quotes, the work beginning with Clara's

Mazurka from her *Soirées musicales*, op. 6, duly identified as 'Motto de Clara Wieck'. The eight *Novelletten* were not named after a novel, but after Clara Novello, Schumann sheepishly explaining to Clara that 'Wiecketten ... sounds [too cumbersome].' Clara also appears in no. 8 in the first edition, where 'Stimme aus der Ferne' denotes the musical quote from her Nocturne, op. 6, no. 2.[37]

While still involved with the *Novelletten* in February and March 1838 Schumann quickly finished off 'about thirty quaint little things, from which I have selected twelve, and called them *Kinderszenen*' (*Scenes from Childhood*, op. 15). These pieces clearly anticipate family life: indeed, he would refer to them years later in 1848 to Reinecke as 'reflections of an adult for other adults'. They evoke a child's dreamings ('Of Foreign Lands and Peoples') and moods ('Important Event'; 'Almost Too Serious'), as well as capturing the domestic scene, with games ('Catch Me if You Can') or descriptions ('By the Fireside'; 'Child Falling Asleep'), until the whole sequence is framed by the poet's closing voice. These must surely recapture Schumann's own youthful improvisations of events and people. Before leaving Vienna in May 1839, he could boast significant progress on another twelve pieces or so. On 11 March 1839 he wrote that he had 'sat at the piano the entire week and composed and laughed and cried all at the same time. You will find all of this nicely depicted in my opus 20, the *Grosse Humoresque* which is already at the printers.' The third line had an inner voice, to be imagined, not played – his own, but identical to Clara's *Romanze* in G minor – heard as evidence of their musical identity: 'It's so strange how our feelings correspond.' This period also included the *Arabesque* and *Blumenstück* (opp. 18, 19), and a *Leichenfanstasie* ('funeral fantasy'): conceived just before he left Vienna, written under the premonition of his brother Eduard's death and published as a four-movement piece under another Hoffmannesque title, *Nachtstücke* (op. 23). In October 1839 Schumann wrote to Clara that he had begun about fifty new works, though many were not completed, or were reworked or issued later.[38]

The originality of the pianism that Schumann produced between 1835 and 1840 still did not translate into significant performance recognition, however. He told Clara 'None of my things are really for public performance.' Nor was this due to Wieck, who never ever prevented Clara playing Robert's works publicly: though perhaps tailoring for Robert's consumption, Clara none the less said to him at the beginning of 1838 '[father] always raves about you to everyone, and he has me play your pieces. Recently he gave a big party (among the people he invited were Vienna's greatest poets) just so they could hear Carnaval.' Rather, the music was largely beyond early audiences and depended entirely on sensitive and imaginative reception for appreciation as single items within larger programmes at private performances. In February 1838 Clara played the Toccata and first Sonata for a private circle during her tours in Dresden and Breslau. In April 1838 she played Carnaval to Liszt, which is how he first heard it. Liszt in turn played Carnaval to Schumann, impressing him greatly, though Clara did not like Liszt's performance. Indeed, Schumann dedicated the Fantasia in C to Liszt and the pianist took the work into the public domain early, giving its first, though incomplete, public performance (of ten selected movements) at the Leipzig Gewandhaus on 30 March 1840. But Liszt also observed that he never received his accustomed public response from Schumann's works, though he reciprocated in dedicating his B minor Sonata to Schumann.[39]

Both Clara and Schumann were acutely aware of the problem of public promotion. He was very firm with her in January 1839: 'You often play Carnaval to those who aren't familiar with anything of mine – wouldn't the Fantasiestücke be better for that? One piece offsets the other in Carnaval, and not everyone can stand that; in the Fantasiestücke, however, one can relax and indulge oneself – but do as you like'. And he had told her in March 1838 'You were wise not to play my [Etudes symphoniques]. That sort of thing is not suited to the general public.' Clara was equally and acutely conscious of the problem of promoting such individual and often strange music by the standards of the time. She wanted works for an audience, something for her to play in Paris:

Listen, Robert, would you compose something brilliant, easy to understand, something that has no titles, but is a complete, continuing piece, not too long and not too short? I would like so much to have something of yours to play at concerts that is suited to a general audience. I know this is humiliating for a genius of course, but expedience demands it.

The *Faschingsschwank aus Wien* (*Carnival Jest from Vienna*), op. 26, of 1839–40 is perhaps a response to this. The first movement has a disguised quotation of the *Marseillaise*: a musical greeting to Clara in Paris, as well as a thumb at the censors. The second movement, Romance, also refers to Clara's piece in the same key of G minor. Responding to Clara's request to simplify the 'far too difficult' last movement of the G minor Sonata he drafted an entirely new finale in mid December 1838. But Schumann was equally resistant to artistic constraint, insisting that he did not want to sacrifice his imagination for popularity.[40]

Schumann pressed on with wider publication opportunities in Leipzig. Buoyed by the completion of *Carnaval* and the *Etudes symphoniques* he tried to make a new start with Breitkopf & Härtel. He wrote to Raimund Härtel on 22 December 1835:

> I should like to know whether you would feel inclined, a little later on, to publish one or more of my compositions; they are short and would not entail much expense. There are some brilliant sonatas, *Variations symphoniques*, *Fasching* [later *Carnaval*] and others. That one cannot make one's fortune with such things, nobody knows better than myself. However, give them a trial. I make no pretensions.

Then, on 22 May 1837, with more focus to Hermann Härtel:

> I take this opportunity of asking you, as I have intended doing for a long time, whether you will publish two of my compositions. One is called *Carnaval*, the other *Phantasien* [*Fantasiestücke*] for pianoforte. The *Carnaval* will appear at the same time, at Schlesinger's in Paris, though in a slightly modified form, and altered to suit the French; so I would ask you to let their name appear on the title page as well as your own. Perhaps you will have a characteristic title-page lithographed according to my own ideas, but we will talk that over. Each composition would consist of between twenty and twenty-four plates.[41]

As well as *Carnaval*, Breitkopf took the *Fantasiestücke*, which appeared as op. 12. On 7 August 1837 Schumann specified to Breitkopf 'it will be best if you bring them out in two books. Each will contain about twelve or thirteen pages. If both books could appear by the last day of September that would oblige me greatly.' When *Kinderszenen* appeared he was thrilled, writing to Hermann Härtel on 2 March 1839 from Vienna: 'I cannot tell you what pleasure the *Kinderszenen* have given me; it is the prettiest thing I have met with in my musical publications. May you be well rewarded. My misgivings about the misprints have been fulfilled but the blame lies with the bad manuscript.'[42]

Schumann was still reticent about exposing his music: 'any artificial instigation of public opinion by the artist himself is an abomination to me. Whatever is strong will make its own way.' He was reserved about receiving reviews of his music in the *Neue Zeitschrift*, stating that his paper existed for the benefit of others (though a review had appeared from Moscheles as early as 1836 of op. 11); and he was very resistant to the suggestion of influencing Fink through Breitkopf & Härtel to receive reviews in the *Allgemeine musikalische Zeitung*. But he was also very aware of what was advertised and known, and prodded his contacts for further exposure. In January 1837 he wrote to Keferstein: '[will you] insert a notice of my compositions in the *Caecilia*. I would rather that you made a regular résumé. The *Caecilia* is the only paper where anything can be said about me.' He was thrilled when Liszt wrote the first French review in the *Gazette musicale de Paris*, and wanted to meet him in Vienna.[43]

At the same time he mentioned to Clara an appreciative letter from Simonin de Sire, commenting: 'I am really quite happy that my compositions are finding acceptance here and there – I'm writing more easily and clearly by far now, and, I think, more gracefully; I used to patch smaller passages together, and the result was many strange things but little that was beautiful.' To the organist W.H. Rieffel: 'I was again delighted with what you said about my piano compositions. If I could but find more people who understood my meaning! I hope in this respect I shall succeed better with songs. One of these days, look at my series of Heine's songs. Some more will follow shortly, also some part songs.' Therefore he had little income, but the pleasure of improving sales, reflecting the exposure of the reviews, though not yet public performance. Of *Carnaval* and *Fantasiestücke*, he quotes 250 to 300 copies; of *Kinderszenen*, 'which have only been out for six months', 300 to 350.[44]

By the late 1830s Schumann wanted to write music other than for piano. Perhaps inspired by Mendelssohn's three string quartets, op. 44 as well as his enthusiasm for the late Beethoven quartets, he had looked forward to his own first quartets, stating 'the piano is getting too limited for me', and telling Fischhof in a letter of 3 April 1838 that his first quartet was underway. Another quartet was contemplated in June, though Clara was here defensive about his expertise, and he again reacted sharply to her desire for accessibility. By 1839 he wanted bigger genres, in January working on a *Konzertsatz* in D minor for piano and orchestra – 'the [*Konzertsatz* is] something between a symphony, a concerto and a grand sonata. I see that I can't write a concerto for a virtuoso: I'll have to think of something else' – though it was never published in Schumann's lifetime. And by 13 March 1840, he was even beginning to plan the extension of his artistic brotherhood into entirely new territory in an opera based on a story in the second part of Hoffmann's *Serapionsbrüder* in which Schumann had long been interested: *Doge und Dogaressa*.[45]

5 Married life: Leipzig 1840–4

Robert and Clara were married at the parish church of the village of Schönefeld (now on the outskirts of Leipzig) on the morning of Saturday 12 September 1840, the day before Clara's twenty-first birthday. The service was conducted by an old school friend of Robert's in Zwickau. After all the pressures they just wanted a quiet and personal service (neither was a dogmatic believer). Clara recalls that:

> it began with a choral[e], then the minister Wildenhahn ... gave a short and simple address but one which spoke from the heart to the heart. My whole heart was filled with thankfulness to Him who had at last led us across so many rocks and cliffs to each other; my most fervent prayer was that it might please Him to preserve my Robert to me for many, many years.

Only close friends were present, including Clara's mother and her stepfather Adolf Bargiel, with Moritz Reuter and E. A. Becker as the witnesses, and socializing continued through the day with visits to and from other close friends. Clara again:

> We danced a little – there was no romping, but all faces showed heartfelt satisfaction. It was a beautiful day, and even the sun, which had hidden itself for many days past, poured its mild rays upon us as we drove to the wedding, as if it would bless our union. Nothing disturbed us on this day, and it shall be inscribed in this book as the happiest and most important of my life.[1]

6 Robert Schumann. Lithograph by Joseph Kriehuber, published by Mechetti, Vienna, 1839.

Schumann's desire for children was consistent with the idealized picture of family life that had emerged so vividly in *Kinderszenen*. In fact he would have a much bigger family than his brothers or parents, and would later comment to Mendelssohn that he had told Clara 'one cannot have enough. It is the greatest blessing we can have on earth.' Clara was to bear him eight children, with at least two miscarriages and one infant loss in a mere fourteen years of married life. Two children were born to them in the 1840–44 period: Marie in 1841 and Elise, in 1843. It was the birth of Elise that now led Wieck to seek reconciliation with the pair, doubtless a calculating move on his part, with Robert's growing reputation and Clara's ability to maintain her independence. An invitation arrived for Robert in Leipzig on 16 December 1843:

> For Clara's sake and the world's, we can no longer keep each other at distance. You are now a family man – is any more explanation needed? Where art is concerned we have always agreed – I was even your teacher – my judgments determined the course of your present career. I don't need to tell you that I will co-operate with your talent and support your beautiful efforts. You are joyfully expected at Dresden by your father Fr. Wieck.

This eased Clara's tensions, though she had doubtless been lobbying in private, and Robert accepted it graciously, at least externally. Robert confirmed the reconciliation 'of Clara and old W[ieck]' to Johann Verhulst in June 1843.[2]

From the start, this was destined to be a great artistic marriage of a pair dedicated to their art and its mutual deepening, and the sharing of a wider culture to the full. Domesticity was initially unknown to either of them. Among the gifts Schumann gave Clara was a marriage diary, maintained with varying regularity for four years for communication and reflection, and including rules of industry, thrift and loyalty. Robert begins the 'First Week': 'only few events, abundant happiness', and Clara: 'this love makes me inexpressibly happy. We rejoice in good fortune never known to me before – my father always scoffed at so-called domestic bliss. How I pity those who are unfamiliar with it! They are only half alive.'[3]

Robert assumed the dominant role, at least initially. He sought to deepen Clara's culture, which had suffered grossly through her development as a child prodigy, according to his own taste, giving her much more confidence. She owed him her first contact with great literature, of which she had read practically nothing: they studied the role of music in Shakespeare's plays, the poetry of Byron, the plays of Victor Hugo (which she disliked: 'the frivolous, vulgar, mutilated and improbable ... these sorts of works are only for the French ... for a healthy German mind such a work is abominable'), though

7 First married home, 5 Inselstrasse (now no. 18), Leipzig. Today the Robert-und-Clara-Schumann-Haus.

she found reading aloud from Jean Paul, with which she must have become rather familiar, tiresome. Her musical tastes continued to change: virtuoso display works, often based on opera arias, which she still played, yielded increasingly to an interest in the symphonies as well as concertos of Beethoven, to the string quartets of Beethoven, Mozart and Haydn, to Bach fugues (studied jointly in September 1840), and to his B minor Mass, as well as to contrapuntal exercises and score reading; their joint studies even took them to the Johanneskirche in Leipzig where they attempted to play the organ (though not to their satisfaction)– 'we did not handle it with any accomplishment'.[4]

The new Schumann home now also became the focus of their professional as well as social and domestic life. Number 5 Inselstrasse (now 18) was situated in the district of Friedrichsstadt, to the east side of the city: newly built elegant houses with gardens. Clara's reference to this as a 'cozy nook' gives perhaps an indication of the high standard of living they both took for granted. The accommodation included a large wide music room – more of the dimension of a small hall, with an ante-room, though not well insulated for sound – as well as spacious living quarters. Access to the beautiful rural environs that Robert already knew well was easy, and they liked to take walks, not least to Connewitz. The high point of their now relatively simple life was home music and reception of musical friends who shared their values and enthusiasms, and with the numerous visitors to Leipzig. 'Sundays have become our music days, alternating between our house and Mendelssohn's. Whatever we bring with us will be played.' Clara recalls her '*debut* as a housewife' with the elite of Leipzig's musical life and Liszt as visitor: 'Among those making up the party were the Freges, the Härtels and the Davids, and Liszt was the life and soul.' And for all their potential musical differences, Liszt became deeply involved in Schumann's compositions, and remained a close friend and visitor.[5]

Now the Schumanns could also entertain the great visiting musicians more easily, and their visitors' book is a *Who's Who* of the musical world. Of composers and writers: William Sterndale Bennett, Robert Franz, Niels Gade, Adolf Henselt, Ferdinand Hiller, Theodor Kirchner, Heinrich Marschner, Ignaz Moscheles, Louis Spohr, Robert Franz and Moritz Hauptmann. Schumann encountered Hector Berlioz many times when he visited to conduct a series of concerts in 1843, and likewise Richard Wagner, a native of Leipzig (three years Schumann's junior) whom they had often met through Dorn and Wieck. (Wagner had been a regular borrower from Wieck's music library as well as being a contributor to the *Neue Zeitschrift*, for which he was always appreciative to Schumann.) Of pianists, Sigismund Thalberg and Anton Rubinstein; of violinists, Ole Bull; of singers, Pauline Viardot Garcia and Wilhelmine Schröder-Devrient; as well as the Dresden painter Eduard Bendemann; the Viennese music publisher Pietro Mechetti and Hamburg music publisher August Cranz; Mozart's son, Franz Xavier Mozart; and Goethe's grandson, Walther von Goethe.[6]

But even apart from the completely new practicalities of their life, it is obvious that such a marriage would generate tensions as well as confer blessings: the deeper drives of the partners were not always complementary, and could not have been so, even without Schumann's temperament and illnesses. Clara insisted on her independent life as a player, and to be able to respond to invitations; Robert needed a calm, uninterrupted environment for his growing compositional ambitions. From the very start this was so. And he realized this as much as she. Clara had to run the home, for which she had not been trained, and of which she had earlier been terrified. Though, as a middle-class family, their house was run with assistance, it did not always run smoothly. They started with a good housekeeper through friends, but she soon left to get married, and Clara, as head of the household, was faced with finding a replacement; and one maid was dismissed for stealing. In February 1843, Clara comments 'the household gave me much unpleasantness this month, I often had to change nursemaids and had much trouble'. She commented stoically of these things: 'Those are the dark sides and it has to be that way! I do have enough happiness with my Robert and child.' The children were looked after by nannies, other than for long trips, when the family were called on.[7]

Clara tried her best to respond to Robert's creative needs: to be sensitive to his comments, to remove distractions, so that he could compose freely. But she could feel absolutely bereft and desperate for signs of his affection. She had to tolerate his 'coldness' towards her whilst he was absorbed in the First Symphony in 1841. Nor could Clara share fully in the achievement of his first great early public success, the premiere of *Das Paradies und die Peri* in Leipzig. She did not hear the work till it was finished, complaining in the diary in April 1843 that 'Robert has completed second part of the *Peri*, but has not told me much about it', even though he then required her to make the piano vocal score and be with him at rehearsals.[8]

The joint diary reflects her restlessness. She wanted to do so much for him – to earn money to relieve him of the tasks that kept him from creation: 'my most terrible thought is that you should have to work for money, because that simply cannot make you happy, and yet if you do not let me work as well, if you cut off every means for me to earn something, I see no other way out. I would gladly earn money, however, to create a life for you that is entirely dedicated to your art; it pains me most deeply when I have to ask you for money, and you give me what you have earned; I often feel as if this must rob your life of all poetry.'[9]

Clara was deeply frustrated. Both knew, as Nancy Reich has pointed out, that she could 'earn more in one three week concert tour than Schumann obtained from composing and editing in a year'. Robert varied in his sensitivity to all this. In October 1840 he wrote after completing the short song cycle to poems by Kerner, op. 35, 'they gave dear Clara pleasure, as well as pain; since she must purchase my love so often with [my] silence and invisibility. Well that's the way it goes in marriages of artists, and if they love each other, that's always good enough.' She only needed his warmth to respond, noting in February 1841 that 'I cannot help mentioning my Robert's most affectionate behavior, and to assure him once more that this is my greatest bliss.' But though he acknowledged the difficulties, he did nothing to alleviate them. He was unhappy when she was away: alone with only the child and servants, he became conscious of it. On 30 March 1842, with three weeks until Clara's return from the Hamburg/Denmark trip: 'Quiet Easter – without Clara – what will those of the future only be like?'[10]

The arrival of children naturally complicated this difficult balance as well as bringing fulfilment to both, and brought things to a point. Indeed, one can sense Robert's self-consciousness when he opines in February 1843 'Clara knows herself her primary occupation to be a mother, however, so that I believe she is happy under these conditions, which just simply cannot be changed.' He knew this compromised her own creative life yet – as a man of his time – had no answer to it nor felt any obligation to provide one. She accepted this role like all women of her class – but made the very most of her opportunities, at least not having to give up playing on marriage, unlike many leading female players. She was completely unwilling, indeed unable, to give up her professional skills on marriage: she had been trained to play professionally not socially. And she barely allowed pregnancy to interrupt her performance schedule (she used wet nurses as soon as possible), playing whenever she could, always with the thought of Robert's interests: for example, before Elise's birth in April 1843, she played publicly in Leipzig up to 9 February, and soon after there and in Dresden.[11]

But Leipzig and Dresden were too limiting: she simply had to tour. In February 1842, six months after the birth of Marie, she started with a tour of north Germany and Denmark to show her continuing pianistic presence, playing in Oldenburg, Hamburg and Copenhagen. Robert accompanied her to Hamburg but then returned home, irritated by the travel and by feeling snubbed in Oldenburg, when he was not invited to a reception for Clara after her concert on 25 February. They bade farewell on 10 March 1842 in Hamburg, 'the most terrible day in our marriage so far', as she put it, and Clara remained in Copenhagen for two months, returning at the end of April. She had long wanted to tour in Russia, the natural extension of her existing concert itinerary, and plans were made for a tour later in 1842, though postponed because of the political situation. When the trip was reconsidered for 1844, Robert again accompanied her, but only after great persuasion first from Clara and then from Mendelssohn in December 1843. The tour lasted from the end of January to the end of April, and they took in Berlin, then travelled via Tilsit and Riga to St Petersburg and Moscow. It was a great success for Clara, but not for Robert, though he put a brave face on it in letters. Though his Piano Quintet was a success with Clara at the piano at a soirée and at her third St Petersburg concert on 12 March 1844, he disliked the formalities and never wanted to be away from his desk.[12]

On marriage, Robert was now ready to move forward professionally. His major commitment was still the *Neue Zeitschrift*. But relative to the vast time it took, the paper actually provided relatively little income – Schumann had always talked it up. The administrative commitment was huge in dealing with his contributors and the financial aspects of circulation: he was always under pressure and got badly behind as his compositional ambitions expanded. Thus he blew hot and cold and was clearly losing impetus. In March 1841 Clara notes 'Robert pores over his journal, which right now bores him terribly'; to Carl Kossmaly he writes on 9 May 1841:

I wish I could do more than my bare duty. But you know that I have a home of my own now, and that circumstances have changed – not for the worse ... In the deepest confidence – would you feel inclined later to take my place as regular editor of the paper? I shall eventually go and live in a larger town and should like this institution of mine to be in competent hands.[13]

But he could always be roused to activity by new stimulus. Indeed, much more of great importance was still to appear up to 1844 and make a major impact on emerging musical culture. The breadth of his vision and generous actions on behalf of musicians had by now made him widely known and esteemed. To Fischhof: 'send me accounts at once of the *Salzburg Festival* [the unveiling of Mozart's statue on 4 September 1842] or ... ask someone else in my name to do so.' But he also stuck to his old commitments, stressing to Kossmaly that Schubert deserved 'a few weighty words ... Of course, his more important works are still unpublished. But his songs and piano compositions alone are quite sufficient for a sketch ... Do you know his Symphony in C? A splendid composition; rather long, but wonderfully full of life and *quite* new in character.' In June 1841 he noted that Mendelssohn 'had brought along a small Song without Words' for the *Zeitschrift* supplement. Further included in his tenure would be reports on Parisian musical life by Wagner and Berlioz in the first half of 1842, and his own contributions continued through the second half of 1845 from Dresden.[14]

Schumann's reluctance to sell the *Neue Zeitschrift* till 1844 was as much to do with status as with money. His compositional reputation was still emerging only slowly and the *Zeitschrift* was increasingly respected. He commented in frustration to Clara in November 1843: 'shall I then never be able to live entirely in my beloved art?' Then, on 5 June 1844, at a low point following the Russian visit, he wrote to Verhulst 'I have given up the management of the paper entirely to Lorenz this year, and do not think I shall take it up again' (Schumann did not do well from the deal, and was in no physical and mental shape to control events). Yet his new domestic setting gave him a newly professional attitude to compositional income and promotion. Not only was he more adroit in promoting his interests, but it is a sign of his change of life that he kept records from 1840, though still insisting even in June 1843 that 'I don't like to write and speak about my own works; my wish is that they may have good effects in the world and assure me of a loving remembrance from my children.'[15]

This insecurity of future income and the ambivalence of his creative position led Schumann to seek public institutional status (an instinct already apparent in his seeking a university degree to advance his professional standing in the legal battle with Wieck). One obvious step forward was through teaching, and a new opportunity arose through his friendship with Mendelssohn. In addition to his achievements as a conductor in Leipzig since 1837, Mendelssohn pioneered the establishment of the new Leipzig Conservatory. Opened on 2 April 1843, it represented a major new initiative in musical education, and was a signal moment in the unification of German musical culture: effectively a response to the traditional centrality of the Paris Conservatoire for France. Schumann commented to Verhulst 'I think it will have an important effect on the musical future of Germany', and discussed it extensively in the *Neue Zeitschrift*. It was, from the start, of the first rank with faculty drawn from leading musicians of Europe, and attracted students from all over. Previously musicians typically learned from family members, were apprenticed, or studied privately: Clara's education with teachers from Leipzig, Dresden and Berlin was not unusual for a talented musician of means.

The idea of participation was first broached in Bonneville in 1842 well before the opening. Mendelssohn's invitation was certainly a token of his esteem. Schumann began his duties as professor of piano and playing from score, and also for exercises in composition, in April 1843. This complemented Clara's life: teaching had become an enticing option in her new domestic setting and fear of the potential financial insecurity; she taught regularly, students coming from far and wide for high fees. But it did not work out; Schumann was not a successful teacher. His quiet, gentle, suggestive but apparently largely uncommunicative manner was inappropriate for teaching. He would sit through a lesson and hardly say a word, even when it was necessary, though Clara comments adversely on the teaching situation that 'I have no idea how one can teach 6 students at the same time.' By midsummer Schumann thought that few of the fifty students he had seen showed any real talent and he soon gave it up; he appears to have regarded only one student, Theodor Kirchner, as having any gifts: 'a significant talent whom I have always treated with great consideration for seeking advice from me'.[16]

Despite these reservations, Schumann had become well settled in Leipzig by 1843. He liked the city and was seemingly quietly confident of his future there: 'to spend some time in a place like Leipzig offers many advantages to the artist', he wrote to Kossmaly from Leipzig on 9 May 1841. It is entirely natural that his growing musical and professional status should have lead him to apply for Mendelssohn's job in 1843/4 when Mendelssohn finally left after eight years of highly productive work in the city to assume new responsibilities in Berlin. But, after Hiller's interregnum, the job went to Niels Gade, a blow that turned Schumann away from the city, and gave the first of many doses of professional/institutional reality. Whilst the city had provided his base, contacts and stimulus – and Schumann's whole mature musical development had taken place there – he had become increasingly frustrated by its limitations in offering performances and professional support. Now, by 1844, having given up his newspaper and his teaching at the Conservatoire, with Mendelssohn gone, and having failed to obtain the Gewandhaus position, Schumann was growing tired of Leipzig and ready for a change.[17]

Marriage and its prospect had released all Schumann's long nurtured ambitions in new genres and large-scale composition. With systematic intensity, he explored, in 1840–1, a year of song; in 1841, of orchestral music; and in 1842 and 1843, of chamber music and of choral music respectively. The sudden burst of song was unexpected. Not only had he not touched the genre since his early efforts, but had apparently long thought it inferior to instrumental music. Yet by August 1842 he was enthusiastically urging a young composer to 'above all, write for the voice. That gets you on more than anything, and brings out the innermost qualities of the musician.' The *Liederjahr* had begun on 1 February 1840, and in twelve months he had produced 125 solo songs with piano, over half his total output, as well as his first vocal duets and male-voice choruses. One motivating factor was that Schumann no longer needed to speak to Clara through the piano. She was now his and freer actively to promote his work. He might also be seen as responding more fully to her earlier pleas for more accessible works – and song-like qualities were already a conspicuous feature of his style.[18]

Now, on marriage, income was also a factor in building a professional position, and song was a most marketable product in the emerging bourgeois musical world. But above all, the major motive for song composition was standing ready in Schumann's vast knowledge of German literature: especially the new Romantic poetry, the innately musical lyricism of which found immediate response in him and to which he responded with one song after another, as well as to established names. He had a conspicuous sense of creating a German art form, as in commenting to Clara that 'Only a German heart that can feel intimately is appropriate for German lieder.' As pianist he had effectively written songs without words – indeed, the dependence of his songs on the piano, which provides not merely expression and support but often completes the musical sense, is characteristic. He certainly anticipated that these songs would advance his public reputation.[19]

Schumann's 1840 songs comprised several planned cycles and many looser groupings of songs. His choice of poets was partly personal and the themes largely autobiographical. As well as their aesthetic qualities, he knew most of his poets personally and the songs reflect both the struggles of his past life and the happiness of the present: love and loss continue to inspire as in the piano works. Schumann's first and chief poetic focus was Heinrich Heine, the most musical of Romantic lyricists, whom Schumann had sought out personally ten years before, in two cycles, *Liederkreis*, op. 24 (February 1840), and *Dichterliebe*, op. 48 (May 1840), drawn from the *Buch der Lieder*. *Dichterliebe* (*The Poet's Love*) is the most obviously autobiographical of his personal struggles for Clara, as of those with his own nature. Heine's verses also appear in a 'garland' of twenty-six settings, *Myrthen* (*Myrtles*), by various authors, chiefly Goethe, Byron, Julius Mosen, Friedrich Rückert, Hans Christian Andersen, and, most notably, Robert Burns. The work was dedicated as a wedding present to his 'beloved bride', and finished in early 1840. These poets all appear in other collections through the year. A second *Liederkreis*, op. 39, was completed in April–May 1840 to texts by Joseph von Eichendorff, Schumann commenting to Clara that this was his most Romantic cycle and that she was to be found in a great deal of it.[20]

Schumann's setting of nine lyric poems from Friedrich Rückert's *Liebesfrühling*, op. 37, was intended as a birthday present for Clara. With her own settings of 1840 now comprising nos. 2, 4 and 11, the work was published as a joint publication by 9 June 1841; Rückert wrote a poem to the Schumann couple in acknowledgment of their settings. In sober contrast, a cool reflection on the future seems implicit in the cycle of eight songs on poems by Adelbert von Chamisso, *Frauenliebe und -leben* (*Woman's Life and Love*), of July 1840, from marriage to widowhood. (Schumann's five settings of Andersen, op. 40, were also translated from the original Danish by Chamisso.) Justinius Kerner, a poet of his youthful settings of 1827–8 and now a friend, provided the texts of the *Zwölf Gedichte* published as op. 35; Schumann had also known Mosen since August 1833. And the quality of the musical substance and textual response represents a direct historical continuity from his youthful devotion to and knowledge of the songs of Schubert, only newly emerging in musical circles. Also apparent in many songs – and to be much more so later – the ballad character manifests itself most strongly in another Heine setting, of *Balsatzar* (*Belshazar*; later published as op. 57). Many of these poets also served for two sets of duets, opp. 34 and 43, and Heine provides two texts, as does Mosen, for six male-voice choruses, op. 33.[21]

Though today the fame of Schumann's texted works lies with the solo songs, public song recitals were unknown in the 1840s. The songs were first given to distinguished singers, friends and visitors, for whom some were written: for example Wilhelmine Schröder-Devrient, Pauline Viardot Garcia and Livia Frege, or the closer home circle of Sophie Kaskel, Emilie List and Clara herself, who had trained in singing. Andersen recalls one Leipzig occasion:

> [A] wonderful, truly poetic evening awaited me at Robert Schumann's. The previous year the composer had astonished me by doing me the honour of dedicating the music he had composed for four of my poems – translated by Chamisso into German – to me. On the evening in question these settings were sung by Mrs Frege accompanied by Clara on the piano, with just the composer and the poet for audience. Her soulful singing would have entranced and delighted an audience of thousands. The evening passed all too quickly as we partook of a festive supper and exchanged our thoughts on art and music.

Public performance was of individual songs within larger concert settings, either in Clara's own recitals, or in concerts of hers where Robert's large-scale music was performed. For example, the ballad 'Die beiden Grenadiere', op. 49, no. 1 received – through its popular character – an early exposure in public at Clara's Gewandhaus concert on 6 December 1841, in which Robert's D minor Symphony and *Sinfonietta* were premiered (under Ferdinand David).[22]

In total contrast, Schumann's reputation as a vocal composer was rather first established by an oratorio: a text of another of the *Myrthen* poets, the Irish writer and collector Thomas Moore's *Das Paradies und die Peri (Paradise and the Peri)*. *Lalla Rookh* (a collection of four 'oriental epic tales' based on Persian legend, published in 1817) facilitated Schumann's entry into dramatic music. The text reflects contemporary operatic themes in the blending of the human and divine through the three attempts of the fallen angel of the title to regain entry to heaven. Schumann had first contemplated it towards the end of 1841; his Zwickau friend Emil Flechsig provided the translation, on which Schumann worked with Adolf Bötger to transform it into a libretto, eventually completing the music by mid June 1843, after four months of intense labour. Schumann's comment that it represented a new genre for the concert hall, 'an oratorio; not for in the [sanctuary], but for

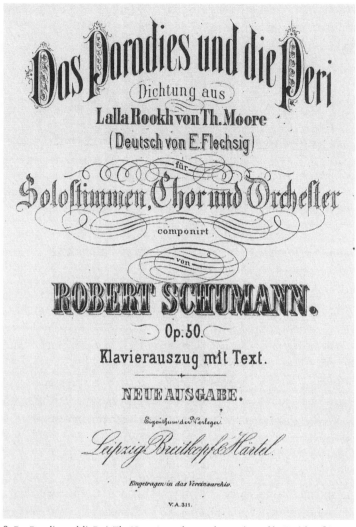

8 *Das Paradies und die Peri*. The Neue Ausgabe vocal score issued by Breitkopf & Härtel, c. 1880.

bright, happy people', refers to the traditionally religious and musical associations of the genre.[23]

Its immediate success from its first performance on 4 December 1843 at the Leipzig Gewandhaus was the foundation of Schumann's reputation as a composer. The social importance of choral societies guaranteed large-scale choral works huge exposure, and this was promoted by the influential Livia Frege, who sang the part of the Peri, with Schumann proving himself apparently adequate if not distinguished in his first public appearance as conductor. It gave him international rather than provincial exposure, with performances as far afield as Amsterdam, Prague, Zurich and even New York. The excitement of choral rehearsals for the Dresden performance was an entirely new and invigorating experience for Schumann. From now on he was constantly thinking of operatic subjects.

Schumann's symphonic aspirations had been rekindled by the discovery of Schubert's C major Symphony in 1839, and he made sketches for works never completed. He sketched the First ('Spring') Symphony in B flat in four days in January 1841, completing it immediately thereafter. Schumann ascribed the rhythm of the opening fanfare, drawn from the following Allegro theme, to a poem of invocation to spring by Adolf Bötger, thus giving the work its title. All four movements also possessed titles, suppressed on publication – and reflecting a background in piano music as well as the symphonic tradition from Beethoven's 'Pastoral' Symphony. The prevailingly dance-like, short-breathed character of the outer movements also reflects Schumann's piano music (as does the scherzo of the *Sinfonietta*).[24]

But the D minor Symphony of March 1841 was very different. First titled a 'Fantasy Symphony', its movements are not only continuous but with an entirely new level of formal integration and thematic concentration, far exceeding Mendelssohn (in the 'Scottish' and 'Reformation' symphonies and the *Lobgesang*). The intense though sombre lyricism of the first movement goes back to the Fantasia in C; and the double trios of the slow movement to the F minor Sonata and other movements. The single movement *Fantasia* in A minor for piano and orchestra was even more a fantasy on a theme of a very new, improvisatory character, though retaining the outline of a concerto first movement. The chamber music was of even greater range. In the *Neue Zeitschrift*, Schumann had required that string quartets be in the classical tradition, and his three quartets of 1842 follow intense studies of Haydn, Mozart and

Beethoven. But much more characteristic are the Quartet and Quintet
for piano and strings, the Quintet not only the first important work
in the genre, but innovative in form, not least in its powerful unify-
ing finale. An entirely new sound world was opened in a set of variations on an original Andante in B flat for pianos, horn and two cellos,
of January–February 1843.

Reception of these works was mixed, though an even greater success than *Das Paradies und die Peri* was the *Patriotisches Lied* for solo voice,
chorus and piano, to a rousing text by Nicolaus Becker titled 'They shall
not have it, the German Rhine', of which Schumann proudly declared
'all Germany is talking about it', and later 'Friese has prepared a school
edition', when Clara noted that it was into its fifth printing, and had
been arranged by Schumann for four-part male choir as well as for
mixed chorus and orchestra. But it was obviously less natural to him
than lieder to refined poetry: 'With that I saw clearly how difficult it is
to write singable things for the people.'[25]

Mendelssohn's new dedication to Schumann's interests gave the
B flat Symphony a fine performance and review, and it immediately
found a publisher, again in Breitkopf & Härtel, in November 1841. But
other large-scale works were more difficult. Schumann reveals new
acumen in marketing them, however, as in taking the initiative in
leveraging the outstanding success of the *Peri* against other works.
To Härtel in December 1843: 'If ... you agree to publish the full score
by December of next year, I will gladly promise to give you another
smaller composition into the bargain, and would propose a concert
allegro for piano-forte with orchestral accompaniment.' Though
the house agreed on the usual condition that the score be printed for
piano, with the *Partitur* to appear later, Schumann never delivered this
allegro movement (which subsequently became the first movement of
the Piano Concerto). And similarly to the publisher Hofmeister on the
symphony, he wrote:

> the sympathy with which the public received my symphony made me
> think of another orchestral work of mine, which I should now like to
> give to the world [the *Sinfonietta/ Suite*]. You may have heard it at our

last concert, but not, of course, in perfection. It is distinguished from
the symphony form, as the different movements can also be played
separately, and I expect that the Overture particularly will make a
good effect ... According to my calculation, the price of the orchestral
parts would be about four Thalers, and that of the piano score, at the
most, two Thalers. I am sure you will do a good business with the
latter.

But Schumann was unsuccessful with this, as with the more demanding D minor Symphony.[26]

Indeed, he now sought to reanimate some publications that were
insufficiently marketed, continuing to Hofmeister that he would like
to sell the entire opus of impromptus, which he had previously published at his own expense, with the plates.

I should like to do the same with my *Davidsbündlertänze*, which were
published by Friese [also at Schumann's own expense], and, as he is
not a music publisher, have hardly become known at all ... I am sure
it would be quite different if a proper publisher took an interest in
them, for pieces of this kind ought to become popular, even among
amateurs. Instead of the mystic title, or beneath it, one might perhaps
put 'Twelve characteristic pieces'. There are still about 170 complete
copies of the *Davidsbündlertänze*.[27]

Schumann was particularly aware of his own limitations as a performer in promoting his works and lack of status. He cultivated contacts and friends who might offer better performances and looked
patiently to the future for them. To Carl Kossmaly in January 1842:

I am pleased to hear you want to perform my symphony. There is no
score. However, the first violin part gives a pretty good idea of the
whole. I will reserve a few hints till later. The two orchestral works –
i.e., a second symphony (D minor) and an overture, scherzo and
finale which were performed at our last concert did not obtain such a
success as the first one. It was almost too much at once, I think, and
then we missed Mendelssohn as conductor. That matters nothing. I
know the things are not a whit behind the first and sooner or later will
assert themselves in their own way.

To Griepenkerl:

Who is the director? I would like to give him, or you, a few hints before it is performed. Take my child under your protection: it was born in a fiery hour.

And to Kahlert:

Many thanks for the criticism of the symphony. A really perfect performance would, I think, make you see it in a different light. But the composer ought to be contented even if he only awakens the sympathy of the critic, and I have awakened yours, as every line of your essay tells me. As to my vocal compositions, I wish you would look at them more carefully. They hint at my future. I don't dare promise better things than I have already accomplished (I mean in song) and am content with that.[28]

In the early 1840s Schumann was becoming acutely aware of his potential, and shows his maturing self-awareness. To Kossmaly in September 1842: 'On looking back, I see much that gives me pleasure, but it is nothing compared to the prospects I see opening out before me in the distance, in my occasional happy hours.' And in May 1843:

I enclose a packet of my older compositions. You will soon find out all that is immature and unfinished in them. They are mostly reflections of my former stormy life. The man and musician within me were always trying to speak at once. Indeed I think that is the case still, only I have learned to control myself more and my art likewise. How many joys and sorrows lie buried in this little heap of notes your sympathetic heart will soon find out ... Indeed, early efforts often contain most germs for the future ... All these things are but little known, and that for very natural reasons: firstly, on intellectual grounds, because of the difficulties in form and matter; secondly, because I am no performer, and cannot play them in public; thirdly, because, being the editor, I could not mention them in my paper; and fourthly, because Fink is editor of the other paper [Allegemeine musikalische Zeitung] and would never mention them.[29]

Schumann knew he was ahead of his time and he knew his worth: he was patient and waited for a sensitive response. He was stimulated by good reviews and could sense acceptance beckoning with new performance interests. Thus to Kossmaly on 9 May 1841 on the new B flat Symphony: 'I wish you knew my symphony. How I enjoyed hearing it performed! And so did other people; for it was received with an amount of sympathy, such as I don't think has been accorded to any modern symphony since Beethoven. I now have ... all sorts of fresh orchestral ideas...'. And again in October: 'the symphony is behind me. I now have other goals'. Then, in sending piano works via Breitkopf to Kossmaly on 25 January 1844, further to an essay on his music: 'A great deal ... gave me the greatest pleasure, but I think you would speak differently on a good many subjects if we could be together for a little while. In any case I am grateful for your thoughtful care. You are the first who has ever said anything significant about me and thoroughness and truth are everywhere apparent.'[30]

Marriage and family brought a sense of security, happiness and fulfilment that gave Schumann a release from emotional tensions for a time. The first three years were, despite setbacks, the happiest of his life, and his sustained periods of composition during this time must be regarded as the high point of his emotional wellbeing. The sense of a new beginning in his diary is transmitted into the ecstatic lyrical 'spring-like' quality of so many of his songs, and extends into the 'Spring' Symphony: moods unique to Schumann. But the emotionally more favorable environment for work also confronted him with the work–exhaustion cycle of his own creativity. And equally threatening was the stress of his outside world – most immediately apparent in Clara's performing and success. The Hamburg/Denmark tour posed the first major problem. When he returned home, prematurely, from Hamburg in March 1842, he whined, putting a lot of manipulative emotional pressure on her. He liked it best when she was at home. But he recognized his situation, and, as earlier, attempted to analyse and control his behavior during the period. Having decided that he should return and Clara continue the tour on her own, he notes in the joint diary on 14 March 1842:

> Shall I then neglect my talent in order to serve as your companion on trips? And you, should you therefore leave your talent unused,

because I simply am chained to my journal and the piano? ... We have hit on a way out. You took a female companion for yourself, I returned to the child and to my work. But what will the world say? ... Yes, it is absolutely necessary that we find the means to use and develop both of our talents side by side.

Anything that reduced the stress of unwanted commitment helped him; thus he had originally happily exchanged the proposed Russian tour for one to Denmark via Hamburg.[31]

The rescheduled 1844 Russia trip was much more difficult to cope with. The purely physical aspect was exhausting enough. The severe weather posed the first problem. The weather at Dorpat was at least ten degrees below freezing and they became stuck in a snow storm. At Dorpat Robert was confined to bed for almost a week with cold, fever and severe anxiety. On 5 June 1844 he almost passed out from the roughness of the roads. In St Petersburg, he felt depressed, and was preoccupied and incommunicative, with attacks of dizziness that impaired his sight, causing him to seek medical advice in Moscow whence they travelled after a month. Viardot Garcia and Henselt acted as Clara's companion on official visits. Schumann only had the strength to conduct his B flat Symphony on one occasion; he complained of no peace and quiet for composing. Moreover, Clara could not count on full halls. The couple reported to Wieck: 'We have given up the journey to Sweden; we have too great a longing to get home to our children again.' By the end of the Russian tour – they arrived back in Leipzig on 24 May – Schumann was in a precarious state physically and psychologically, and continued very ill through August.[32]

Throwing himself into the continuation of his music for Goethe's *Faust* (begun in Dorpat) on his return to Leipzig was a natural reaction to these frustrations. But the illness in Russia represented the beginning of a coming major breakdown in August, which now took far longer to resolve than any earlier event. His letter to Dr Krüger of October 1844 states that he had been very ill for three months, unable to listen to music at all, and feeling 'quite hopeless'. He had consulted doctors to no apparent effect throughout the travelling; their diagnoses were as previously: the effects of an artistic temperament. One doctor even suggested that Schumann give up composition for a time, or at least develop other interests, to break the work connection. The only positive response was an attempt to relieve the symptoms with rest, hydrotherapy and long walks. A brief holiday in the Harz Mountains from 10 to 18 September 1844 brought little relief. Consultation on 1 October 1844 with a homoeopathic doctor did little good. But Schumann was also capable of rationalizing to disguise his real condition to friends, having returned from Russia 'quite well and sound', and preparing for a trip to Holland, then to England (he also 'dreamed' of resettling in America on more than one occasion during this period).[33]

It was in his exhausted state that he at last decided to give up the *Zeitschrift*.[34]

6 Growing ambitions: Dresden 1844–50

The move to Dresden was not part of any larger professional plan. The Schumanns decided to stay for the winter of 1844–5 having visited Wieck there for a week from 3 October, and with Robert still on the rebound from his Leipzig rejection, and exhausted after the Russian trip and needing recuperation. They took an apartment on 17 October and finally left Leipzig after a farewell concert on 13 December: and Leipzig was easily reached by train so that their connections remained intact. But, coincidentally, Dresden had important creative attractions for Schumann, with his growing interest in operatic composition. Its court had one of the greatest Italian stages in Germany, deriving from a long and distinguished tradition, yet had also been the location of the development of German opera, with Weber as director from 1816 to his death in 1825 and, since 1843, Richard Wagner. Dresden also had significant choral traditions in its major churches and through the prominent Liedertafel tradition of male-voice choirs.[1]

But Schumann was still an outsider to court culture and intimidated by it: though the couple made many friends they never really settled. Clara quickly observed that Dresden was a 'musical backwater' and a miserable existence for artists; they were soon reminiscing about music and friends in Leipzig, with Clara commenting on an early return visit that 'the life and people here certainly do cheer us up considerably. Sooner or later I really think we shall settle down here again.' Again, it was Clara who was acknowledged through invitations

9 Dresden. The old city and Elbe Bridge.

to perform, and played several times at the court. But throughout the residence Robert made little or no progress in official circles, and also, again, felt snubbed, galling to his pride – though this was probably more a matter of court etiquette and musical ignorance than disparagement (Clara's Viennese honour had given her court status). For her part, Clara always sought to include him and his music as a condition of her appearance.[2]

Shortly before they left Dresden Clara would observe 'How much there is of Robert's which we have not yet heard! it is dreadful! The want of sympathy among the artists here goes so far that not one of them so much as asks what Robert may be working at ... such nature here, and such human beings.' But Dresden was to be a very important transition in Schumann's professional life. It introduced him to a wider sphere of contacts, and to musical activities and the realities of professional life, not least that of the theatre. Most important/formative of the musical contacts was Ferdinand Hiller, a now prominent musician of private means, who had conducted the Gewandhaus

10 The Piano Concerto in A minor. Title page of the first edition, July 1846.

concerts of 1843–4 (replacing Mendelssohn), and whom Schumann had probably met first in Leipzig in 1832 and then in the Mendelssohn circle. Schumann entrusted him with conducting the first performance of the Piano Concerto with Clara as soloist on 4 December 1845 in Dresden, and dedicated it to him 'in friendship' ('freundschaftlich zugeeignet').[3]

The artistic community was to be more important than public musical recognition to Schumann (many associated with the important Zwinger Art Gallery), and Clara soon observed the artists to be more interested in music than the court musicians. Wagner affirms Schumann's observation of the vitality and support of this circle in which Hiller was also prominent, and through whose regular exchange he met the historical painter Eduard Bendemann (1811–89); the sculptor Ernst Rietschel (1804–61), who made a plaster of Robert and Clara; the painter Julius Hübner (1806–82); the poet Robert Reinick (1805–52); the actor Eduard Devrient (1801–77); and the writers Berthold Auerbach (1812–82) and Otto Ludwig (1813–65). Notable also was the natural philosopher, painter and leading medical doctor Carl Gustav Carus (1789–1869), a relative of his youthful friends. Musicians included those he already knew and esteemed, notably the singer Wilhelmine Schröder-Devrient, who had been famed at Dresden since 1823 for her performance as Beethoven's Leonore, and visitors such as Berlioz: 'we all meet once a week now … and there is always something either to read or talk about, and the proceedings are very lively'. As ever, the Schumann home was always open for musical visitors to the city. In the summer of 1846, for example, they had received the young pianist Hans von Bülow, and the critic Eduard Hanslick; as well as David, Liszt and Jenny Lind. His hospitality to Nils Gade after Gade's appointment to the Gewandhaus is a sign of Schumann's strong and collegiate character. Clara was very close to Devrient as a great artist; less predictably, in view of her popular stardom, Clara was also drawn to Lind, who became a close friend for a time.[4]

Schumann's musical ambitions interacted with this environment through its orchestral activity – the attempts to establish subscription concerts – as well as dramatic productions at the court opera: especially Wagner's new works, which Schumann could discuss and observe first-hand through attendance at opera rehearsals and personal contact with Wagner. The paucity of public orchestral music was still typical of court cities at the time, by comparison with the 'free' commercial and artistic vibrancy of Leipzig (whose pioneering public concerts since 1784 had been organized by businessmen in the Cloth Hall (Gewandhaus) for which they are named). Schumann bridled

11 Robert and Clara Schumann. Plaster relief by Ernst Rietschel, Dresden, 1846, reproduced in lithographic copy.

against the quality of the orchestral performances to Mendelssohn a year after his arrival: 'one symphony of Beethoven a year, with ornamentations by the band *ad libitum* ... Will the Leipzig people help us sometimes?'And later: 'our orchestra is really quite first rate and the wind capital [but] our audience consists almost entirely of the aristocracy – I fear we often give them too good music.' Hiller was the driver of change and sought to establish more regular concert series as well as special concerts, for example for the Weber memorial. Schumann followed his attempts with enthusiasm, if pessimism. To Mendelssohn:

they want to arrange some subscription concerts here, but I
doubt... they will come to anything. There is nothing to be done
with the band – and nothing without it either. They are still in an
awful groove here. For example, the band will never play Beethoven
symphonies in extra concerts, because it might not be advantageous
to their Palm Sunday concert and Pension Fund [the traditional major
annual concerts at the time].[5]

Wagner's activities were much more dynamic and offered more
stimuli to Schumann's developing ideas, though Schumann's first
reactions were negative. To Mendelssohn: 'a clever fellow, but full of
crazy ideas ... he cannot write or imagine four consecutive bars that
are melodious, or even correct ... the full score lies beautifully printed
before us, and its [consecutive] fifths and octaves into the bargain ...
[*Tannhäuser*] is not a shade better than Rienzi [but] the aristocracy is
still raving about Rienzi'. Schumann changed his mind with experience in the theatre, however. Thus to Heinrich Dorn:

I wish you could see *Tannhäuser*; it contains much that is deep and
original, and a great deal of it is a hundred times better than his
former operas, though some of the music is certainly very trivial. In
short, he may become of immense importance to the stage, and as far
as I know him he has got the courage for it. I consider the technical
part, the instrumentation, excellent, and it is all far more masterly
than it used to be. He has already finished another new text, *Lohengrin*.

Wagner had completed *Tannhäuser* during 1844, and soon after meeting
Schumann in Dresden in 1845 he presented him with a lithographed
copy of the score and a friendly greeting. But at the personal level,
Schumann was totally alienated from such a bristling and political
personality, an anarchical friend of Michael Bakunin, who espoused
an entirely different kind of Romanticism and who offended a man of
Schumann's reflective temperament. Added to this was Wagner's deni-
gration of Mendelssohn, akin to that of Liszt.[6]

Rather than Wagner, it was Ferdinand Hiller who moved Schumann
forward professionally in this period by offering him the directorship of the Dresden Liedertafel, the male voice choir that he had

conducted since 1844. Its first rehearsal took place on 20 November 1847, and though it carried no salary, this practical experience was an invaluable stimulus, giving his first extended conducting experience, 'which is a pleasure to me, and incites me in many ways'. But he gave it up in October 1848, tired of the limitations of the genre, having meanwhile been inspired to found a full choral society, his Verein für Chorgesang. Schumann had founded the Verein by placing a public advert for an introductory meeting. Choir member Marie von Lindemann recalls that 'On 5 January 1848 a group of musical ladies and gentlemen answered a written invitation by Dr Robert Schumann and assembled in the garden room of the Harmonic Society in Dresden to found a new choral society.' Schumann records '117 members ... 57 actual and the rest subscribers', telling Verhulst in November that the Society was 'most flourishing'.[7] He had clear ideas of his task. Lindemann continues:

> Schumann said that the foundation of a choral society lies in voice training – we sang a choral *solfeggio* written by him. He expressed the wish to cultivate modern music without ignoring earlier works ... [It met] every Wednesday evening and welcomed more and more members. The first performance was on 26 March 1848 in the hall of the former Coselsches Palais behind the Frauenkirche. All present were electrified by Schumann's songs.

Schumann was clearly confident in his direction, and introduced large-scale new works. He wrote to Franz Brendel (now editor of the *Neue Zeitschrift*) that his society was studying Gade's *Comala*: 'It really seems to me that the Leipzig people have underrated this work. I am sure that it is the most important composition of modern times.' He conducted the Verein until he left Dresden in October 1850.[8]

The loss of the *Neue Zeitschrift* left a vacuum in Schumann's life that could not be filled solely by composition. Two aspects of that activity now emerge more strongly in his life: the dedication to the revival of earlier music as well as its study, and a commitment to the music of the younger generation. The *Neue Zeitschrift* had engaged with emerging

study of Baroque and Renaissance composers, and Schumann's repertory with the Verein even included Palestrina – an advanced interest ('at
times it really sounds like music of the spheres, and, then, what art! I
really believe he is the greatest musical genius Italy has ever produced',
he wrote to Brendel). But the main focus of his attention was the music
of Bach and Handel, especially the former. Of his many interests the
most pressing during this time was the creation of a new, correct edition of *Das wohltemperierte Clavier* (*The Well-Tempered Clavier*). To Hermann
Härtel in January 1845 he wrote:

> I have had an idea in my head for a long time, about which I should
> like to know your opinion. The fact is, I consider that we lack a
> really good edition of J. S. Bach's *Wohltemperirtes Clavier*. Czerny's
> edition, with its unnecessary fingering and really idiotic marks of
> execution, appears to me like a caricature; and the older ones are, for
> the most part, incorrect. Then there are the various readings, which
> complicate matters still more, so that nobody knows which edition to
> depend upon. But as many of the different readings are Bach's own,
> I think it would be of great interest to be able to compare them in
> print. Above all, take the advice of Mendelssohn and [Franz] Hauser
> in Vienna, who possess many numbers of the *Wohltemperirtes Clavier* in
> the original MS – at least, I am sure Hauser does – and Mendelssohn
> has, at all events, got the oldest edition of his works. My object is
> to obtain as correct an edition as possible, based upon the original
> manuscript and the oldest editions, and quoting the various readings
> … I am firmly convinced that this undertaking would also prove
> profitable to the publisher.[9]

Although Schumann thanked Mendelssohn later in the year 'for the
trouble you have taken about the *Wohltemperirtes Clavier*', Schumann
never produced this edition. But the benefit of his commitment would
eventually appear in the *Bach Werke* issued by Breitkopf & Härtel
beginning in 1851, consequent upon the foundation of the Leipzig
Bach Gesellschaft the preceding year, the centenary of Bach's death, by
Schumann and others of his circle (Moritz Hauptmann, Julius Rietz,
Otto Jahn, C. F. Becker and Ignaz Moscheles), though he never served

on the board. The edition was a signal moment in nineteenth-century music, and commanded wide interest and editorial support from leading musicians. It was inaugurated by choral music, not instrumental, beginning with the least-known repertory: that of the cantata. The St Matthew and St John Passions and the Mass in B minor followed only some years later. Schumann's interest in the Passions was now as deep as in the keyboard works. A lengthy letter to the Hamburg musician G. D. Otten suggests the level of his knowledge of editorial and textual issues in the dating of the St John and St Matthew Passions, and he performed individual parts of the St John with the Verein at different times. And his interest appears to have been wide: he responded enthusiastically to the receipt of the new Breitkopf & Härtel edition of C. P. E. Bach's religious odes and songs to texts by Gellert. By comparison with that of J. S. Bach, the choral music of Handel was infinitely more widely known, especially in England, where its immense initial impact had spread quickly to Germany. Schumann was very keen to obtain the latest critical editions of the Handel Society in London, writing to Hermann Härtel 'have you not yet obtained for me any of the new English edition of Handel's works? I am much looking forward to it.'[10]

The rapidly growing reputation of Schumann's works during the Dresden period attracted many young composers to his cause. He responded to them keenly, either by offering advice or openings to those recommended by friends, or even by replying at length to total strangers. His reply to a young composer – Emil Büchner – clarifies and vindicates his sensitivity as a teacher, and a sense of shared dedication to the highest ideals that confirms his own value system at this time of growing maturity in his own life. Of a sonata he writes:

> the piece bears ample testimony alike to your industry, your aspirations and your talents. But there are some shallow parts in it, and here and there you have obviously felt this yourself. A good deal would bear alteration, but not all of it; I am thinking of some of the motives in the adagio and scherzo. However, instead of correcting and rewriting it, look upon this composition as a study, and begin something new with fresh energy. I think you will find this more improving. As I said before there is much in your composition that

I like and sympathize with; and then, you possess knowledge of the instrument and its most beautiful effects, such as one does not often meet with in modern pianoforte works. But every now and then the pianist is too much to the fore. As a composer you must throw him overboard altogether, if you aim to a more than merely ephemeral effect. Only that which comes from the heart and is inspired from within, will hold its own and outlast time. Please don't be offended at my remarks. It is so difficult to discuss the mysterious powers of creative capacity; indeed, one can but indicate one's meaning. Whatever you do, don't give up working steadily on, even though the world should withhold its approbation for a long time. The other day I read: 'An artist should daily combat his vanity, his ambition', if he would emerge from the struggle bright and strong. So I will address these words to you as a conclusion, and with the assurance of my sincerest sympathy, I remain, Yours faithfully, R.Sch.[11]

Schumann's professional and compositional life in the Dresden period was dominated by his health to a much greater extent than previously, and shows an uneven contour of gradual acceleration towards restoration and a major creative emphasis over several years. His state is described by Dr Helbig, his physician during the years at Dresden:

[He] came to Dresden in October, 1844, and labored so unceasingly on the music for the epilogue to Goethe's *Faust* that he fell into a very morbid condition, manifested by the following symptoms: as soon as he began to use his brain, shivering, faintness and cold feet set in, together with great pain and a peculiar fear of death, which took the form of a dread of high hills or houses, all metallic substances (even keys), medicine and infection. He suffered much from loss of sleep and felt worse at dawn than at any other time. As he studied every prescription until he found some reason for not taking it, I ordered him cold plunge baths, which so far improved his health that he was able to return to his usual (only) occupation, composition … I [advised] that he should employ himself and distract his mind with something else than music.[12]

It took upwards of two years to get through the worst. But Schumann's comments show his constant awareness of his condition and attempts to cope with it. At first, in autumn 1844, he recalled to Krüger a 'kind of general nervous disorder ... [in which music] went through my nerves like a knife'. Then in January 1845 to Härtel: 'I am still not at all well: the attacks of great nervous prostration have unfortunately rather increased than decreased, and so I often look very anxiously into the future.' In May 1845 he wrote to Verhulst: 'I have had a bad time of it since you last heard from me. I was often very ill. Gloomy demons possessed me. Now I am rather better, and am beginning to work again, which for months has been out of the question.' But, alarmingly, he had developed new and more radical symptoms during this period: as well as acute depression, insomnia, exhaustion and phobias, he experienced bodily tremors, irritations all over, auditory disturbances and hallucinations. To Kahlert he admitted his 'distressing mental condition ... I lost every melody ... as soon as I conceived it'. His friends had thought him close to death.[13]

Again he sought many doctors, but medical help in Dresden was no different from before. The primary recommendation was for water therapy, which took the standard form of sea bathing as well as long walks: the benefit felt from this was certainly real – an escape from the grime and possible infection of cities – though not inspired by any understanding of his deeper condition. The Schumanns stayed a month during July and August on the north German coast overlooking the beach at Nordeney, where Clara miscarried their fifth child. Dr Carl Gustav Carus recommended hypnosis as treatment for Schumann's nearsightedness and blurring of vision, given by Dr Helbig. Schumann also subjected himself, for a second time in his life, to phrenological examination, a fashionable analysis of the skull to determine personality characteristics; and he gave up smoking.[14]

Schumann's self-awareness led him to begin to use music therapeutically on limited tasks that gave him pleasure. By May 1845 he had written fugues on BACH and other subjects, and canonic studies for the pedal piano, published as opp. 60, 72, 56 and 58 respectively (Clara also published a book of Preludes and Fugues). Then, feeling more strength from December 1845 to October 1846, he embarked on

a vastly bigger project with another symphony, in C major: 'I wrote the
symphony in December 1845, when I had hardly got over my illness,
and it seems to me as though the music betrayed as much. Only in the
last movement did I begin to feel myself again, and I really began to get
better after having finished the whole work.' He later associated parts
of the D minor Trio with this new energy.[15]

By 1848–9 he was again relatively stable and back to full activity,
though still defensive. At the end of 1849 he wrote to Hiller: 'I have
been extremely industrious this year, as I have probably told you; one is
bound to work as long as it is daylight.' And he was rational as well as
creative in his response. So, bluntly to Hiller at the same time:

> I have to be very careful in guarding against all melancholy
> impressions [he was recalling the effect of the sight of a mental
> institution near Maxen in 1848]. And though, as you are aware, we
> musicians often dwell on sunny heights, yet when the unhappiness of
> life comes before our eyes in all its naked ugliness, it hurts us all the
> more. At least, that is my case, with my fervid imagination. I am sure I
> remember having read something similar about Goethe.[16]

Schumann's need to keep a low profile for much of the Dresden
period, and his vulnerability to disturbance, were balanced by a growing sense of security through family responsibilities. This period
marks a significant change in the Schumanns' family circumstances.
He was now 34. For the first time in his adult life he had no outside
professional obligations beyond those arising from his compositions,
and took the opportunity for greater seclusion. Towards the end of the
period he would recall this as having been the ideal situation for creative work, even whilst contemplating institutional employment: 'I
never can forget the last few years, when I was able to devote myself
exclusively to composition ... I am well aware that such a fruitful, and
in this respect happy, time will probably not come again in a hurry.'[17]

It is abundantly clear that he wanted a young family around him,
and did not regard it as an encumbrance to his creative life. In the
Dresden years, another daughter and then three sons were born to the

couple: Julie in March 1845, Emil in February 1846, Ludwig in November 1848 and Ferdinand in January 1849. After Ludwig's birth he wrote to Verhulst: 'I possess great treasures in my own home – such a dear wife, such satisfactory children.'[18]

But Robert's detachment from the pressures of children rebounded directly on Clara and her creative aspirations. Though, as before, he continued to realize the pressures on Clara, he also continued to take them for granted and rationalize them. One almost wonders at his bland statement to Verhulst: 'We have a boy now, too. His name is Ludwig and he is the delight of his mother.' But the births put her under immense pressure, which manifested itself in poor health, of which Schumann often spoke to Mendelssohn (the correspondence reveals a bond as family men). Thus Clara inevitably gave fewer concerts and it was her decreasing ability to support him financially as she wished that weighed her increasingly down – as did thoughts of the economic future: for she had more foresight than Robert. But she continued to support him in the most practical way by running the home, and artistically through music making. But her fears were correct: by 1848, with a large family to support, their savings had fallen drastically low, and Schumann now wrote to his brother Carl to cash in his investments in Carl's business, a sure sign of his problems. Thus there were also financial reasons for Schumann's industry as he recovered his health through the Dresden years.[19]

The couple soon settled into a regular pattern. Every day at 11 a.m. they took an hour's walk together; they ate lunch with the children; they spent an hour in a café before dinner. They both enjoyed nature as they had always done. They stressed its attractions to their friends: Schumann writes to Verhulst encouraging him to come to enjoy the beautiful environs as well as the company of colleagues 'like Julius Becker and Gustav Nottebohm'. But as life went by they faced more personal losses. In their own family, the first son Emil died after a year, and Schumann's surviving sibling Carl, to whom he was closest, died in April 1849, preceded by his son, Schumann's nephew 'little Carl'. Moreover, there was the loss of close musical friends and supporters, and of major contemporaries with whom he had been significantly connected. First there was the shock of the death of Fanny Mendelssohn followed quickly by that of Felix, both succumbing to strokes in May and November 1847 respectively; then of Chopin in October 1849. Indeed, these deaths were as much a blow to Clara, who was musically much closer to them than was Robert, and had formed a very close artistic bond of sympathy with Fanny. In turn, these deaths changed Schumann's position in the world of music. Now his greatest contemporaries were of a different stamp: Liszt and Wagner. And he had already shown his impatience with both in different ways, despite their support for him.[20]

Schumann's irritation at Dresden court etiquette and the ignoring of his work by its officialdom must have received some small vindication in the events that unfolded in 1848. The elegant aristocratic façade of the 'Florence of the North' could not hide the political vulnerability of its leaders. Dresden was, by the time Schumann arrived, a seedbed for political reaction. Responding to the insurrections elsewhere in Germany, and the demands of his own parliament, the Landtag, the king of Saxony, Frederick Augustus II, dissolved the body on 30 April, appointing an ultra-conservative government. Fearful of its military support by Prussia, popular protest became violent on 3 May and the city was briefly held by the revolutionaries until the arrival of Prussian troops, with new hand-held guns that inflicted terrible casualties in house-to-house fighting for four days.

Though he was clearly of liberal and republican sentiments (he read the paper daily to keep abreast of contemporary events) stemming from his early home and schooling, Schumann's disposition was far too passive to permit his expressing his opinion openly and frankly, far less of taking an active share in politics. He therefore stood in contrast not only to Wagner, but to other musicians such as Wilhelmine Schroeder-Devrient, who took an active part in the protests and fighting (women were newly prominent in political action in 1848); Schumann continued to compose fluently despite the vast disturbance outside their home. Clara describes these terrifying events at length, as well as the attempt to involve Robert in the local street defence group, and their very dramatic escape from the city via the train station where they talked themselves through. With the eldest daughter, Marie, they travelled to the estate of their friends the Serres at Maxen. Clara went through the whole ordeal again the next day to fetch the other children, Elise, Julie and Ludwig, who had been left with the maid. On 9 May the royalists recaptured the city and the next day Schumann and Clara returned to collect belongings. But they had been offended by the anti-republicanism of some aristocrats at the Serre estate, and went to Bad Kreiska where they lived quietly until 12 June. By contrast, Wagner, who had manned the barricades with the radical Michael Bakunin, was banned by the royalists, and fled to live in exile in Zurich.[21]

Though Schumann's illness of 1844 and his slow recovery constrained his compositional energies, they did not prevent him from working, save during the worst periods. Indeed, the time now available for composition and the new artistic stimuli in Dresden prompted a huge development in Schumann's compositional range in the later Dresden years: as he pointed out himself, by 1849 he enjoyed his 'greatest year ever', with a fifth of his total output in many new genres – choral, dramatic, orchestral and instrumental – that carried straight through into the Düsseldorf years. And the change of location made his current goals clearer to him: on the one hand, great ambitions in dramatic music; on the other, concerns for more marketable works, more directly influenced by his own musical's activities. His comment from 1842 that his 'prayer … morn and eve' was German opera was as much an expression of idealism as of the status attached to operatic success, and he now pursued it with as much dedication as Wagner: indeed, their projects overlapped. Early on in Dresden, to the *Lohengrin* text, Schumann reacted 'it was a double surprise to me for I had been contemplating this story for the last year – or, at any rate, a similar one from the period of King Arthur and the Round Table – and now I must throw it overboard. The majority of us, especially the painters, admired [it] extremely.'[22]

His first operatic (and oratorio) plans for his longest dramatic pre-occupation, Goethe's *Faust*, soon yielded to a lesser generic result. His initial work, whilst resting at Dorpat on the Russian tour, had been to set the final scene of Goethe's Part II, the *Chorus Mysticus*, for eight-part chorus and soloists. Back in Leipzig, months before completion, he had written disheartened to Mendelssohn on 24 September 1845: 'I do not know whether I shall ever publish it.' But the Goethe centenary of 1849 and the prospect of the involvement of his Dresden Liedertafel in the celebrations gave public occasion for its exposure: it had been completed in nine individual scenes, summarizing the two parts of Goethe's work, with no attempt at continuity of narrative or action and no intention that they should be presented as a whole, and as yet without the overture. Nonetheless it was unique in attempting to capture the entire spirit of the two parts of *Faust* rather than the more familiar drama and characterization of the first part, with supernatural and love interest focused on Mephisto and Gretchen, as most recently in Berlioz's *La Damnation de Faust* of 1845–6 (based on his *Huit scènes de Faust* of 1828–9).[23]

Prior to this, in 1848–9, Schumann had decided on another dramatic challenge of Faustian character, yet completely different in genre: incidental music to accompany Byron's pre-eminently Romantic anti-hero *Manfred*, the lofty and defiant loner haunted by remorse for an undisclosed act, and seeking forgiveness from the spirit of the dead Astarte. Again he saw this dramatic compromise as innovative, calling it 'not an opera, *Singspiel* or melodrama but a dramatic poem with music', and claiming it as 'quite new and unprecedented'; it comprises fourteen numbers falling into three sections following an overture, and includes entr'actes and melodrama.[24]

Meanwhile he had warmed to a much more realistic operatic scheme, the medieval romance *Genoveva*, recounting the misfortunes and eventual vindication of the virtuous Genevieve of Brabant, doubtless inspired by the recent publication of Christian Friedrich Hebbel's play of the same name. But Hebbel himself refused to be involved in producing a libretto for Schumann, who was never happy with his friend Robert Reinick's reconciling of Hebbel's version with Tieck's much earlier story, and Schumann wrote Act III himself, completing the composition within a year. But its production was bedevilled by delays and court opera politics over a two-year period from 1848 to 1850, and it was withdrawn after only three performances between February and April 1850. Though it contains much truly dramatic music, it lacks theatrical sense, mainly as a consequence of its libretto. It was the libretto that was the main cause of Wagner's reserve when Schumann discussed the work with him, though we only know so from Wagner himself, who 'pointed out the great effects in it and pointed out the necessary changes', Schumann resisting 'any interference with his work and his inspiration in a most stubborn and prickly fashion. So we left it at that.'[25]

Connected much more closely with his practical circumstances were his choral works. By January 1846 Schumann had expressed to Carl Reinecke his belief in the importance of writing for chorus, and over the next five years his output completely transcended his initial contributions of 1840. His interest in the Liedertafel movement is already apparent in the Gesänge for male voice chorus, op. 62, and the Ritornelle in canonic form, op. 67, the latter reflective of his contrapuntal preoccupations in the canonic studies and sketches published as op. 56 and 58, and the fugues on BACH, op. 60 for pedal piano or organ, all of 1845. Two sets of Romanzen, opp. 69 and 91, of 1849 for women's voices alone reflect his work with the mixed-voice Verein. And likewise drawing again on many favoured poets is the much larger number of works for mixed voices: these include eight opuses, published with chorus and solo settings (beginning before he founded the choir) in 1846 (opp. 55, 59) and in 1849 (opp. 67, 75, 138, 142, 145, 146), comprising upwards of forty settings, including four sets of Lieder und Romanzen. Impressive double-choir writing for male voices appears in the motet Verzweifle nicht im Schmerzenthal (Despair not in the Vale of Sorrow), op. 93, and in the mixed choruses, op. 141. Though some of these are stylized for social function (the Jagdlieder with horns, and the posthumously published three Deutsche Freiheitsgesänge, WoO 4 (1937) reflect his sympathy with the political events of 1848–9, as do the Marches, op. 76 that he referred to as his 'Republican Marches'), most pieces clearly illustrate his comments on having achieved a new directness and melodiousness in his work, and his manifest pleasure in training and directing voices. They show a constant exploration of possibilities of ensemble though mixing of solo and chorus (the arrangement of the solo song 'Talismane', op. 25, no. 8 as op. 141, no. 4 is especially striking) and imaginative use of instruments, as well as exotic styles, for example in the *Spanische Liebeslieder* with piano duet, and the *Spanisches Liederspiel* with a Bolero number.[26]

Work with the Verein inspired much larger works with orchestra: in 1847, *Beim Abschied zu singen* (*To Be Sung on Parting*), op. 84, for chorus and double wind orchestra; in 1848, the *Adventlied*, op. 71, to a sacred poem by Friedrich Rückert (employing the chorale *Nun danket alle Gott*); in 1849, the evocative *Nachtlied*, to a text by Hebbel for chorus and orchestra, op. 108. The Goethe year of 1849 inspired focus on the *Wilhelm Meister* lyrics: the *Requiem für Mignon* of 1849 is a cantata- like presentation of Mignon's funeral passage for solo voices, mixed choir and orchestra. The return to the piano was also strongly educational in motive. He drew particular attention to his *Album für die Jugend* (*Album for the Young*), op. 68. This work, published in 1848, intended for the composer's own children, is presented in order of increasing difficulty. It is divided into two parts – *Für Kleinere* and *Für Erwachsene* – the first edition stating that 'the Album seeks not only to train the fingers but to shape musical taste'. And a new simplicity also characterizes many of the nine *Waldszenen*, op. 82, of 1848–9, which evoke Germanic Romanticism's love of country and forest scenes; similar qualities inform the piano duets *Bilder aus Osten* (*Pictures from the East*).

These trends also appear in a second era of solo song from March 1849 continuing into the early 1850s, in which Schumann produced another 120 songs in 14 opuses. The *Liederalbum für die Jugend*, op. 79, complement the piano works of op. 68: 28 settings of poems of folk-like character drawing on familiar sources, notably from *Des Knaben Wunderhorn*, and Geibel translations of Spanish texts, as well as of poets already set by Schumann. And in the same vein, entire sets of Spanish folk poetry to Geibel translations (opp. 74, 138). But by this time Schumann had set a vast number of poets, and overall the stylistic range represents, like the choral works, an impressive repertory of great stylistic variety, with many of the opuses comprising duets and choral pieces as well as solos. Rückert's *Liebesfrühling* provides texts for another group of eight pieces: *Minnespiel*, op. 101. The Goethe focus of 1849 yielded further settings from *Wilhelm Meister*: seven of the Mignon and Harper songs, op. 98a. But he also turned to entirely new poets: Nikolaus Lenau (op. 90); 'Wilhelm von der Neun' ('Wilhelm of the Nine [Muses]': F. W. T. Schöpff; op. 89); the teenage Elisabeth Kullmann, who died at 17, with whose verse Schumann became obsessed (op. 104, of 1851); poems attributed to Mary, Queen of Scots (op. 135, December 1852); and those of Julius Buddeus, Karl Candidus, Ferdinand Braun, Paul Heyse and Titus Ulrich.

Before this wave of vocal settings, and following his therapeutic keyboard works of 1845, Schumann's attempt to regain control of creative life had become manifest in the concern to revise and elaborate earlier large-scale unpublished works. In the summer of 1845 he added to the Fantasia for piano and orchestra of 1841 an Intermezzo and Finale to create the Piano Concerto in A minor, his first full concerto. He also revised the three-movement *Sinfonietta*, written at the same time. These successes doubtless helped him to embark on the C major Symphony, of bigger dimensions and scoring than previous orchestral works: his most obvious response to the 'Great' C major Symphony of Schubert from its broad and cumulative introduction and finale. But he also continued with single-movement or continuous concerted works: the Introduction and Allegro Appassionato (known as the *Concertstück*, op. 92) for Clara in 1848 and, in 1849, the *Konzertstück*, op. 86, for four horns and orchestra in three uninterrupted movements. Dresden was also fruitful in chamber music. His contact with the two concert masters of the Court Orchestra, Franz Schubert and Friedrich Kummer, stimulated his first published Piano Trio, in D minor, op. 63 (clearly in the line of the Mendelssohn Trio in this key); and he followed it with the Piano Trio in A minor that he had offered to Peters in 1844 but not delivered, now appearing through Kistner as *Fantasiestücke*, op. 88, a suite of four individual movements. Further instrumental works found important new openings in the literature, marketable in alternative scorings: for clarinet (also viola or cello) and piano, the *Fantasiestücke*, op. 73; for oboe (also violin or clarinet) and piano, the three *Romances*, op. 94; for horn (also violin or cello) and piano, the Adagio and Allegro, op. 70; for cello and piano, *Fünf Stücke im Volkston*, op. 102.

But Dresden was no place for the public performance of major orchestral works: rather Mendelssohn and the Leipzig Gewandhaus were at hand for superior performance. They gave the C major Symphony its first performance on 5 November 1846. Not even works written for Dresden players were given there first. The *Konzertstück*, op. 86, written for the Dresden horn section, was performed first in Leipzig. The D minor Piano Trio, presented to Clara on her twenty-eighth birthday on 13 September 1847, was, though played privately with Schubert and Kummer, premiered at Leipzig Tonkünstlerverein on 13 November 1848 with the pianist Heinrich Enke, Wasielewski and Andreas Grabau.

The high point of Schumann's public presence as a musician in Dresden must be judged the performance of the *Faust* music, under his direction in Dresden, given simultaneously in Leipzig under Julius Rietz, and in Weimar under Liszt, on 29 August 1849. Schumann had commented humorously to Härtel earlier 'I should like to have Faust's cloak for just that day, so as to hear it everywhere.' It was received well in Weimar, and Schumann remarked to Brendel that 'the performance here [Dresden] was as good as could be after only two short orchestral rehearsals. The choruses were excellent, and they sang with the greatest enjoyment. The solo parts, too, were first rate … The audience listened with rapt attention.' But Leipzig was less successful. Schumann considered it a mistake to have put the work in the first part of the programme since 'the character of the entire [last] scene is one of conclusion'; also relevant was that the original rather than revised form of this movement was used, since the parts had not been copied.[27]

By the later 1840s Schumann was confident with his progress in letters to his circle. To Brendel: 'as I have said before, I am quite content with the recognition I have so far met with in an ever widening sphere. No doubt, chance does sometimes throw one together with narrow minded folks and mediocrities, but one must not mind them.' Indeed, in response to adverse reviews he had said that he did not understand the so called lack of appreciation of his works: 'Where are the composers whose works are all equally popular?' Yet Schumann could also be sensitive: he became extremely irritated in 1850 about a biography provided in the *Allgemeine musikalische Zeitung*: '[it] is almost entirely a translation of an article which appeared in the *Gazette Musicale* in 1836. What the author has added at the end of it might quite well also have been written in 1836: to my mind it but inadequately expresses my present position as an artist.'[28]

He sought constant news of his performances and kept in contact with performers through the publisher and independently. To Härtel, before he had begun conducting, on 20 March 1846 he wrote: 'Has there been another *Liedertafel* since the first, and did they, perchance, try one of my songs? Did they make a good impression? Write to me quite openly – I always like that best.' To Otten, who had given the C major Symphony with the Philharmonic Orchestra in Hamburg in 1849: 'I have long heard of your activity in promoting good music, particularly by your *Concertverein*. Anything that is thoroughly good gets known without newspaper articles.' But this reticence was not absolute: he also remarked to Härtel: 'you know me well enough not to believe that I am friend of those trumpet calls which many publishers send out into the world; but the public is naturally forgetful, and wants reminding of things now and then'. In fact he kept his eyes open and was always appreciative of support. To Hiller: 'Reinecke ... told me that you had performed a symphony of mine. Is that the second? If so, I should like to know what you think of it. For although it is printed, there is always much to be gained for the future by comparing opinions in that way.'[29]

Schumann was especially active in motivating reviews through his circle, where an easy relation existed between publishers. He wrote to Härtel: 'Herr Whistling [who had published the Piano Quintet and Studies for pedal piano] is anxious that some of my compositions published by him should be discussed in your paper [AMZ] and begged me to intimate this to you. Perhaps Dr Krüger would undertake to criticize them: he is a very estimable critic, my favourite among the newer ones' (though they would subsequently fall out). To C. F. Becker: 'If you find the opus [Fugues, op. 72] of sufficient interest say something about it in one of the two papers ... I have not filed and worked so much at any of my compositions, and have endeavored to render it to some extent worthy of the great name it bears.' And to Härtel in 1846: 'I think it will be necessary for you to call attention to the Album [*Liederalbum für die Jugend*, op. 79] just before Christmas in the local and Leipzig papers, especially in the Dresden *Advertiser [Anzeiger]*.'[30]

Schumann was realistic about what would and would not sell – of the balance between sales and artistic value. Though he acknowledged to Härtel that pieces for male-voice choir could only command a small circulation ('if only I could write you something that would bring you real profit') and realized that the Fugues, op. 72, were naturally less popular (though he called them 'characteristic pieces [though] their form is severe'), he knew that many small-scale choral works commanded a large market in the often convivial choral culture of the time: this combined with his opportunity for rehearsal to motivate the large choral output. Schumann's financial records reveal the considerable increase in his compositional income and his establishment as an important figure, even if he did not have the popular status of Liszt and Chopin, nor the media attention of Wagner. And his big works were getting attention: the *Adventlied*, op.71, no. 1 for soprano solo, chorus and orchestra, was given its first performance after rehearsal with the Dresden choir at the Leipzig Gewandhaus under Julius Rietz in December 1849 – though, to get things in economic perspective – none ever rivalled the 1,500 copies published of his *Patriotisches Lied*. And nor, indeed, could sales of orchestral scores ever reach those of the four-handed arrangements that Härtel was especially keen to obtain.[31]

Before their marriage, Schumann had told Clara firmly that she would 'never be the wife of a *Kapellmeister*' (he had even earlier told her the same of a professor). But by the later 1840s, his natural desire for professional acknowledgment together with pressing economic circumstance had quelled these elevated reservations, and he was now in the market for musical directorship, spurred by his recent experience in conducting. In 1847 he had already responded to news that the directorship of the Vienna Conservatoire was becoming vacant, and had written to Nottebohm that 'the post is just such a one as I should like, as I am full of strength and energy now, and am longing for an active sphere of life', asking for details of the circumstances before making formal application, though nothing came of it. And after Wagner's vacation of the Dresden Opera directorship consequent upon his political exile from Dresden in 1848 Schumann also enquired about this. By 1849 he was again keen for a change. In July Härtel had informed him of the probability that Rietz, now the conductor of the Leipzig Gewandhaus, would receive the Berlin conductorship in succession to Otto Nicolai. Schumann's interest in Leipzig rekindled and he asked quickly that his name be put forward, only, however, to be put out by what he saw as Härtel's subsequent disingenuousness in the matter: 'I am gradually coming to the age of self-knowledge, and am learning how far an offence touches me, if, indeed, one was ever intended ... Have I been mistaken in the opinion I always thought you had of me hitherto?'. But Schumann was by any means a contender in this larger world of performance.[32]

It was again Hiller who moved Schumann forward. In mid November 1849, Hiller informed Schumann of his own likely appointment to Cologne and enquired whether Schumann would accept the Düsseldorf position that he would vacate if Cologne were offered. This posed a problem: Düsseldorf was certainly not a first choice among leading positions. But, equally, it represented an opportunity. The choir and orchestra had been well trained: and such a position meant a steady income. Schumann replied to Hiller with pointed requests for information on 19 November 1849. Though the Düsseldorf post

offered half the financial status of Liszt or Wagner as musical directors (the salary was to be 750 thalers, whereas Liszt received 1,000
thalers plus 300 for concerts, and Wagner 1,500 thalers as Court Opera
director), Schumann eventually felt bound to accept Hiller's offer.
Returning to Dresden after visiting Clara's relatives in Berlin, he officially accepted on 31 March 1849 to begin in September 1850. Officially
musical Dresden took no notice of Schumann's departure in August
1850, though the Verein acknowledged it with a farewell dinner. The
transition had included important exposure of his works in Clara's
concerts in Bremen and Hamburg in March 1850, when Clara had col-
laborated with Jenny Lind.[33]

7 Triumph and decline: Düsseldorf 1850–4

With the move to Düsseldorf, Schumann had, despite initial reservations, every reason to feel deep satisfaction with his achievements and status. His growing body of large-scale works and the growing familiarity of smaller works had placed him as the natural successor to Mendelssohn in many eyes. Once decided Schumann came to Düsseldorf with an upsurge of spirits and energy because the post gave completely new opportunities and support for his creations. Here Schumann might come into his own as a rounded public figure as composer, performer and artistic leader. The easy-going life in the Rhineland was totally different from the formalities of Dresden. The Rhinelanders were open to modern works, and Hiller had seen to it that every welcome was given him: the couple were greeted at the station on the evening of 2 September and the first week was a celebratory reception that exceeded anything in Schumann's own previous experience. Nothing, it seemed, could have promised more (indeed, he commented to Zwickau friend Carl Klizsch after the first season 'I am very contented with my situation, and as it does not tax my physical strength too much (conducting certainly is very fatiguing), I really don't know of any I should like better'). His responsibility was to be in charge of the Allgemeine Musikverein, a professional orchestra, excellent for a small town (previous conductors had been Mendelssohn, Julius Rietz and Hiller), and the Gesangverein, a highly proficient and enthusiastic amateur choral society, which presented in association

12 Robert and Clara Schumann in Hamburg. Daguerreotype taken on 20 March 1850 by Johann Anton Völlner.

around ten subscription concerts annually in a season from October to May in the Geißler Hall, including a benefit concert for the Director of Music and the traditional charity concert. A major choral work occupied the entire programme for at least two concerts, and the series also included chamber concerts held in the smaller Cuteschen Hall.[1]

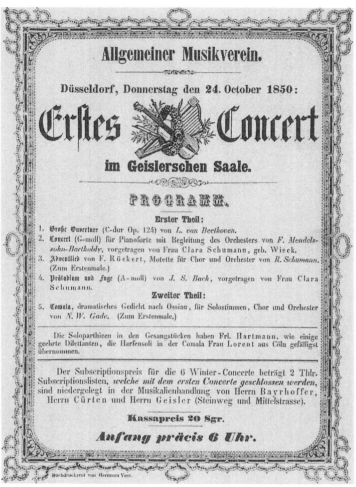

Allgemeiner Musikverein.

Düsseldorf, Donnerstag den 24. October 1850:

Erstes ☙ Concert

im Geislerschen Saale.

PROGRAMM.

Erster Theil:

1. Große Ouverture (C-dur Op. 124) von *L. van Beethoven.*
2. Concert (G-moll) für Pianoforte mit Begleitung des Orchesters von *F. Mendelssohn-Bartholdy,* vorgetragen von Frau Clara Schumann, geb. Wieck.
3. Adventlied von F. Rückert, Motette für Chor und Orchester von *R. Schumann.* (Zum Erstenmale.)
4. Präludium und Fuge (A-moll) von *J. S. Bach,* vorgetragen von Frau Clara Schumann.

Zweiter Theil:

5. Comala, dramatisches Gedicht nach Ossian, für Solostimmen, Chor und Orchester von *N. W. Gade.* (Zum Erstenmale.)

Die Soloparthieen in den Gesangstücken haben Frl. Hartmann, wie einige geehrte Dilettanten, die Harfensoli in der Comala Frau Lorent aus Cöln gefälligst übernommen.

Der Subscriptionspreis für die 6 Winter-Concerte beträgt 2 Thlr. Subscriptionslisten, *welche mit dem ersten Concerte geschlossen werden,* sind niedergelegt in der Musikalienhandlung von Herrn Bayrhoffer, Herrn Cürten und Herrn Geisler (Steinweg und Mittelstrasse).

Kassapreis 20 Sgr.

Anfang präcis 6 Uhr.

Buchdruckerei von Hermann Voss.

13 Schumann's first concert with the Allgemeine Musikalische Gesellschaft Düsseldorf, 24 October 1850.

As the civic musician, Schumann had also every year to oversee several choral performances at mass on saints' days in the two main Catholic churches, St Maximilianus and St Lambertus, of this Catholic city with the Gesangverein. Moreover, a leading role was required

14 The Geißler Hall, Düsseldorf.

in the very important Lower Rhine Music Festival when it rotated to Düsseldorf (the other venues were Aachen and Cologne), a major showcase for choral performance and new works every May, and in which the choral society played a very prominent part. The Schumanns immediately became part of the leading circle of the town, which included many painters, a number of whom were musical, notably Friedrich Wilhelm Schadow (brother-in-law of Eduard Bendemann in Dresden); Ferdinand Theodor Hildebrandt; Christian Köhler; and C.F. Sohn; as well as C. F. Lessing (nephew of G. F. Lessing); and Schumann's two doctors, Wolfgang Müller of Königswinter and Richard Hasenclever, a member of the Board of Health, much admired by Clara as a 'universal man'.[2]

Schumann threw himself into the first year's work and conducted all nine orchestral and choral subscription concerts of the season, his choice of repertory reflecting his idealism with support for both new composers and significant older music, as well his own and the emerging foundational concert repertory. Indeed, he was now able to express his commitments in a more direct way than as a writer

15 The 'Rhenish' Symphony in E flat. Four-handed arrangement by Karl
Reinecke.

and editor, and draw on his experience and achievements as a choral
conductor in Dresden. He was initially extremely impressed with the
choir and the potential of the orchestra. Every mixed concert save
one of the first season included a Schumann work, mainly for chorus
and orchestra, all recently composed: *Adventlied*, *Requiem für Mignon*,
Neujahrslied and *Nachtlied*, as well as the 'Rhenish' Symphony – given

a second time by request – the new overture *Die Braut von Messina*, the Introduction and Allegro Appassionato (op. 92) with Clara as soloist, and songs. The benefit concert on 13 March was almost entirely given to his music (Clara added Beethoven's 'Moonlight' Sonata). The music of close musical colleagues in Düsseldorf featured: notably orchestral overtures by Hiller, by his assistant conductor Julius Tausch, by Rietz and by Carl Reinecke, as well as items from Mendelssohn's *Elijah*. Schumann's particular admiration for Gade's *Comala* emerges again in his placing it as the second part of his first concert.[3]

The two fully choral concerts were given to Handel's *Israel in Egypt* at Christmas 1850 and Bach's St John Passion at Easter 1851 (the latter for the first time in Düsseldorf). The instrumental soloists were also mainly from Düsseldorf. Clara's was the most frequent solo presence, with the Mendelssohn G minor Concerto (complemented by Bach's A minor Organ Prelude and Fugue, BWV 543 in transcription) and Weber's *Konzertstück*. Tausch played the first Beethoven Piano Concerto, whilst Wasielewski as concert master gave the Mendelssohn Violin Concerto and a Beethoven Romance. Reinecke gave Mendelssohn's Second Piano Concerto. Another first Bach performance in Düsseldorf was of his 'Triple Concerto', BWV 1064, by three female pianists. A selection of concert and operatic overtures and operatic and choral/vocal solos and solo songs filled out the programmes, in which a planned complete cycle of the Beethoven symphonies as concluding items gave coherence (nos. 7, 5 and 6 in this season). The two chamber concerts followed similar repertory, introducing Schumann's D minor Trio and his Andante and Variations for two pianos, with Clara also presenting Mendelssohn's *Variations sérieuses* and Beethoven's 'Appassionata' Sonata, as well as smaller pieces: songs by Mendelssohn, Hiller and Rietz completed the programmes.

To external observers and Schumann's supporters the first season may have seemed successful. Hiller celebrated the first concert on 24 October with a reception, and Clara was very happy with her Mendelssohn concerto on the same occasion: 'it was the first time for many years that I had played an orchestral piece from memory'. But Hiller was committed to see the best in Schumann. In pitching hope against experience he turned a completely blind eye not only to his limited directorial skills, but to his temperament. But a much more objective observer, Schumann's concert master Joseph von Wasielewski (specifically appointed by him in 1850) saw at first hand through the veneer of appreciation that '[Schumann] lacked the ability to put himself in close rapport with others ... he also lacked the physical energy and endurance requisite for a director ... nor did he exercise any ... care or oversight.' Benefiting from the inherited discipline of his performing forces, 'most of the performances under his direction were satisfactory if the measure of technical perfection was not applied'. Events bear him out. Criticism soon began to surface in the press: a review appeared in the *Düsseldorfer Zeitung* at the end of March criticizing Schumann's direction as vague and too retiring for the whole season; and even his own concert on 13 March was seen as below par.[4]

Thus nothing had changed since Livia Frege's comment to Clara during the rehearsals for *Das Paradies und die Peri* in 1843 that 'if only you could persuade your dear husband to scold a little and insist on greater attention, all would go well at once', and Wagner's reference to Schumann's concert performance of the work in Dresden as 'quite extraordinarily incompetent'. But, quite apart from backing Robert in all circumstances, Clara's own comment in the early 1840s that conducting had to be more 'relaxed and expressive' suggests that she too did not take the technical aspects too earnestly and looked for other qualities: indeed, conducting in this period was still a nascent art and very variable in standards. This is clearly borne out in Schumann's earlier comments on conducting in the *Neue Zeitschrift*. Taking issue with the 'vanity and self-importance' of conductors as a 'distraction and necessary evil', he states plainly that 'a good orchestra ... needs to be conducted in symphonies, overtures and such, only at the start and at changes of tempo. For the rest, the conductor can quietly stand on the podium, following the score and waiting until his direction is again required', and where other time-beating is essential 'it must not become affected', most effort being devoted to rehearsal, with the emphasis on the commitment of the players to technical mastery. This, in summary, is exactly what was observed at Düsseldorf, and stands at the extreme opposite to the methods of Wagner. Thus in Düsseldorf Clara still praised Schumann for conducting 'perfectly quietly and yet with such great energy', and claimed that his performance of the 'Pastoral' Symphony was the best since Mendelssohn's time: and that the choruses of the St John Passion 'were most successful'.[5]

Schumann's first year had been of remarkable creative energy in composition clearly inspired by access to his own orchestra with its proficient principal players, a full choral society and guaranteed performance, as well as private music making, artistic exchange and study (plus opportunities for smaller-scale choral works). Indeed, the buoyant 'Rhenish' Symphony was written in specific celebration of his circumstances, composed between September and October 1850 in only five weeks, of which he commented 'I have attempted to capture the popular tone', apparent in the folk-like melodies, especially of movements two, three and four: the cathedral evocation movement. The three concert overtures inspired by classical plays – and intended first for operatic or oratorio treatment (he added to the overture to Schiller's *Die Braut von Messina* of 1850 overtures to Goethe's *Hermann und Dorothea* and Shakespeare's *Julius Caesar*) – were equally an attempt to explore and show off the orchestra. A cello concerto followed the symphony in November and was first read through and then rehearsed by the first cellist at Düsseldorf, Christian Reimers, at Schumann's home on 27 October 1851 (Wasielewski played the violin version at the same time), though set aside for further revision.[6]

But the choral society offered much bigger opportunities than Dresden. He drew most notably on the ballad genre (already explored in solo songs with piano). Using Romantic poetic versions of medieval stories as texts, he now claimed his choral ballads with orchestra as a new genre, the first of which was op. 116, a setting of Ludwig Uhland's *Der Königssohn*, in 1851. But his largest goal was something grand of the scope of *Israel in Egypt*, which he regarded as the ideal form, further to his strong objections to the poor state of the genre in the *Neue Zeitschrift* (and which he conducted on 21 December 1850), though he also wished to employ free poetry rather than religious and biblical texts. Again, his ambitions were of the loftiest kind, an oratorio on the subject of Martin Luther. But rather he settled for a work in clear succession to *Das Paradies und die Peri: Der Rose Pilgerfahrt (The Pilgrimage of the Rose)*, a text sent to him by August Horn in 1851, which recaptures its popular idiom with a similarly naïve fairy tale of a rose that aspires to the human condition, and thus to love. Written first with piano, Schumann then orchestrated it in 1851–2 to gain wider performance.[7]

It was the preparations of the 1851–2 season that brought the problems of Schumann's direction suddenly to a head. On 25 August 1851 a meeting of the Gesangverein levelled criticism at his conducting, finding him uncommunicative and even indolent as a conductor, and on 6 September Schumann had a 'stormy confrontation' with Wilhelm Wortman – the deputy Burgomeister, who was secretary of the committee of the Allgemeine Musikverein – apparently over the selection of repertoire and artists for the coming season, Wortman claiming Schumann's repertory was considered to include too much of his own music and that of his friends. But the deeper reason was the decline of morale. Clara's diary for the same day indicates the lack of attendance and interest in hard and new work of at least some of the members; the choral society was beginning to fall apart, with serious non-attendance for the new season and the orchestra not even fully manned, and this brought the suppressed reservations of the Schumanns to the surface: 'Robert thinks that few people – or, rather, no one – here is capable of entering easily into the deeper music; but I think there are as many people here as in Dresden, at least people here have more enthusiasm and more desire to find out what is good.'[8]

Schumann was certainly angry because of inattention (even chattering) in rehearsal. But whilst ready to leave, he was also aware that things might improve. So he forged ahead, obviously focusing on his supporters and better singers in forming a *Singerkränzchen*. Fired by a performance of *Der Rose Pilgerfahrt* at his home (just completed by the end of November, 1851), thirty singers agreed to meet every two weeks from autumn 1851 to sing items that the majority in the choral society (who wanted a more immediate musical experience) could or would not perform; he introduced them to church music of the sixteenth to eighteenth centuries. In a similar spirit he founded a *Quartettkränzchen* for significant modern chamber music from his leading players, depending on Reimers, Wasielewski and Becker, though this collapsed for lack of time.[9]

Schumann had scheduled only one major work of his own for the second 1851–2 season of subscription concerts: the premiere of *Der Rose Pilgerfahrt* as the second half of the fifth concert on 5 February 1852 (though he premiered his *Spanisches Liederspiel* in the charity concert on 20 May). Music of his contemporary circle of composers was again featured, with Gade's Symphony no. 4 and Mendelssohn's Symphony no. 4 (both for the first time); as well as overtures by Rietz and Sterndale Bennett (*Concert Overture* and *The Naiads* respectively); and instrumental and vocal works by Hiller, Stephen Heller and Mendelssohn. Clara played only once owing to pregnancy (the second Chopin Concerto), Tausch and Wasielewski also again playing concertos (Weber's E flat Piano Concerto; and Viotti's A minor Violin Concerto, no. 22 and Spohr's *Gesangsthema* respectively); and Schumann's special connection was acknowledged with the Schubert 'Great' C major Symphony, as well as Spohr's popular *Die Weihe der Töne* Symphony. Choral works reflected the greater study possible with the *Singerkränzchen* as a core, comprising major Baroque works little known, if at all, to his audiences: Handel's *Joshua* and movements from the 'Dettingen' *Te Deum*, Bach's St Matthew Passion and movements from the B minor Mass ('Et incarnatus' and 'Crucifixus'), the latter prompting particular resistance from some of the choir.

Schumann conducted concerts 1 to 6 from 23 October 1851 to 4 March 1852. But his absence from concert 7 on 18 March in order to direct his works at a festival of his music in Leipzig accelerated the movement of events. For Tausch's direction of the concert (including the Mass movements), illuminated Schumann's inadequacies, since they had been rehearsed by him, prompting the view that Tausch should take rehearsals for the forthcoming performance of the St Matthew Passion on 4 April (a more demanding work than the St John Passion) to lighten Schumann's burden. Quite apart from the challenge to Schumann's artistic authority, this also had financial consequences, since Tausch had to be paid from Schumann's salary, though Schumann conducted the Passion.

The drive to compose, especially for voice and choir, continued to consume Schumann. Now drawn further to ballad texts, in the summer of 1852 he set the declamation ballad, *Die Flüchtlinge* (*The Fugitives*); then a second and third choral ballad, *Des Sängers Fluch* (*The Minstrel's Curse*) to a text by Uhland, and *Vom Pagen und der Königstochter* (*The Page and the King's Daughter*) to a text by Geibel. A fourth choral ballad with men's voices, *Das Glück von Edenhall* (*The Luck of Edenhall*), also by Uhland, but adapted by Hasenclever, followed in 1853. All continue the earlier Romantic medieval/chivalric themes of curse and redemption. Then followed the first evidence of the liturgical music he was required to provide for the city in settings of the Mass, in C minor, and the Requiem Mass, in D flat major, for chorus, soloists and orchestra, Schumann commenting to Strackerjan that religious composition was the composer's 'highest aim'. He sketched the Mass within ten days in February 1852 during the Carnival season, and immediately turned to instrumentation, completing on 30 March 1852, and revising in the spring of 1853. His models were those of current study and performance: Bach's Mass in B minor, Cherubini's C minor Requiem and Beethoven's *Missa solemnis*. But, as with oratorio, he was clearly looking for a broader market, if not interpretation of the genre, in telling Schott in a letter that both the Mass and the Requiem were for 'church and concert hall'. The Mass was first rehearsed on 18 April 1852 with the *Singerkränzchen*, but the performance was deferred by ill health. He never directed a church performance of the Mass or Requiem; he planned to submit the Mass to an English choral competition advertised early in 1853.[10]

From late 1851, a new surge of chamber music also complemented that of the Dresden period (1848–9), again prompted by the leading instrumentalists to hand. The first two Violin Sonatas (in A minor and D minor: 'Grand' Sonata) and a third Piano Trio appeared through September to November, first rehearsed in Düsseldorf by Clara and Wasielewski, with Reimers as cellist. Wasliewski also gave the first reading of the new *Märchenbilder* (*Fairy Tale Pictures*) written earlier between 1 and 4 March 1851 for viola and piano – further evidence of Schumann's interest in unusual combinations. But it was old colleagues in Leipzig who were the Schumanns' preferred performers, and on their last visit to the city in March 1852, after several rehearsals at musical soirées, Clara, together with Ferdinand David, gave premieres to the A minor Sonata and, with Andreas Grabau, the new Trio on 21 March, during musical morning entertainments at the Gewandhaus (with Liszt in the audience). The second Sonata was also apparently premiered, at a private matinée on 15 March by Clara and David, the dedicatee, though it was publicly played only in 1853 by Clara and Joachim. For solo piano, Schumann's *Fantasiestücke*, op. 111, recapture the intensity of some of the pieces of the same title in his op. 12 of 1836, and continuing interest in piano composition for four hands appears in two sets of *Ballszenen*.[11]

Despite the background of opposition to his direction, Schumann pressed on with the 1852–3 season, now responding to the committed support of a much younger concert master, Ruppert Becker (Wasielewski having now apparently taken his cue from the deteriorating situation and gone to a new post). Schumann had again planned a technically demanding season with many Düsseldorf first performances. Of his own works, the new ballad *Vom Pagen und der Königstochter* was well received at its first performance and repeated at his benefit concert along with the first performance of the revised version of the D minor Symphony from manuscript (with the 'Kyrie' and 'Gloria' from the still incomplete Mass). The chamber concert of the series also began with his work: the Piano Quintet. Support for contemporaries continued in Gade's Symphony no. 2, Overture *Im Hochland*, and his *Frühlingsfantasie* for four vocal soloists, piano and orchestra (for the first time); the last concert comprised Hiller's Symphony *Im Freien* and Karl Müller's lyric scenes *Tasso in Sorrento*, both for the first time. Mendelssohn was also prominent, with *Lobgesang* as the second part of the first concert, and the finale to the opera *Lorelei* (first time). Other major choral works were Beethoven's cantata *Meeresstille und glückliche Fahrt* and Haydn's *Die Jahreszeiten*. Of instrumental music, Symphonies 4 and 7 completed the Beethoven sequence of nos. 1–8, and programmes included overtures by Weber (*The Ruler of the Spirits*) and Spontini (*Ferdinand Cortez*), and concertos played by Clara (the Henselt, and Beethoven in G major) and Becker (Mendelssohn Violin Concerto).[12]

But Schumann was not equal to the commitments. Owing to his continuing physical exhaustion following a summer vacation/cure in June–July 1852 in Bad Godesberg, he had to entrust Tausch with the first two concerts; the choir continued to prefer rehearsals under the deputy and the concerts went better. His first appearance was for the premiere of *Vom Pagen und der Königstochter* in the second part of the 2 December concert. But the audience was hostile and Schumann's confidence gone; there were calls for his resignation after a sluggish performance and another stormy meeting with the Allgemeine Musikverein on 11 December, followed by what Schumann called a *freche Briefe* ('cheeky letter') from Wortmann on 14 December suggesting that he limit his conducting. Though he was given a vote of confidence the next day by twenty-two members of the Allgemeine Musikverein, including Tausch, his pupil Albert Dietrich, Joseph Euler and Hasenclever (who objected to the tone of the letter), the damage had been done. There was now a tacit agreement that Tausch should train the choir and Schumann take orchestral rehearsals and public concerts. On 30 December Schumann returned to the podium to conduct Beethoven's Symphony no. 7 and the Gade *Frühlingsfantasie*, in which Clara was piano soloist. Problems for the rest of the season were largely resolved by substitution (Hiller and Müller conducting their own works).[13]

Düsseldorf had no interest in losing Schumann and the society was now involved in a damage limitation exercise to save its reputation by whatever means. With the pressure of the Lower Rhine Music Festival approaching in May 1853 in the city, Schumann was stimulated to renewed effort, but only managed with the aid of Hiller and Tausch. Though the featured choral work, Handel's *Messiah*, was not successful, Schumann garnered public acclaim for a second performance of his revised D minor Symphony on the opening day, the Piano Concerto with Clara and recent Festival Overture on the *Rheinweinlied* for tenor, choir and orchestra, op. 123.

The situation was now so grave that Schumann could not realistically survive another year of criticism: first the choir had declined, now the orchestra. The first disaster was at the religious choral concert at the St Maximilianus performance of Moritz Hauptmann's Mass on 16 October 1853, which, rehearsed by Tausch, Schumann had taken over at the last minute: on this occasion he was so absorbed that he continued conducting after the music had finished and the priest had begun intoning. The members of the Gesangverein now flatly refused to sing under his direction, which was to include Mendelssohn's *Erste Walpurgisnacht* at the first subscription on 27 October. It was agreed instead that Tausch would conduct short choral works – Mendelssohn's extensive choral ballad now being conveniently defined as a short work. Schumann had already pre-planned this concert to accommodate his admiration for Joseph Joachim – whom he had just heard again in Mendelssohn's Violin Concerto at the Lower Rhine Festival – through a performance of Schumann's new *Fantasia* in C, op. 131 (the Schumanns had first met the 13-year-old Joachim in November 1844 through Mendelssohn in Leipzig). The concert was also to include Joachim's overture *Hamlet*, a work new to Schumann and requiring his focused direction. Rehearsal proved a problem, the concert was very poorly received, and was the last Schumann ever conducted in Düsseldorf.

Facing the third subscription concert on 3 November 1853 with severely reduced options, the chairman and two members of the executive committee suggested to Clara on 7 November that Schumann conduct only his own pieces and leave other duties to Tausch; and that the choir should no longer appear in public unless conducted by Tausch. Clara immediately saw this as a conspiracy by the tactful Tausch, who had done everything to avoid confrontation in this most delicate situation. Schumann thought it a breach of faith and warned Tausch not to conduct the following concert. But it did not come to this, as Schumann failed to attend rehearsals or conduct the concert. Within a week the administration announced that Tausch would take over for the rest of the season. Schumann's blunt letter of 19 November now broke off relations with the committee. Niecks gives an apparently balanced first-hand account of the events from November and the report of the committee at that time, showing their very rational response and their reprimanding of the orchestral player who had angered Schumann by leaving a rehearsal.[14]

One reason for Schumann's growing impatience and increasingly resistance to criticism was his growing compositional reputation and success elsewhere. Attaining the Düsseldorf position had emboldened him. With the first scent of trouble at the end of his first year he was prepared to think of moving, always, as previously, with Vienna primarily in mind. With the problems of the third season he wrote to Carl van Bruyck on 17 December 1852 that he wanted to go to Vienna if an opening for a conductor could be found, and then again at the climax of his directorial problems in 1853: 'we intend to cut ourselves loose the winter after next (54/55), and are thinking of remaining some time in Vienna. Life in a small town no longer agrees with us; everything repeats itself as in a circle and powers and means always remain the same ... [do not] speak to a third person until it is decided.' This was all pure fantasy, as his comment at the same time to Joachim that 'I have an offer, though only through a third person' suggests. Schumann was completely unproven as a director and his reputation already dimmed as such: he had no basis for a professional move. But he had certainly sought to develop his contacts during this difficult time. The visit to Hamburg in the spring of 1850 had been highly successful, and Leipzig was by now a strong base through his long association with the Gewandhaus: the Leipzig festival from 5 to 22 March 1852 had consisted of three concerts featuring a broad selection of his choral, orchestral and chamber music, in which he conducted, and had been very successful and important.[15]

Schumann wrote to Verhulst on 9 November 1853 'my music is spreading more and more, and in other countries too, especially in Holland and England [and has found] harmonious echoes in men's hearts'. The accessibility of Holland prompted the tour on which the couple embarked after Schumann's resignation at Düsseldorf, from 24 November to 22 December 1853: twelve highly acclaimed concerts included songs, and nine major orchestral and choral works of Schumann. Clara played a very wide repertory, including the Piano Quintet; the Piano Concerto; and the Introduction and Allegro, op. 134; and most of the song accompaniments as well. Schumann even commented that he was better known in Holland than Germany. He also had a supporter in Belgium (de Sire), where he had adjudicated, and a longstanding invitation to England through Bennett.[16]

With the growing distribution of his works, a younger generation was drawn to Schumann as a major progressive figure in German music. Many sent their works, or even offered to make arrangements or editions of his own in tribute and in search of recommendations. He writes to Breitkopf & Härtel in February 1851 of the future editor of his letters: 'A young composer from Göttingen, G. Jansen, has sent me an arrangement of my first symphony for eight hands on two pianos which is admirably effective', and inviting publication. Schumann often recommended young composers and new works to his publishers: for example, Albert Dietrich's Piano Trio and Tausch's piano *Fanatasies*, both published by Breitkopf & Härtel (though Brahms uncharacteristically had had his compositions returned unopened in Hamburg in 1850). With Schumann's directorship Düsseldorf also became a place of pilgrimage for the young: Dietrich himself (1829–1908: a pupil of Moscheles, Rietz and Hauptmann in Leipzig) in 1851; [Fürchtegott] Theodor Kirchner (1823–1903): a pupil of C. F. Becker in Leipzig as well as of Schumann; Woldemar Bargiel (1828–97): Clara's half-brother as the son of her mother's second husband Adolf Bargiel; and Brahms's youthful Hamburg friend, Louise Japha (1826–1910).[17]

In retrospect it seems remarkably fortuitous that the two most intimate figures of the future Schumann circle came into his life so soon before his final breakdown. Two of the four concerto pieces of the Düsseldorf period were written for Joachim: of the *Fantasia*, Schumann commented 'there is a complete lack of brilliant concert pieces for the violin. This one in particular has a cheerful character.' But the Violin Concerto, composed for him soon after in November 1853, was more of a challenge to Joachim, and only ever rehearsed in his lifetime, on the Schumanns' visit to Hanover in January 1854. And Brahms arrived at the Schumanns' door on 30 September 1853 with the recommendation of Joachim. Both Robert and Clara were overwhelmed by his talent. Though Schumann did not write a piece for him, he did change the dedication of the Introduction and Allegro in D minor written for Clara and published as op. 134 for their thirteenth wedding anniversary with Clara's enthusiastic approval. More important, though, was the article in which he wrote his last and certainly most prescient endorsement of a young composer: 'Neue Bahnen' ('New Paths') for the *Neue Zeitschrift*, his first contribution for ten years, hailing Brahms as the prophet of new music. Schumann also wrote directly to Breitkopf & Härtel to recommend Brahms's compositions for publication.[18]

The celebration of Joachim's arrival in October 1853 brought the three composers and Albert Dietrich, now to be a close friend of Brahms, together. Schumann proposed to Dietrich that they and Brahms compose a sonata, the so-called 'FAE' Sonata. This was never intended for publication as such, and on 29 October Schumann began to write two more movements to complement his own and complete his third sonata, in A minor. The interest in unusual ensembles continued in the *Märchenerzählungen* (*Fairy Tale Stories*) scored for clarinet, viola and piano (violin ad lib), dedicated to Dietrich. Utility piano music continued in the three *Sonaten für die Jugend*, dedicated to Marie, Julie and Eugenie Schumann; and further piano duets, now titled *Kinderball*. The only works to follow these in 1853 were the Overture to complete the *Scenes from Faust* (finally added 19–23 December); the seven *Fughetten* for piano; the *Songs of the Dawn* (*Gesänge der Frühe*, op. 133), his last piano cycle, dedicated to Bettina von Arnim; and a single canon, 'An Alexis'.

Despite the creative stimulus of Schumann's new friends, there is clear evidence that Schumann's increasing public acceptance was accompanied by stocktaking, practical as well as mental – perhaps also recognition that he had now completed all he wished. He had by now not only written in every genre, but often multiple works within them. This is manifest in the related activities of revising his compositional list and earlier compositions; and also reflected growing confidence, and the need to look to posterity's judgment.

He wrote to Breitkopf & Härtel in 1853 'as one gets older one begins to look back on one's past life and is anxious to put one's mental affairs in good order. There already exists a catalogue of my compositions, but there is much fault to be found in the arrangement; and I think it would interest one's friends to know the dates of composition.' In fact Schumann had first discussed a published catalogue of works as early as 1847 with Whistling, though it did not appear until 1851 (through opp. 1–92), also listing arrangements and other items, though without thematic incipits. Breitkopf now offered him one on the lines of the Beethoven and Mendelssohn catalogues, and Schumann proofread it in January 1854, though they never published it. The first Schumann catalogue did not appear until 1860 from Schuberth, compiled by Alfred Dörfell.[19]

Listing of his works naturally triggered the desire for revisions. In addition to the most important of these – the innovative Symphony in D minor of 1841 – the revision of earlier piano cycles also became possible when publishers required new editions in the 1850s, and his extensive changes surely reflect the less Romantic atmosphere of reception and his mature need for the works to be seen as musically self-sufficient. In some cases he now removed evocative titles and expression markings (in op. 5 he also changed the movements). Equally, he now felt confident to release a number of unpublished earlier small piano works: 1852 saw the *Bunte Blätter* as collections of fourteen previously unpublished pieces from 1832 to 1837 as op. 99, and they were followed by the twenty *Albumblätter*, from the 1830s and 1840s, as op. 124 in late 1854. Another aspect of this earlier creativity was the critical writing that had occupied so much of this period. Schumann now assembled his complete writings, likewise subjecting them to a revised perspective, and describing them to his publisher Wigand as 'a record of myself, which might perhaps be of interest to many who only know me as a composer'.[20]

In retrospect, Schumann's failure to direct performances successfully was – at least to begin with – entirely predictable, recalling a pattern of work pressure leading to anxiety and illness. He had never had such public responsibilities and been under such technical scrutiny. By tragic irony, his attainment of the sought-for public status coincided with his final decline, a sad mixture of physical illness, depression, fear of failure, frustrated ambition and ideals – the inability of the mere mortals in his choir to grasp the greatness of the music with which he sought to inspire them. It clearly took very little to draw out old tendencies to arrogance and superiority, echoed by Clara, who simply encouraged them: she was equally frustrated and angry. Clara could do no more than support him, as she too was wholly committed to his creative world, if independent in many other regards. Deeply overworked by the end of the first year, he would clearly need medical care and his aggressive public behaviour tracked his declining physical condition, of which most of the audiences knew little or nothing. But Niecks confirms the definitely casual dimension of Schumann's attitudes, and there seems little doubt that the couple were soon considered outside their social circle to be standoffish and superior.

At the end of the first season on 11 June 1851, Schumann had told Wasielewski 'I am the victim of occasional nervous attacks, which sometimes alarm me; especially a few days ago, when I fainted after hearing Radecke playing the organ.' Wasielewski stresses that everyone noticed a change as 'symptoms of terrible, slowly developing, and anxiously watched disease appeared'. The couple sought relief by a summer holiday trip, from 19/20 July to 5 August 1851, down the Rhine to Rüdesheim. They spent a day in Heidelberg revisiting old haunts, then went on to Baden-Baden, Geneva, Chamonix and Vevey, returning on 5 August; it was recalled by both as an extremely happy time. But by the end of the second season, 1851–2, Schumann had suffered attacks of rheumatism, dizziness, apparent paralysis, convulsive coughing, coldness and insomnia, and could not go to Weimar for Liszt's premiere of the complete music to *Manfred* on 13 June. But rather the couple travelled again to the Rhineland for the eleven-day vacation/cure at Bad Godesberg from 26 June to 6 July, which included long walks and climbing up the Arthal and Siebengebirge – in very hot weather. Schumann was not protective of his exposure to the sun, and on an evening walk he again fainted. He returned to Düsseldorf on 7 July, very ill. The condition worsened through the summer of 1852 with difficulty of enunciation, which he had always suffered, though now more extreme.[21]

Since the beginning of 1852, Schumann had thought the music he conducted too fast, insisted upon slowing it when he led, and had a sad demeanor and inner apathy. Doctors again advised water treatment, and he began a series of daily river plunges in the Rhine, again briefly beneficial. Arrangements were now made to excuse him from his responsibilities for the imminent Lower Rhine Festival, as he was exhausted mentally and physically by the slightest exertion. Following the festival, Dr Müller persuaded Schumann to convalesce at the spa of Scheveningen on the Dutch coast for more of the daily immersion regimen. The couple left on 12 August and shared time there with Johannes Verhulst and Jenny Lind. There Clara had another miscarriage. Though himself still ill with various complaints and dizziness, and deeply concerned about Clara at the time, Schumann played down his own condition to Verhulst, suggesting that perhaps the fates 'will give me back my strength'.[22]

The season 1852–3 brought new features. His concert master Ruppert Becker was with him in a beer salon one evening when Schumann put down the paper and commented 'I can read no more. I hear an incessant A.' Dividing responsibilities for the summer festival he commented to Hiller 'My strength is not what it used to be', and to Strackerjan on 24 July 1853 'I have not yet got my strength back, either, and have to avoid any lengthy and fatiguing work.' Visiting Bonn in July 1853 he believed he had had a paralytic stroke one morning when he got up: his doctor could not persuade him otherwise. By the time of Schumann's final acrimonious exchanges with the Düsseldorf authorities in the autumn, he appears to have been resigned to failure there. Niecks's father, a member of the orchestra, confirmed that he was completely undiplomatic towards officials, could not brook contradiction and was almost childish with the orchestra. And this was without the fact that Clara kept many problems with the committee out of his way in acting so vociferously for him, though he also criticized her as rehearsal pianist.[23]

This was only one of the pressures Clara had to put up with. She was never really happy in Düsseldorf. Though initially taken with the openness of the people, especially the women, she increasingly found their informality – and that of the 'lower classes' as she put it – offensive ('rude, conceited, pretentious'). Clara continued to worry about money (they had incurred many expenses with the move). Though their instinct to move on was far from unnatural, the post offered many advantages: notably a secure income (Clara realistically observed 'when one has 6 children [moving] is not so easy'); and access to the rich musical life of the region, especially the Gurzenich concerts of Cologne, to compensate for that lack of artistic commitment she found in Düsseldorf. Her defensiveness, even paranoia, was a mirror of her constant need to be supportive and to compensate for Schumann's social deficiencies in many ways for years, and increasingly so at Düsseldorf.[24]

Though both were in denial, it was much more difficult for Clara to detach herself from circumstances. Schumann's professional and personal crises placed mounting pressure on her, as mother, head of the house, to say nothing of the pursuit of her own career. To their six surviving children, two more were added with the arrival of Eugenie in 1851 and then Felix in 1854, several months after Schumann's hospitalization. His creative detachment continued: he told her nothing about the 'Rhenish' Symphony. She embraced her role as muse with increasing determination: 'How magnificent is a mind like his, with such a power of incessant creative activity, and how fortunate I am that heaven has given me sufficient intelligence and feeling to understand his mind and character': one must suspect that this was written partly for posterity and in compensation for her frustrations, for it inevitably affected her own health: Robert now reports Clara as regularly unwell.[25]

Clara's performing life was completely compromised by circumstances. In the first two years they had four family homes. Their first apartment was on the Alleestrasse, but they soon had to leave it quickly when the house was sold, and made a disastrous move to a house with constant disturbance from noisy neighbors and building construction at 252 Königsallee. After the Rhine tour in the summer of 1851 they settled more comfortably into a house in Herzogsstrasse: a quiet neighbourhood to Robert's great relief, Clara observing him as 'joyful as he seldom is'. Finally, on 19 September 1852, they moved to a spacious new residence – a town house at 1032 Bilkerstrasse (now no. 15) – prompted by the growth of the family. Though they had had a fine music room in the second house, holding between twenty and seventy people and where the first performance of *Der Rose Pilgerfahrt* was given, it was not until the last house that Clara had a room of her own for practice, commenting that for the first time Robert could not hear her practising: 'When I am able to work regularly like this, I really feel in my element; quite a different feeling seems to come over me, I am much freer and lighter … Music is, after all, a good piece of my life, and when it is wanting I feel as if I had lost all physical and mental elasticity.' Clara's pupils were an important part of their income; and Robert bought her a new grand piano, to her immense surprise and pleasure, in September 1853.[26]

Throughout the pressures of professional life in Düsseldorf, Schumann appears to have remained at ease with his professional friends, in a natural alliance with people who understood him, especially Joachim and Brahms. He wrote to his old mentor Kapellmeister Kuntsch a most generous letter to acknowledge his professional jubilee early in July 1852. Wasielewski recalls of Schumann that:

> His habits during the last years of his life were exceedingly regular. In the morning he worked till about twelve o'clock: he then usually took

a walk with his wife and one of his intimate friends. At one o'clock he dined; and, after a short rest worked until five or six. He then generally visited some public place or private club of which he was a member, to read the papers, and drink a glass of wine or beer. At eight he usually returned to sup at home.

They continued to welcome musical visitors, as of old.

> He sometimes assembled a few of his musical friends and acquaintances at his own house, and could, if in the mood make a very agreeable host. While in Düsseldorf he was uncommonly gay and good natured. Once, after music and supper, he even proposed a general dance, in which he took a brisk share, to the great astonishment of all present.[27]

Wasielewski also furnishes a vivid description of Schumann in later years:

> Robert Schumann was of middling stature, almost tall and slightly corpulent. His bearing, while in health, was haughty, distinguished, dignified, and calm; his gait slow, soft, and a little slovenly. When at home he generally wore felt shoes. He often paced his room on tiptoe, apparently without cause. His eyes were generally downcast; half closed and only brightened in intercourse with intimate friends, but then most pleasantly. His countenance produced an agreeable, kindly impression; it was without regular beauty and not particularly intellectual. The fine cut mouth, usually puckered as if to whistle, was, next to the eyes, the most attractive feature of his round, full, ruddy face. Above the heavy nose rose a high, bold, arched brow, which broadened visibly at the temples. His head, covered with long, thick, dark brown hair, was firm and intensely powerful, we might say square. The expression on his face, although firm, was sweet and genial; the rich soul-life was hardly mirrored there. When he assumed a friendly, confidential manner – as he but seldom did – he could work upon his friends at will.[28]

8 The end: 1854–6

The year 1854 began quietly with family in Düsseldorf. The Allgemeine Gesellschaft continued to pay Schumann's salary, pending his own formal resignation, which had not been given, softening its tone and awaiting recovery. The committee was completely unwilling to face the embarrassment of seeking an immediate replacement in the circumstances, and Tausch continued to conduct. The only event was the brief visit in mid January to Hanover for treasured music making with Brahms and Joachim, who was Kapellmeister there. Schumann now worked unceasingly at his *Dichtergarten*, a collection of quotations of poets old and new on music (another of his lifelong interests), researching much of the time in the municipal library, commenting to Joachim, that '[it] is growing more and more [imposing], and I have put up signposts here and there so that people should not get lost, i.e. explanatory notes. I am now among the ancients, with Homer and the Greeks. I have discovered particularly splendid passages in Plato.'[1]

The darkness now finally came in the climax of events sadly chronicled by Clara through Litzmann's commentary, and no less disturbing for their familiarity. On the nights of 10 and 11 February:

> Robert suffered from so violent an affliction of the hearing that he did not close his eyes all night. He kept on hearing the same note over and over again, and at times he heard chords. By day it became merged in other sounds ... every noise, he says, sounds to him like music, a

16 The Schumann children, *c.* 1854–5. From left: Ludwig, Marie (with Felix on her lap), Elise, Ferdinand, Eugenie. Julie is absent.

music more wonderful and played by more exquisite instruments than ever sounded on earth.

This continued so that he could only work by day with

the most terrible effort. He said frequently, that if this did not cease, his mind must give way ... The affection of his hearing has

so increased that he hears whole pieces from beginning to end as if
played by a full orchestra, and the last chord goes on sounding until
Robert thinks of another piece. Ah! and one can do nothing to ease
him.[2]

On the night of 17 February:

Robert suddenly [got] up and wrote down a theme, which, as he said,
an angel had sung to him ... he was firmly convinced that angels
hovered around him revealing glories to him in wonderful music
... they bade us welcome and before a year had passed we should be
united with them ... Morning came and with it a terrible change. The
angel voices turned to those of demons and in hideous music they
told him he was a sinner and they would cast him into hell.

In the following days:

he felt himself surrounded alternately by good and evil spirits [and]
often they spoke. At the same time his mind was so clear that he
wrote touching, peaceful variations on the wonderfully, peaceful,
holy theme which he had written down on the night of the 10th ... as
well as two [business] letters. At night there were often moments
in which he begged me to leave him, as he might do me an injury ...
[but then] it was all right again ... He often complained that his
head was spinning, and then would assert that it would soon be all
over with him, and he would take leave of me, and make all sorts
of arrangements about his money and his compositions etc. ... On
Sunday [26 February] he felt a little better and in the evening he played
a sonata by a young musician Martin Cohn, to Herr Dietrich, with
the greatest interest, but worked himself into such a state of joyous
exaltation that the perspiration poured down from his brow.[3]

Despite all this Schumann was fully aware of his condition, and
still looked in his own way to cope with it. On 26 February, he suddenly
demanded to be removed to a psychiatric clinic for fear of his inadequacies and capacity to do harm. He sent for a carriage, arranged his papers
and prepared to depart. Clara calmed him, after challenging him with
the separation from his wife and children, to which he replied that he
would soon return home, cured. A doctor was called and Schumann

agreed to spend the night. Clara continues on the 27th: 'Robert got up, but he was more profoundly melancholy than words can say. If I so much as touched him he said "Ah! Clara, I am not worthy of your love." *He* said this; he whom I always looked up to with the greatest, the most profound reverence ... ah! and all that I could say was of no use.' A noonday visit from Dr Hasenclever and Albert Dietrich saw him completing a fair copy of the variations; when he had done this he

> suddenly left the room and went sighing into his bedroom. I had left the room for only a few minutes, in order to say something to Dr Hasenclever in the next room, and had left [little Marie] sitting with him (for 10 days I had never left him alone for a minute). Marie thought he would come back in a minute but he did not come, but ran out into the most dreadful rain, in nothing but his coat, with no boots and no waistcoat. Bertha [the maid] suddenly burst in and told me that he had gone – no words can describe my feelings, only I know that I felt as though my heart had ceased to beat. Dietrich, Hasenclever and in fact all who were there ran out to look for him, but could not find him; an hour later two strangers brought him back; where and how they found him I could not learn.[4]

In fact he had gone to the nearby toll bridge, given the collector his silk handkerchief in payment, had thrown himself into the Rhine, had attempted to do so again after initial rescue by tugboat men, and had been recognized. Clara was indeed not told about this, nor permitted to see him. Only much later did she find out the facts. A second physician was called in. Schumann had a paroxysm, which then calmed. In response to his persistent demands to be institutionalized, plans were now laid. Dr Hasenclever took the responsibility of executing his wish through his existing professional acquaintance with Dr Franz Richarz and his private sanatorium at Endenich near Bonn.[5]

Schumann travelled to Endenich with Hasenclever and two attendants on 4 March, with no parting message to his wife, a messenger confirming his safe arrival. From the first Clara was forbidden to visit him since Richarz believed that separation from the family was essential, and she wrote in anguish to Wasielewski several days later: 'My dearest friend. How can they do this to me? Not writing me a single word about my husband. It breaks my heart not to know how he lives and what he does, if he is still hearing voices, any word from him would be balm to my wounded heart. I do not look for any definitive result, just how he is sleeping, what he does each day, and if he asks for me.' She wasn't to see him again until just before his death in July 1856.[6]

Relative to the time, Richarz was progressive in avoidance of restraint, force-feeding or drugs: he prescribed baths, diet and purges, designed to contain symptoms. Schumann had a room of his own with a twenty-four-hour attendant, and had a piano and the means of composition his room. As emerges, he played and extemporized, at least during the first year, was generally free to wander in the grounds and was allowed accompanied visits to Bonn, which he treasured.[7]

For six months Schumann did not mention Clara's name. It was not until 12 September 1854 (their wedding day and the day before her birthday) that she records receipt of a letter from Dr Richarz indicating Robert's wish to hear from her. Her reaction suggests that she had been discouraged from doing this earlier, because she was hurt by the letter, quoting Richarz as stating 'Robert was beginning to doubt the existence of me and the children as it was so long since he had received a letter ... The doctor asked me to write him a few lines – they wished to see what impression it would make on him.' Though, having 'suffered so unspeakably for 6 months ... it was torture', she wrote two letters immediately. Schumann replied directly on 14 September initiating a semi-regular correspondence. This letter was overflowing with frustration about the location of his things – scores, and their letters and memories over many years – and his desire again to hear her 'wonderful' playing: 'Is it a dream that we were in Holland last year?'. He was practical as well: his letter of 18 September, which also confirms receipt of the news of the birth of their eighth child in June 1854, provisionally named Felix after Mendelssohn for Schumann's confirmation, tells her: '8 pm just got back from Bonn where I paid my regular visit to Beethoven's statue; the organ started playing; now stronger; will you ask Dr. Peters to give me some money from time to

time when I want it. And let me pay it back to him. It makes me so sad
to have nothing to give to a poor person.'[8]

But Schumann's mind was increasingly going back to happier times
as he sensed them departing completely. Since 27 February his life had
been radically changed; he was now living in a suspended state of reality: 'my life is less eventful than it used to be. How different everything
was then.' But Clara longed for every message about him, though she
was always disappointed. Thus on 30 December, 'a letter from Robert
at once cheering and depressing'. When she eventually asked Brahms
for Schumann's letters to him, she was severely disappointed. There
was not enough communication for her needs: we rather learn of what
she sent Robert – of news, musical scores and books, anything to support him and make a link – largely through his letters to Joachim and
Brahms.[9]

Indeed, Schumann's contact with Clara had stimulated his desire to
make contact with their circle of friends; though Clara was not allowed
to visit, Richarz allowed friends. Schumann wrote to Joachim, who
replied directly on 17 November 1854. The subject of Joachim's letter
was largely the D minor Violin Concerto:

> If I could only play your D minor concerto to you; I know it better
> now than that time in Hannover when, to my great annoyance, I did
> it such injustice at the rehearsal, because my arm was so tired with
> conducting. The ¾ time sounds much more stately now. Do you
> remember how pleased you were, and how you laughed when we
> said the last movement sounded as though Kosciusko were leading
> a Polonaise with Sobiesky: it was so stately? Those were glorious
> days!

Joachim also promised copies of his own overtures *Demetrius* and *Henry
IV*, noted Clara's performance of the Brahms variations on Schumann's
own theme in F sharp minor, that he had heard the Piano Quintet and
the enthusiasm for Schumann's music in Hanover.

Schumann replied on 25 November: 'if I could only hear my D minor
concerto played by you; my Clara wrote so enthusiastically about
it', asking for an enclosed letter to be sent to Brahms and to Clara,

wishing to see them all, and saying that he was still working on his *Dichtergarten* (Clara had just sent his recently published compositions and the first volume of his *Gesammelte Schriften*). On 27 December 1854 Clara received a letter from Richarz stating that Joachim's visit had pleased him. And Joachim and Brahms had said that complete recovery was on the way: but she was wary. This was Schumann's first visit in ten months.[10]

Schumann now wrote to Brahms on 27 November 1854. Again Schumann's preoccupation was with their music. He wanted to hear the Variations in F sharp minor, and talks about the music that Clara had sent in detail. Schumann further wrote of the variations to Brahms on 15 December asking what else he had published since they had parted; he was glad that they remembered him in Hamburg, and pleased to hear about the talent of his little girls Marie, Eugenie and Julie.[11]

On 11 January 1855 Brahms went to see Schumann and played him the Variations and Ballades, which Schumann had described vividly from the music to Clara in his letter of 8 January. But Schumann's letter of 22 January 1855 was now ominous: 'My Clara, I feel as if something terrible were before me. Woe is me if I am never to see you and the children!' Brahms wrote on 30 January to thank him for the dedication of the *Konzertstück* in D minor and with general news. On 19 February Brahms gave Clara a book of remembrance for Robert into which to press a flower from every city in which she stayed.[12]

Schumann's enthusiasm for Brahms and his music continued to be intense: in a letter of 20 March Robert says to Brahms of the Piano Sonata no. 2 'I live in your music. I can play most of it at sight.' He offers criticisms of Joachim's Variations on an Original Theme for viola, and requests the poems of Elisabeth Kullmann and an atlas. Schumann continued his concern about his own publications. In March–April 1855 he corresponded with Karl Joseph Simrock about the four-handed arrangement of the *Rheinweinlied* and arrangements for the translation of his *Maria Stuart* songs, and with Brahms concerning proofs of *Gesänge der Frühe*. Schumann's awareness of events continued through the newspapers: he had heard about his Düsseldorf position being offered to open competition, asking whether Brahms or Verhulst might apply, and then knowing that it had fallen to Tausch in that May. On 22 March a letter from Robert welcomed Clara home from touring.[13]

But these positive connections took place against a background of increasing decline, with chronic memory failure (insistence on his correct recollections even when they were faulty), and the fear that he was being poisoned. Brahms spared Clara the worst of what he had seen on his visits of 11 January and 14 February. After his visit on 2 April 1855, Brahms reported that Schumann now wanted to leave the sanatorium, and on 24 April Richarz noted to Clara that he was fearful that Schumann wanted to work too much. Wasielewski gave the most vivid description of his condition, writing to Eduard Hanslick that in the summer of 1855 he had listened with a friend to Schumann extemporizing at the keyboard from a side room 'like a machine whose springs have broken but which still tries to work, jerking convulsively'. But Schumann's friend Bettina von Arnim had a more robust response to his situation, noting on her visit in May 1855 that his treatment was inappropriate and that he should come home.[14]

But through the rest of 1855 his condition steadily deteriorated and he wrote to Clara on 5 May a spring greeting enclosing a picture of Mendelssohn with, however, another prophetic comment that 'there [was] a shadow hovering over' the next letter she would shortly receive. He then sent Brahms birthday greetings for 7 May, as we learn from Brahms's reply, which also informs us that Schumann had sent Brahms the original score of the *Braut von Messina* Overture. On 8 May 1855 Clara received a letter from the doctor telling her that Schumann was sleeping uneasily. She was concerned that she had not received his promised letter further to 5 May. She never received it; that was his last letter. On 4 September, oppressed by his silence, Clara wrote to Robert begging 'for one word … It is now four months since I received his last lines.' On 10 September 1855 a letter from Richarz arrived 'to deprive her of all hope of complete recovery'. Schumann's body no less than his mind revealed the strain of living; now he suffered disorders of taste and smell, and even deeper depression. It is from this point that the ineffectiveness of Richarz's treatment comes to the surface. Ostwald, whilst acknowledging the difficulties of treating the withdrawn Schumann, stresses other facts: a rash of suicides through self starvation at the clinic, suggesting declining care and the loss of Richarz's early ideals. He may have given up under the purely physical affront.[15]

By April 1856, Richarz wrote to Clara that Schumann was ill beyond help. Brahms saw him on 10 April and on 8 June, his birthday, and found him thin, oblivious to everything outside, now long preoccupied with picking names out of an atlas and putting them in alphabetical order; he was confined to bed with swollen feet. Hearing Brahms's report, Clara, who had been touring England since April, returned on 14 July. On 23 July, Clara received a telegram from Dr Richarz that he was nearing the end: 'the pain, the longing, just to have one more glance from him, to let him feel that I am near – I had to go'. She hurried to Endenich, but the crisis passed.[16]

Summoned again on the 27 July, Clara now saw Robert for the first time in over two years, at between 6 and 7 in the evening.

> He smiled, and put his arm around me with great effort, for he can no longer control his limbs. I shall never forget it. Not all the treasures in the world could equal this embrace. My Robert, it was thus that we had to see each other again, how painfully I had to trace out your beloved features. What a sorrowful sight it was. Two and a half years ago you were torn from me without any farewell, though your heart must have been full, and now I lay silent at your feet hardly daring to breathe; only now and then I received a look, clouded as it were, but unspeakably gentle.

On Monday 28 July Clara and Brahms spent the whole day at the clinic, and Clara helped Robert take a little wine, licked from her fingers. He died the following day at 4 in the afternoon, whilst they had gone to collect Joachim from the station: Clara did not see him till half an hour later. She records 'His head was beautiful, the forehead so transparent and slightly arched. I stood by the body of my passionately loved husband, and I was at peace. All my feelings were absorbed in thankfulness to God that he was at last set free, and as I kneeled by his bed I was

filled with awe, it was as though his holy spirit was hovering over me ...
If only he had taken me with him.'[17]

Clara's failure to visit Schumann and its possible effect on his condition has inevitably attracted attention: could she not have ignored Richarz and insisted on closer contact? But there seem obvious explanations. First, Clara, at least initially, totally relied on Richarz's medical authority and counsel in a situation that she could hardly comprehend, still less accept. Also she had her close circle to act for her in keeping the lines of communication open: and she continued to hope for at least a year that Schumann would recover and come home. She thus had no reason to consider moving closer to him; Endenich was some distance from Düsseldorf, not an easy visit. Equally important was the emotional impact on her: she also had to think of herself. There must have been a limit to her capacity to cope with the emotional upheaval of a visit when she needed above all to keep her sanity. And she admitted that she could not bear to see him like that: a barrier must inevitably have grown up in her against an impossible situation. She must have seen it all coming for years. She was constantly trying to reach him and maintain such contact as was permitted. Her deep frustration, false hopes and growing anguish come through every comment.

And then there was money. The clinic was expensive, costing 50 thalers a month, and she did not want to draw on his investments, now accruing in value to 5,000 thalers. She was fiercely independent and turned down all offers of help except from Paul Mendelssohn (her personal banker), from whom she took a large loan of 400 thalers, but which she soon repaid. She wanted to provide for herself and the children on her own, but by September 1854 declared 'my money is at an end'. Her sure way of resolving this was to greatly augment her teaching income by public performance, especially touring, which enabled her to use her talents to the full and promote Robert's music. But she kept her touring accessible (Leipzig, Weimar, in October 1854, then Rotterdam in January 1855), and turned down a lucrative British tour in case Robert should wish to see her. On 16 March 1856 she took her daughters Marie and Elise, now 15 and 13, to boarding school in Leipzig (12-year-old Julie was already living with Clara's mother in Berlin; Eugenie, 4, and Felix, 2, were being looked after at home; while Ludwig, 8, and Ferdinand, 7, were entered into an academy in Düsseldorf). Only then, with Robert out of communication, did she accept the British tour for three months, from 8 April to 6 July, though returning on reports of Robert's decline on 14 July. In July 1855, she happily recorded

> [concert profits] of 1,340 Thaler sufficient to bring my family through the summer and leave something over. I added another 500 Thaler to the 500 which I sent Paul Mendelssohn last winter. Now he had 1,000 Thaler of mine, and it will be a great joy when I can tell Robert of this. It would give me some comfort for all that I have suffered.[18]

Perspective and legacy

A quiet funeral was quickly arranged for two days later on the evening of 31 July at 7 in Bonn. Crowds gathered as they passed through the city, and Klaus Groth, the north German poet and recent friend of Brahms, asserts the cemetery suddenly became 'dark with people, as if there had been news of a great disaster'. The procession through the churchyard was led by Clara's close circle: her new young friends Joachim and Brahms, and Dietrich were the pall bearers, with members of the Düsseldorf Concordia, who had serenaded the Schumanns on their arrival there, bearing the coffin to burial in the (now Alter) Friedhof at the Sternetor for a simple ceremony. The various obituaries skirted around the cause of death: its circumstances and nature, which had naturally been the subject of rumour throughout musical Germany, were embarrassing. Mental health was not a subject for open discussion in 1856, nor for a century more in many settings; illness that would today be alleviated by medication was then socially catastrophic. The public assumption remained as it had been largely diagnosed by his doctors: that Schumann was possessed of an extraordinary creative energy and imagination, and that these forces had progressively exhausted and finally destroyed him.[1]

However, the circumstances inevitably fed the sense of curiosity. Wasielewski quickly pressed Richarz for an account of Schumann's illness and death including an account of the post mortem, which appeared in the first, 1858 edition of his biography. Richarz reproduced his diagnosis in the press in 1873, repeating the findings of brain ossi-fication and atrophy, and concluding that Schumann had suffered from organic disease from youth, which had only manifested itself in mental disturbance many years later under the pressure of excessive mental effort. But Richarz knew little of Schumann's lifelong mental disposition, and his post mortem was unilluminating of deeper expla-nations, as had been his notes: a reflection of the conventional view that he, at least for the record, accepted. Any other thoughts he had – and we now know that he knew about Schumann's claim of syphilitic infection – he kept to himself, as doubtless did others of Schumann's circle who may have suspected it. And thus the situation essentially remained until the modern times outlined in the Introduction.

But in 1856, the first task of the close circle round Schumann was the preservation of his artistic reputation: to safeguard the musical legacy by removing or protecting anything that might be thought of as displaying a diminution of powers. After his hospitalization, Clara's total dedication to Schumann's genius had already made her highly defensive, as well as suspicious of anyone wishing to probe his secrets, beginning with Wasielewski. She had already apparently destroyed five Romances for cello of November 1853 (successors to the *Fünf Stücke im Volkston* of 1849), which are noted in his writings and were rehearsed in the violin version by Joachim at the Schumann house on 29 January 1854. Most important was the Violin Concerto in D minor, over which she had perhaps exaggerated concerns about the finale, wanting Joachim to write another. Joachim's humorous recollections to Schumann of the movement in the Endenich period may also have masked deeper concern. However, Clara still looked for a publisher in the later 1850s but finally deferred to Joachim, its dedicatee, who kept the manuscript unpublished. At his death in 1907 it went to the Prussian State Library with obligation not to publish for 100 years after 1856, though in 1936 descendants withdrew the publishing injunction leading to its public performance.[2]

Though Schumann's other late instrumental music had the advan-tage of promotion by its dedicated performers as well as others, and was all published by 1854, many other unperformed and unpublished works were suspended by his hospitalization early in that year. It took until the mid 1860s for all to be published as the posthumous opp. 139–41 and 143–8, as well as *Faust*; even the *Neujahrslied*, very popular when first performed in Düsseldorf on 11 January 1851, had to wait till 1861 (as op. 144). Most problematic were the largest works: the Mass and Requiem Mass, which appeared last in 1862 and 1864 respectively. Brahms arranged a performance of the Mass to convince Clara to overcome her scruples about publication. None of Schumann's choral works gained a part of the status accorded Mendelssohn's two oratorios, or later Brahms's *Ein deutsches Requiem*. Most successful was the *Neujahrslied* of 1849–50, though the *Fest-Ouverture* with choral conclusion on the *Rheinweinlied* was not well received, despite Schumann's hopes for its wide popularity.[3]

The appearance of the collected *Robert Schumann Werke* in the 1880s was a marker in the acknowledgment of Schumann as a great figure. Here the canon on which Schumann's familiar reputation is based was largely complete. But problems of judgment were not over. Clara leant a great deal on Brahms as anonymous editor, and the nine items of the supplementary volume of 1893 included some rejected and original versions of works (notably the original version of the Variations, op. 46 and the five variations omitted from the *Etudes symphoniques*, as well as the *Geisterthema*). But they disagreed on publishing the original version of the D minor Symphony, Brahms regarding the original 1841 version as vastly superior. It was not included. Clara's desire to embody her views and experience of interpreting the piano music over a period of forty years led her additionally to produce her own performing edition of the piano music, as was customary for great performers before the age of recordings, to give a definitive view of the work through added editorial markings.[4]

But in the decades after his death, Schumann's reputation had grown unevenly. The piano music of the 1830s naturally had a head start, and the later piano music quickly joined it. But Clara, as its foremost promoter, was still highly selective in promoting Schumann's music to the best advantage: its technical as well as aesthetic challenges held it far behind Chopin and Mendelssohn, who were infinitely more firmly established in the repertory at the time of their deaths. But its popularity is evident in the collected editions of the piano works that were already beginning to appear in 1875 published by Breitkopf & Härtel, and especially in publications in England, a major economic market through Clara's annual concertizing after Robert's death. And soon the domestic side of this music found echoes in France: Bizet's *Jeux d'enfants* (1871) and Fauré's *Dolly Suite* (1894–5) for four hands are unimaginable without *Kinderszenen*; Bizet and Debussy also arranged the Canonic Studies for Pedal Piano, op. 56, for solo piano and two pianos respectively, and these very appealing pieces immediately became standards of the organ repertory. The Piano Concerto was far and away Schumann's best known orchestral piece and completely outperformed all his other orchestral works – symphonies, concertos and concert pieces – into the twentieth century. But the dissemination of other works was tied to the more constrained emergence of public recitals and instrumental and orchestral concerts. Thus the vocal works, especially cycles, emerged contemporaneously with those of Schubert in the growth of the public vocal recital: the baritone Julius Stockhausen pioneered performances of both composers, often accompanied by the young Brahms, and soon adding Brahms's own songs to the tradition. Because of their late publication, the symphonies of Schubert also appeared in the same years as those of Schumann, as public concert life evolved more broadly; and the works of many composers, beginning with Brahms, Dvořák and Tchaikovsky, and later Mahler and Berg, are unimaginable without Schumann's new poetic impulse in orchestral and instrumental music.

Schumann's reputation as a difficult modern was related especially to the later music: the increasingly introverted quality – uniquely apt for *Faust* and *Manfred* – posed more of a problem in the non-dramatic instrumental sphere. It is certainly easy to see the intense struggle of such minor-key works as the A minor and D minor Violin Sonatas, and notably the rugged first movement of the Violin Concerto, as a musical

equivalent of physical struggle. This was certainly the case with critics and was doubtless feared as reflecting decline by his circle. Thus,
the Trio in G minor was seen by the *Leipziger Signale* as possessing
'gloomy, concentrated passion, only here and there making room for
a gentler sentiment, restless surging and pressing and almost painful
wrestling that only rarely smoothes out to peaceful flowing motion'.
Conservatism was especially clear in England. The few leading supporters apart, critics in the leading journals through the 1860s all regarded
Schumann in the words first expressed as early as the 1840s by H. F.
Chorley (who had visited the Schumanns in Leipzig) in the *Athenaeum*
as 'a sincere but most unmelodious mystic'. It was not until a change of
heart by the more enlightened J. W. Davison of *The Times*, occasioned by
a performance of the E flat Symphony by the pioneering August Manns
at the Crystal Palace in 1869 that views began to change.[5]

But the 'mystical' character identified by Chorley was a reflection of
a resistance to change: in fact, later Schumann has a new quality of passionate inwardness undoubtedly drawn from the growing influence of
Bach (especially his choral music, only slowly becoming known to the
general musical audience), of Schubert and of later Beethoven. Brahms
would have to suffer from criticisms as 'the brooding Schumannite
Brahms' before his art was accepted for itself as a new aesthetic – and
no one ever accused Brahms of being depressive. It was perhaps predictable, though still ironical, that the search for a new musical sensibility on which Schumann had built his professional life as a critic
should in his own music have been interpreted as depressive. But the
creation of an audience for music of inward character, free of external
show and display, has become a vital part of the modern concert aesthetic. Schumann stands at the very centre of this sensibility: he would
surely have considered it the ultimate vindication of his work. Today
most listeners incline much more closely to Menuhin's initial response
to Schumann's Violin Concerto as 'the bridge between the Beethoven
and the Brahms concertos' than to the negative press reaction at its
first performances.[6]

But only towards the end of the twentieth century did these traditional prejudices recede. And by the 1970s interest had also begun to extend beyond instrumental music into choral music, long neglected in the twentieth-century reaction against this socially central nineteenth-century genre. The *Scenes from Goethe's Faust* found a major sponsor in Benjamin Britten and a classic recording in the 1970s. Major conductors have since presented the beauties of many of these works, not least the hitherto completely neglected *Nachtlied*; almost all the lesser-known large choral works and all the minor choral works have now been recorded. Even *Genoveva* has found new support as new broader attitudes to the function of music in drama have re-evaluated it in relation to the long-accepted Wagnerian values. In the view of Nikolaus Harnoncourt it is 'a work of art for which one should be prepared to go to the barricades ... not dramatic events but a glimpse into the soul ... a type of opera in which music has a greater say'. In the documentary field the commencement of the second collected edition of his works – *Robert Schumann Sämtliche Werke* – and the accompanying *Werkverzeichnis* of source materials have presented hitherto unparalleled detail in systematically accessible form. And the first decade of the century has seen fresh aspects of Schumann's literary/musical knowledge in the full publication of his *Dichtergarten*.[7]

Thus only at the start of the twenty-first century has it become possible through both performance and documentation to begin to see Schumann's life and music as a whole: to fully appreciate the very high quality of much of the lesser known music, and thus to see the unity of his complete artistic personality – a major figure who responded richly to the exciting and changing times in which he lived, and gave both vital critical and compositional impetus to the new directions in music and its communication to new audiences.

NOTES

Introduction: inherited images

1 The greatnieces of Joseph Joachim, the violinists Jelly and Adila d'Arányi,
claimed his authority in 1933 to release the Violin Concerto, which had
been embargoed for 100 years from 1856: see further for the entire history Michael Struck, *Die umstrittenen späten Instrumentalwerke Schumanns*,
Hamburger Beiträge zur Musikwissenschaft 29 (Hamburg: K. D.
Wagner, 1984), pp. 291–366. The 'dictated' theme (subsequently known
as the *Geisterthema*, F39) is, however, essentially that of the slow move-
ment of the Violin Concerto itself, written only four months before, in
November 1853: thus simply a memory.
2 The full account of the Endenich hospitalization is given in Bernhard
R. Appel (ed.), *Robert Schumann in Endenich (1854–1856): Krankenakten,
Briefzeugnisse und zeitgenössische Berichte*, Schumann Forschungen 11
(Mainz: Schott, 2006). Richarz's papers first appeared in F. H. Franken,
'Robert Schumanns letzte Lebensjahre: Protokoll einer Krankheit',
Stiftung Archiv der Akademie der Künste, *Archiv-Blätter* 1 (1994); par-
tially translated with commentary by Judith Chernaik, 'Guilt Alone
Brings forth Nemesis', *Times Literary Supplement* 5135 (31 August 2001).
3 Berthold Litzmann, *Clara Schumann: Ein Künstlerleben*, 3 vols.
(Leipzig: Breitkopf & Härtel, 1902–8; 1925); trans. and abridged by Grace
Hadow, *Clara Schumann: An Artist's Life*, 2 vols. (London: Macmillan, 1913).
Peter Ostwald, *Schumann: The Inner Voices of a Musical Genius* (Boston,
MA: Northeastern University Press, 1985); simultaneous British edition
as *Schumann: Music and Madness* (London: Gollancz, 1985).

4 Litzmann, *Ein Künstlerleben*, Vol. II, p. 301 (Litzmann, *An Artist's Life*, Vol. 2, p. 59); Robert Schumann, *Robert Schumann: Tagebücher*, 3 vols., Vol. I [1827–38], ed. Georg Eismann (Leipzig: VEB, 1971), p. 330; Vol. III.I: *Haushaltbücher: Teil I* [1837–47], ed. Gerd Nauhaus (Leipzig: VEB, 1982), p. 276; Vol. III.2: *Haushaltbücher: Teil 2* [1847–54], ed. Gerd Nauhaus (Leipzig: VEB, 1982), p. 648. The syphilitic dimension is discussed in great detail in John Worthen, *Robert Schumann: Life and Death of a Musician* (New Haven and London: Yale University Press, 2007), *passim*.

5 For typical conditions see J. Raymond dePaulo, Jr, *Understanding Depression: What We Know and What You Can Do about It* (Hoboken, NJ: Wiley, 2002), pp. 6–70. See further for perceptive discussion of Schumann's contemporaries with depression: Kate Redfield Jamison, *Touched with Fire: Manic-Depressive Illness and the Artistic Temperament* (New York: Simon and Schuster, 1994). Friedrich Niecks gives examples of Schumann's and his father's physical quirks from his acquaintance with the composer: Friedrich Niecks, *Robert Schumann: A Supplementary and Corrective Biography*, ed. Christina Niecks (London: Dent, 1925), pp. 299–302.

6 It seems significant that when Brahms published the *Geisterthema* (commonly known in English as 'Schumann's Last Thought') in the supplementary volume to the *Robert Schumann Werke* in 1893 (Leipzig: Breitkopf & Härtel, 1881–93), Series 14, he did not include the variations: they were only published in 1939 (see Robert Schumann, *Thematisch-bibliographisches Werkverzeichnis*, *Robert Schumann: Sämtliche Werke*, Series 8, *Supplemente 6*, ed. Margit McCorkle (Mainz: Schott, 2003) [F39], pp. 691–2). However, Brahms had previously used it for his own duet Variations on a Theme of Schumann, op. 23 in 1861 (published 1863).

7 Letter to Hermann Härtel of 28 July 1849, in Robert Schumann, *Robert Schumanns Briefe: Neue Folge. Zweite, vermehrte und verbesserte Auflage*, ed. F. Gustav Jansen (Leipzig: Breitkopf & Härtel, 1904), p. 308; trans. from *Neue Folge* by May Herbert, *The Life of Schumann: Told in His Letters*, 2 vols. (London: Bentley, 1890), Vol. II, p. 104.

1 A favourable upbringing: Zwickau 1810–28

1 Georg Eismann, *Robert Schumann: Ein Quellenwerk über sein Leben und Schaffen*, 2 vols. (Leipzig: Breitkopf & Härtel, 1956), Vol. I, p. 10. See

Heinrich A. Pierer, ed., *Universal Lexicon der Gegenwart und Vergangenheit*, 2nd edition, 34 vols. (Altenburg: H. A. Pierer, 1840–6), Vol. XXVII, p. 378. No mention is made in any source documentation of the second name, Alexander, often ascribed to Schumann.

2 Joseph von Wasielewski, *Robert Schumann: Eine Biographie*, ed. Wilhelm W. Wasielewski (Leipzig: Breitkopf & Härtel, 1906), 'Vorwort', pp. 3–5; trans. A. L. Alger, *The Life of Schumann*, repr. with new introduction by Leon Plantinga (Detroit: Detroit Reprints in Music, 1975), pp. 11–14.

3 *Salomo der Weise und sein Narr Markolf* ('Jerusalem' [= Zwickau?], 1797); *Handbuch der Merkantilisch-geographischen Gewerb- und Produktenkunde, für Kaufleute, Geschäfftsmänner und Statistiker, etc.* (Erfurt, 1797). Other mercantile books are *Die Handling von Hamburg* (Leipzig, 1803); and *Versuch einer vollständigen systematisch geordneten Warrenkunde* (Leipzig, 1807), dedicated to the 'Kaiser' [Tsar] of Russia.

4 *Walter Scott's Romane, aus dem Englischen* (Zwickau: Gebrüder Schumann, 1822–30); *Vollständiges Staats-, Post- und Zeitungs-Lexicon von Sachsen ... verfasst von A. Schumann [fortgeführt und vollendet von Albert Schiffner ...]*, Bd 1–18 (Zwickau: Gebrüder Schumann, 1814–30); *Bildnisse der berühmtesten Menschen aller Völker und Zeiten etc.* (Zwickau: Gebrüder Schumann, 1819–32).

5 Friedrich Niecks claims a young tutor was employed in the Schumann house in exchange for board and lodging for two years before preparatory school: Friedrich Niecks, *Robert Schumann: A Supplementary and Corrective Biography*, ed. Christina Niecks (London: Dent, 1925), p. 28; Eismann, *Ein Quellenwerk*, Vol. I, p. 11; the school is described by Emil Herzog (of Zwickau), *Geschichte der Zwickau Gymnasium* (Zwickau: 'Im Commission der Richters'chen Buchhandlung', 1869); Eismann, *Ein Quellenwerk*, Vol. I, pp. 10–11.

6 August Schumann is quoted from *Vollständiges Staats-, Post- und Zeitungs-Lexicon*, in Eismann, *Ein Quellenwerk*, Vol. I, p. 9. Emil Herzog's account in *Chronik der Kreissstadt Zwickau*, 2 vols., Vol. II (Zwickau: Kessinger, 1845), pp. 752–61 is translated in Niecks, *Robert Schumann*, pp. 16–17.

7 Eismann, *Ein Quellenwerk*, Vol. I, p. 14.

8 Ibid., pp. 18–23; Niecks, *Robert Schumann*, pp. 41–5.

9 Niecks, *Robert Schumann*, pp. 41–5; Eismann, *Ein Quellenwerk*, Vol. I, p. 28.

10 Eismann, *Ein Quellenwerk*, Vol. I, pp. 12, 18; Eugenie Schumann, *Ein Lebensbild meines Vaters* (Leipzig: Koehler and Amerlang, 1931), p. 20; Wasielewski, *Eine Biographie*, pp. 11 (Wasielewski, *Life of Schumann*, p. 18).

11 Eismann, *Ein Quellenwerk*, Vol. I, p. 13 note; Niecks, *Robert Schumann*, p. 33–5.

12 Eismann, *Ein Quellenwerk*, Vol. I, pp. 17–18; Wasielewski, *Eine Biographie*, p. 14 (Wasielewski, *Life of Schumann*, pp. 21–2).

13 Wasielewski, *Eine Biographie*, pp. 14–15 and note (Wasielewski, *Life of Schumann*, p. 22 and note); Eismann, *Ein Quellenwerk*, Vol. I, p. 44.

14 Eismann, *Ein Quellenwerk*, Vol. I, p. 21 and note. Letter of Kuntsch to Schumann of 1830 [n.d.], in Eismann, *Ein Quellenwerk*, Vol. I, pp. 67–8. Letter of Clara Schumann to Friedrich Niecks of 28 May 1889, in Niecks, *Robert Schumann*, p. 32. Letter to Kuntsch of beginning of July 1852, in Robert Schumann, *Robert Schumanns Briefe: Neue Folge. Zweite, vermehrte und verbesserte Auflage*, ed. F. Gustav Jansen (Leipzig: Breitkopf & Härtel, 1904), p. 358; trans. May Herbert, *The Life of Schumann: Told in His Letters*, 2 vols. (London: Bentley, 1890), Vol. II, p. 158).

15 Eismann, *Ein Quellenwerk*, p. 15.

16 Robert Schumann, *Thematisch-bibliographisches Werkverzeichnis, Robert Schumann: Sämtliche Werke*, Series 8, Supplemente 6, ed. Margit McCorkle (Mainz: Schott, 2003) [B1–4], pp. 658–70; the Kerner and other early song settings are listed as M1–2 in Robert Schumann, *Thematisch-bibliographisches Werkverzeichnis, Robert Schumann: Sämtliche Werke*, Series 8, Supplemente 6, ed. Margit McCorkle (Mainz: Schott, 2003), pp. 727–31). Letters to Wiedebein of 15 July 1828 and 3 August 1826, in Schumann, *Briefe*, pp. 6–8 (Schumann, *Life*, Vol. I, pp. 10, 12 (given as 5 August)); also in Eismann, *Ein Quellenwerk*, Vol. I, pp. 38–40.

17 Eismann, *Ein Quellenwerk*, Vol. I, pp. 15–16.

18 Letter on Schumann's twenty-fifth birthday quoted in E. Schumann, *Ein Lebensbild meines Vaters*, pp. 18–20. Joseph von Wasielewski (1822–96): subsequently a widely experienced conductor and writer on the violin.

19 See letter to Emil Flechsig of 1 December 1827, in Robert Schumann, *Jugendbriefe*, ed. Clara Schumann (Leipzig: Breitkopf & Härtel, 1886), pp. 11–13; trans. May Herbert, *Early Letters of Robert Schumann Originally Published by His Wife* (London: Bell, 1888 [repr. 1970]), pp. 10–11. Emil

Flechsig (1808–78): theologian, priest and later teacher at the Zwickau Gymnasium.

20 Eismann, *Ein Quellenwerk*, Vol. i, p. 14; Wasielewski, *Eine Biographie*, p. 19 (Wasielewski, *Life of Schumann*, p. 24); Robert Schumann, *Tagebücher*, 3 vols., Vol. i [1827–38], ed. Georg Eismann (Leipzig: VEB, 1982), p. 22.

21 Eismann, *Ein Quellenwerk*, Vol. i, pp. 15–16.

22 Letters to Flechsig of 'July', 29 August 1827, in Schumann, *Jugendbriefe*, pp. 1–11 (Schumann, *Early Letters*, pp. 1–10).

23 Carl Ernst Richter, *Biographie von August Schumann* (Zwickau: Gebrüder Schumann, 1826), p. 54; Schumann, *Briefe*, p. 564, note; E. Schumann, *Ein Lebensbild meines Vaters*, p. 60.

24 E. Schumann, *Ein Lebensbild meines Vaters*, p. 20.

25 Eismann, *Ein Quellenwerk*, Vol. i, pp. 31–2; Wasielewski, *Eine Biographie*, pp. 18–19 (Wasielewski, *Life of Schumann*, p. 16).

26 Letter to Johanna Schumann of 21 May 1828, in Schumann, *Jugendbriefe*, pp. 22–33 (Schumann, *Early Letters*, p. 22).

27 Letter to Flechsig of 17 March 1828, in Schumann, *Jugendbriefe*, pp. 13–19 (Schumann, *Early Letters*, p. 13).

2 Undirected student: Leipzig and Heidelberg 1828–30

1 Letter to Julius Schumann, 25 April 1828, in Robert Schumann, *Jugendbriefe*, ed. Clara Schumann (Leipzig: Breitkopf & Härtel, 1886), pp. 19–20; trans. May Herbert, *Early Letters of Robert Schumann Originally Published by His Wife* (London: Bell, 1888 [repr. 1970]), p. 19. Letter of 9 June 1828 to the Kurrer family, in Georg Eismann, *Robert Schumann: Ein Quellenwerk über sein Leben und Schaffen*, 2 vols. (Leipzig: Breitkopf & Härtel, 1956), Vol. i, p. 35. Letter to Gisbert Rosen of 5 June 1828 in Hermann Erler (ed.), *Robert Schumann's Leben: Aus seinen Briefen* 2 vols. (Berlin: Ries and Erler, 1886), Vol. i, pp. 4–6.

2 Letters to Johanna Schumann of 21 May, 13 June, 24 October 1828, in Schumann, *Jugendbriefe*, pp. 22, 25, 40 (Schumann, *Early Letters*, pp. 22–5, 38).

3 Letter to Johanna Schumann of 22 August 1828, in Schumann, *Jugendbriefe*, p. 32 (Schumann, *Early Letters*, p. 31); Robert Schumann, *Tagebücher*, 3 vols., Vol. i [1827–38], ed. Georg Eismann (Leipzig: VEB, 1982), p. 93.

4 Letter to Rosen of 5 June 1828, in Erler, *Robert Schumann's Leben*, Vol. I,
pp. 4–6; letter to Johanna Schumann of 29 June 1828 in Schumann,
Jugendbriefe, pp. 27–9, 24–6 (Schumann, *Early Letters*, pp. 27–8).

5 Letter to Johanna Schumann of 13 June 1828, 24 May 1829, in Schumann,
Jugendbriefe, pp. 25–6, 45 (Schumann, *Early Letters*, pp. 25, 43); letter
to J. G. Rudel of 4 July 1828, in Robert Schumann, *Robert Schumanns
Briefe: Neue Folge. Zweite, vermehrte und verbesserte Auflage*, ed. F. Gustav
Jansen (Leipzig: Breitkopf & Härtel, 1904), p. 6; trans. May Herbert,
The Life of Schumann: Told in His Letters, 2 vols. (London: Bentley, 1890),
Vol. I, p. 9. Julius is quoted in Robert's letter to Johanna Schumann of
24 February 1830, in Schumann, *Jugendbriefe*, pp. 105–6 (Schumann,
Early Letters, p. 102) (n.d., but following 11 February 1830). In assessing
monetary value, 800 thalers was a good salary for a civil servant; lodgings for a single man in a city like Dresden, 400 thalers a month: quoted
in Ronald Taylor, *Schumann: His Life and Work* (London: Granada, 1982),
p. 19.

6 Letters to Johanna Schumann of 21 May, 13 June 1828, in Robert
Schumann, *Jugendbriefe*, pp. 22–6 (Schumann, *Early Letters*, pp. 21–6).

7 Eismann, *Ein Quellenwerk*, Vol. I, p. 43; letter to Rosen of 5 June 1828,
in Schumann, *Briefe*, pp. 3–5 (Schumann, *Life*, Vol. I, p. 1); letters
to Johanna Schumann of 29 June 1828, 21 May 1828, in Schumann,
Jugendbriefe, pp. 27–9, 22–3 (Schumann, *Early Letters*, pp. 27, 22).

8 Letter to Johanna Schumann of 3 August 1828, in Schumann,
Jugendbriefe, pp. 29–31 (Schumann, *Early Letters*, pp. 28–30); letter to
Rosen of 7 November 1828, in Erler, *Robert Schumann's Leben*, Vol. I,
p. 11; A. F. J. Thibaut, *Über Reinheit der Tonkunst* (Heidelberg: J. C. B.
Mohr, 1825: revised and enlarged, 1826).

9 Letters to Johanna Schumann of 3, 31 August 1829, in Schumann,
Jugendbriefe, pp. 67–69, 74–5 (Schumann, *Early Letters*, pp. 65–7, 72).
Emphasis in original.

10 Letter to Johanna Schumann of 17 July 1829, in Schumann, *Jugendbriefe*,
p. 62 (Schumann, *Early Letters*, pp. 60).

11 Schumann, *Tagebücher*, Vol. I, p. 82. Schumanns analysis is quoted and
translated in Peter Ostwald, *Schumann: The Inner Voices of a Musical Genius*
(Boston, MA: Northeastern University Press, 1985), pp. 38–9.

12 Letter to Friedrich Wieck of 6 November 1829, in Schumann,
Jugendbriefe, pp. 78–9 (Schumann, *Early Letters*, p. 77).

13 Eismann, *Ein Quellenwerk*, Vol. 1, p. 81; letter to Wieck of 6 November 1829, in Schumann, *Jugendbriefe*, pp. 82–4 (Schumann, *Early Letters*, pp. 80–3).

14 Schumann, *Tagebücher*, Vol. 1, p. 179–182; Flechsig is quote in Eismann, *Ein Quellenwerk*, Vol. 1, pp. 43–5. Letter to Wieck of 6 November 1829, in Schumann, *Jugendbriefe*, pp. 81–5 (Schumann, *Early Letters*, pp. 79).

15 Töpken is quoted in Eismann, *Ein Quellenwerk*, Vol. 1, p. 55; letter to Wieck of 6 November 1829, in Schumann, *Jugendbriefe*, pp. 79–85 (Schumann, *Early Letters*, pp. 77, 83).

16 Letter to Johanna Schumann of 17 April 1832 in Schumann, *Jugendbriefe*, pp. 167–8 (Schumann, *Early Letters*, p. 160); letter to Ludwig Rellstab of 19 April 1832, in Schumann, *Jugendbriefe*, p. 176 (Schumann, *Early Letters*, p. 161).

17 Letter to Johanna Schumann of 22 August 1828, in Schumann, *Jugendbriefe*, pp. 31–2 (Schumann, *Early Letters*, p. 31); Eduard Röller is quoted in Eismann, *Ein Quellenwerk*, Vol. 1, p. 69; letter to Johanna Schumann of 31 August 1828, in Schumann, *Jugendbriefe*, p. 34 (Schumann, *Early Letters*, p. 33); letter to Wilhelm Götte of 2 October 1828, in Schumann, *Jugendbriefe*, p. 36 (Schumann, *Early Letters*, p. 34).

18 Schumann, *Tagebücher*, Vol. 1, p. 83. Joseph von Wasielewski, *Robert Schumann: Eine Biographie*, ed. Wilhelm W. Wasielewski (Leipzig: Breitkopf & Härtel, 1906), pp. 56–7; trans. A. L. Alger, *Life of Schumann*, repr. with new introduction by Leon Plantinga (Detroit: Detroit Reprints in Music, 1975), p. 49.

19 Letters to Johanna Schumann of 29 June, 3 August 1828, in Schumann, *Jugendbriefe*, pp. 27–30 (Schumann, *Early Letters*, pp. 26–8).

20 Schumann, *Tagebücher*, Vol. 1, pp. 110, 152, 156, 330.

21 Ibid., p. 201.

22 Ibid., pp. 252, 257, 261, 279.

23 Schumann's essay is quoted in ibid., pp. 242–3.

24 Letters to Johanna Schumann of 1, 30 July 1830, in Schumann, *Jugendbriefe*, pp. 115–16, 116–19 (Schumann, *Early Letters*, pp. 112, 113–14).

25 Letter to Johanna Schumann of 22 August 1830, in Schumann, *Jugendbriefe*, pp. 118–20 (Schumann, *Early Letters*, pp. 115, 117) (emphasis in original); Eismann, *Ein Quellenwerk*, Vol. 1, p. 15.

26 Letter of Johanna Schumann to Friedrich Wieck of 7 August 1830, in Eismann, *Ein Quellenwerk*, Vol. I, pp. 62–3; letter of Friedrich Wieck to Johanna Schumann of 9 August 1830, in ibid., pp. 63–5.

27 Letter of Johanna Schumann of 12 August 1830, in Ibid., p. 65; letter to Friedrich Wieck of 21 August, 1830, in Schumann, *Briefe*, pp. 25–6 (Schumann, *Life*, Vol. I, p. 32); Letter to J. F. Rudel of 21 August 1830, in Schumann, *Briefe*, pp. 26–7 (Schumann, *Life*, Vol. I, pp. 33–4).

3   A career in music: Leipzig 1830–5

1 Wieck's approach is evident in Friedrich Wieck, *Clavier und Gesang: Didaktisches und Polemisches* [1853] (Brussels: Almire, 1995); trans., ed. and annotated by Henry Pleasants, *Piano and Song: Didactic and Polemical* (Stuyvesant, NY: Pendragon, 1988); and the piano method of his second daughter, Clara's half-sister Marie Wieck (1832–1916): Marie Wieck (ed.), *Pianoforte Studies*, Peters Edition no. 375 (n.d.).

2 Letter to Johanna Schumann of 12 December 1830, in Robert Schumann, *Jugendbriefe*, ed. Clara Schumann (Leipzig: Breitkopf & Härtel, 1886), p. 134; trans. May Herbert, *Early Letters of Robert Schumann Originally Published by His Wife* (London: Bell, 1888 [repr. 1970]), p. 130. Letter to Johann Hummel of 31 August 1831, in Robert Schumann, *Robert Schumanns Briefe: Neue Folge. Zweite, vermehrte und verbesserte Auflage*, ed. F. Gustav Jansen (Leipzig: Breitkopf & Härtel, 1904), p. 31; trans May Herbert, *The Life of Schumann: Told in His Letters*, 2 vols. (London: Bentley, 1890), Vol. I, p. 34.

3 Letters to Johanna Schumann of 26 May 1832, 15 December 1830, in Schumann, *Jugendbriefe* pp. 179, 137–8 (Schumann, *Early Letters*, pp. 172, 133).

4 Christian Theodor Weinlig (1780–1842): theory teacher and Cantor at St Thomas's, Leipzig, 1823–42; Heinrich Dorn (1804–92), composer: Director of the Leipzig *Hoftheater* 1829–32. Georg Eismann, *Robert Schumann: Ein Quellenwerk über sein Leben und Schaffen*, 2 vols. (Leipzig: Breitkopf & Härtel, 1956), Vol. I, p. 74.

5 Eismann, *Ein Quellenwerk*, Vol. I, pp. 78–9; Robert Schumann, *Tagebücher*, 3 vols., Vol. I [1827–38], ed. Georg Eismann (Leipzig: VEB, 1982), p. 222. [Albert] Theodor Töpken (1808–80); Moritz Semmel (1807–74): brother of Therese Schumann.

6 Schumann, *Tagebücher*, Vol. I, p. 409 (13 June 1832); Wieck, *Didactic and Polemical*, p. 73; Schumann, *Tagebücher*, Vol. I, p. 386 and n. 392. Reuter is quoted in Peter Ostwald, *Schumann: The Inner Voices of a Musical Genius* (Boston, MA: Northeastern University Press, 1985), p. 89. Logier's 'Hand Director' or 'Chiroplast' is illustrated in S. Sadie (ed.), *The New Grove Dictionary of Music and Musicians*, 2nd Edition, 29 vols. (London and New York: Macmillan, 2001), Vol. II, p. 132. For further speculation on this topic, including the possible effects of arsenic treatment, see Ostwald, *Inner Voices*, p. 89; John Worthen, *Robert Schumann: Life and Death of a Musician* (New Haven and London: Yale University Press, 2007), pp. 64–9.

7 Eismann, *Ein Quellenwerk*, Vol. I, pp. 78–9; letters to Johanna Schumann of 9 August, 6 November 1832, in Schumann, *Jugendbriefe*, pp. 188, 194 (Schumann, *Early Letters*, pp. 179–80 and note, p. 185); letter to Töpken of 5 April 1833, in Schumann, *Briefe*, p. 40 (Schumann, *Life*, Vol. I, pp. 37–8).

8 Letters to Clara of 3 December 1838, 24 January 1839, in Eva Weisweiller (ed.), *Clara und Robert Schumann Briefwechsel: Kritische Gesamtausgabe*, 3 vols. (Frankfurt am Main: Stroemfeld/Roter Stern, 1981–2001), Vol. I, p. 307; Vol. II, p. 366; trans. Hildegard Fritsch and Ronald L. Crawford, *The Complete Correspondence of Clara and Robert Schumann: Critical Edition* 3 vols. (New York: Lang, 1994), Vol. I, p. 318; Vol. II, p. 29. Letter to Simonin de Sire of 15 March 1839, in Schumann, *Briefe*, pp. 148–51 (Schumann, *Life*, Vol. I, p. 207).

9 Eismann, *Ein Quellenwerk*, Vol. I, p. 75; letter to Wieck of 11 January 1832, in Schumann, *Jugendbriefe*, p. 162 (Schumann, *Early Letters*, p. 155); letter to Dorn of 25 April 1832, in Schumann, *Jugendbriefe*, pp. 168–9 (Schumann, *Early Letters*, p. 162). Schumann's use of Friedrich Marpurg's *Abhandlung von der Fuge*, 2nd Edition (1806), is discussed by Wolfgang Boetticher, *Robert Schumann: Leben und Werk* (Wilhelmshafen: Noetzel, 2003), pp. 533–4.

10 Schumann, *Tagebücher*, Vol. I, p. 349 (13 July 1831); letter to Kuntsch of 27 July 1832, in Schumann, *Jugendbriefe*, pp. 186–7 (Schumann, *Early Letters*, pp. 178–9); letter to Dorn of 25 April 1832, in Schumann, *Jugendbriefe*, pp. 168–9 (Schumann, *Early Letters*, p. 162).

11 Letter to Christian Gottlob Müller of 2 November 1832, in Schumann, *Jugendbriefe*, pp. 192–3 (Schumann, *Early Letters*, p. 184). Christian

GottlobMüller(1800–63):violinistandcomposer;Statdtmusikdirektor in Altenburg from 1838. Symphony in G minor: Robert Schumann, *Thematisch-bibliographisches Werkverzeichnis, Robert Schumann: Sämtliche Werke*, Series 8, *Supplemente* 6, ed. Margit McCorkle (Mainz: Schott, 2003) [A3].

12 Ernst Theodor Amadeus Hoffmann (1776–1822): poet, composer, conductor, designer and painter. The character of Johannes Kreisler in *Kreisleriana* is described in the translation of Hoffmann's *Fantasy Pieces in Callot's Manner: Pages from the Diary of a Travelling Romantic*, trans. Joseph M. Hayse (Schenectady, NY: Union College Press, 1996), pp. 15–53, 253–84.

13 Schumann, *Tagebücher*, Vol. I, pp. 339, 344 (8 June; 1 July 1831); letter to Dorn of 14 September 1836, in Schumann, *Briefe*, pp. 77–9 (Schumann, *Life*, Vol. I, p. 100); letter to Clara of 29 November 1837, in Weisweiller, *Clara und Robert Schumann Briefwechsel*, Vol. I, p. 53 (Weisweiller, *Complete Correspondence of Clara and Robert*, Vol. I, p. 52).

14 Frédéric Chopin, Variations for Piano and Orchestra, 'Là ci darem la mano' (from Mozart, *Don Giovanni*), op. 2. Letter to G. W. Fink of 27 September 1831, in Schumann, *Jugendbriefe*, pp. 154–5 (Schumann, *Early Letters*, p. 148). Robert Schumann, 'Von K. Schumann: Ein Opus II', review, *Allgemeine Musikalische Zeitung* 49 (7 December 1831), pp. 805–11. Schumann republished this in *Gesammelte Schriften über Musik und Musiker von Robert Schumann*, 4 vols. (Leipzig: Wigand, 1854), Vol. I, p. 3; trans., ed. and annotated by Fanny Raymond Ritter, *Music and Musicians: Essays and Criticisms by Robert Schumann*, 2 vols. (London: Reeves, 1877), Vol. I, pp. 4–7.

15 The *Kaffeebaum* survives to this day as the *Coffe Baum* in Kleine Fleschergasse (See Figure 3) and preserves the 'Schumann corner'. Letters to Johanna Schumann of 28 June 1833, 4 January 1834, in Schumann, *Jugendbriefe*, pp. 211, 229 (Schumann, *Early Letters*, pp. 201, 218).

16 The essays *Die Davidsbündler* appeared in three instalments in *Der Komet* on 7, 14 December 1833 and 12 January 1834, reprinted only in later editions of *Gesammelte Schriften*: see Robert Schumann, *Gesammelte Schriften über Musik und Musiker von Robert Schumann*, ed. Martin Kreissig, 2 vols, (Leipzig, Breitkopf & Härtel, 1914–15), Vol. I, pp. 260–72 (Schumann, *Music and Musicians*, p. 2). The

idea of an artistic brotherhood would have been most familiar to Schumann through E. T. A. Hoffmann's *Serapionsbrüder (Serapion Brotherhood)*, which he also identifies to Clara on 13 March 1840: Schumann, *Jugendbriefe*, pp. 309–10 (Schumann, *Early Letters*, p. 297); Schumann subsequently described the *Davidsbündler* in a letter to Dorn of 14 September 1836, in Schumann, *Briefe*, p. 78 (Schumann, *Life*, Vol. i, p. 100).

17 Schumann, *Gesammelte Schriften* (1854 edition), Vol. i, p. 3 (Schumann, *Music and Musicians*, p. 1); quoted in Eismann, *Ein Quellenwerk*, Vol. i, p. 86; Schumann, *Tagebücher*, Vol. i, p. 420; letter of Carl Schumann of 5 August 1833, in Schumann, *Jugendbriefe*, p. 221 (Schumann, *Early Letters*, p. 210); letter to Wieck of 6 August 1833, in Schumann, *Jugendbriefe*, p. 218–19 (Schumann, *Early Letters*, pp. 207–8); letter to Friedrich Hofmeister, n.d. (dated editorially after 9 August 1833), in Schumann, *Jugendbriefe*, pp. 224–5 (Schumann, *Early Letters*, p. 213; Robert Schumann, *Schumann Briefedition*, [40 vols.] (Cologne: Christoph Dohr, 2008–), Series 3, Vol. iii, p. 229).

18 See further Leon B. Plantinga, *Schumann as Critic* (New Haven and London: Yale University Press, 1967), pp. 4–8.

19 Letter to G. A. Keferstein of 8 July 1834, in Schumann, *Briefe*, p. 50 (Schumann, *Life*, Vol. i, p. 48). Gustav Adolf Keferstein (1799–1861): writer on music and priest.

20 Schumann, *Tagebücher*, Vol. i (2 December 1834), p. 419.

21 Letter to 'The Family Schumann', n.d. (editorially dated between 27 September and 14 October 1831), in Schumann, *Jugendbriefe*, pp. 155 (Schumann, *Early Letters*, p. 149).

22 The family financial details emerge in the course of the 1830s in correspondence. They are assembled and critically evaluated and detailed in Friederike Preiss, *Der Prozess, Clara und Robert Schumanns Kontroverse mit Friedrich Wieck*, Europäische Hochschulschriften, Reihe xxxvi: Musikologie 239 (Frankfurt am Main: Lang, 2004), pp. 120–31.

23 Letter to Clara of 10 May 1838, in Eva Weissweiller (ed.), *Clara und Robert Schumann Briefwechsel: Kritische Gesamtausgabe* (Frankfurt am Main: Stroemfeld/Roter Stern, 1981–2001), 3 vols., Vol. i, pp. 166–7; trans. Hildegard Fritsch and Ronald L. Crawford, *The Complete Correspondence of Clara and Robert Schumann: Critical Edition* (New York: Lang, 1994), 3 vols., Vol. i, p. 171.

24 Letters to Johanna Schumann of 5 May 1832, 4 January 1834, in Schumann, *Jugendbriefe*, pp. 177, 229 (Schumann, *Early Letters*, pp. 170, 218).

25 Letter to Töpken of 18 August 1834, in Schumann, *Briefe*, p. 51 (Schumann, *Life*, Vol. I, p. 54).

26 Eugenie Schumann, *Ein Lebensbild meines Vaters* (Leipzig: Koehler and Amerlang, 1931), p. 223.

27 All Schumann's Leipzig locations are identified on a contemporary map reproduced on the back cover of Hans Joachim Köhler, *Robert Schumann: Sein Leben und Werken in den Leipziger Jahren* (Leipzig: Edition Peters, 1986).

28 Letter to Johanna Schumann of 8 May 1832, in Schumann, *Jugendbriefe*, p. 175 (Schumann, *Early Letters*, p. 168). Henriette Voigt (1808–39); Carl Voigt (1805–81): Eismann, *Ein Quellenwerk*, Vol. I, pp. 95–6.

29 Letters to Julius Schumann of 5 September 1831 and to Johanna Schumann of 21 September 1831, in Schumann, *Jugendbriefe*, pp. 148–50 (Schumann, *Early Letters*, pp. 143–5).

30 Letter to Clara of 11 February 1838, in Weisweiller, *Clara und Robert Schumann Briefwechsel*, Vol. I, pp. 95–6 (Weisweiller, *Complete Correspondence of Clara and Robert*, Vol. I, p. 97); Joseph von Wasielewski, *Robert Schumann: Eine Biographie*, ed. Wilhelm W. Wasielewski (Leipzig: Breitkopf & Härtel, 1906), p. 110; trans. A. L. Alger, *Life of Schumann*, repr. with new introduction by Leon Plantinga (Detroit: Detroit Reprints in Music, 1975), p. 79 and note. Letter to Johanna Schumann of 27 November 1833, in Schumann, *Jugendbriefe*, pp. 227–8 (Schumann, *Early Letters*, pp. 215–16).

31 Letter to Joseph Fischhof of 14 December 1834, in Schumann, *Jugendbriefe*, pp. 263–4 (Schumann, *Early Letters*, p. 251); letter to Johanna Schumann of 2 July 1834, in Schumann, *Jugendbriefe*, p. 243 (Schumann, *Early Letters*, p. 230). The friendship with List is chronicled in Eugen Wendler (ed.), *Das Band der ewigen Liebe: Clara Schumann's Briefwechsel mit Emilie und Elise List* (Stuttgart and Weimar: Metzler, 1996).

32 Letter to Johanna Schumann of 2 July 1834, in Schumann, *Jugendbriefe*, p. 243 (Schumann, *Early Letters*, p. 230–1). Berthold Litzmann, *Clara Schumann: Ein Künstlerleben*, 3 vols. (Leipzig: Breitkopf & Härtel, 1902–8; 1925), Vol. I, p. 93; trans. and abridged by Grace Hadow, *Clara Schumann: An Artist's Life*, 2 vols. (London: Macmillan, 1913), Vol. I, p. 64.

33 Letter to Clara of 11 February 1838, in Weisweiller, *Clara und Robert Schumann Briefwechsel*, Vol. I, pp. 95–6 (Weisweiller, *Complete Correspondence of Clara and Robert*, Vol. I, p. 97).

34 Schumann, *Tagebücher*, Vol. I, p. 420.

35 Letter to Töpken of 5 April 1833, in Schumann, *Briefe*, pp. 39–44 (Schumann, *Life*, Vol. I, p. 37); Schumann's recollections are quoted in 'Musikalische Lebenslauf bis 1833' (manuscript), quoted in Schumann,*Werkverzeichnis*, Series 8, *Supplemente* 6, p. 18; letter to Breitkopf & Härtel of 2 November 1832, in Schumann, *Briefe*, pp. 413–14 (Schumann, *Life*, Vol. II, p. 217).

36 Robert Schumann, 'Franz Liszt', in *Gesammelte Schriften*, Vol. I, p. 484 (*Music and Musicians*, Vol. I, pp. 153–4). Schumann's reference to 'Bach's example' is to the use of the BACH motive in *The Art of Fugue*, which he was currently studying and probably knew before: it thus appears to provide the precedent for all his musical anagrams.

37 Letter to Breitkopf & Härtel of 2 November 1832, in Schumann, *Briefe*, pp. 413–14 (Schumann, *Life*, Vol. II, p. 217); letters to Hofmeister of 29 January, 31 July 1833, in Schumann, *Briefe*, pp. 414–17 (Schumann, *Life*, Vol. II, pp. 218, 220–1; Schumann, *Briefedition*, Series 3, Vol. III, p. 229).

38 Letter to Breitkopf & Härtel of 2 November 1832, in Schumann, *Briefe*, pp. 413–14 (Schumann, *Life*, Vol. II, p. 217); letter to Fink, August 1833, in Schumann, *Jugendbriefe*, p. 225 (Schumann, *Early Letters*, p. 214).

39 Letter to Töpken of 5 April 1833, in Schumann, *Briefe*, p. 40 (Schumann, *Life*, Vol. I, p. 37); Letter to Hofmeister of 29 January 1833, in Schumann, *Briefe*, p. 500 (Schumann, *Life*, Vol. II, p. 218); letters to Ludwig Rellstab of 19 April, 7 December 1832, in Schumann, *Jugendbriefe*, pp. 167–8, 195–6 (Schumann, *Early Letters*, pp. 160–1, 186–8); letter to Wieck of 10 January 1833, in Schumann,*Jugendbriefe*, pp. 199–200 (Schumann, *Early Letters*, p. 190); letter to Johanna Schumann of 2 July 1834, in Schumann, *Jugendbriefe*, pp. 240–1 (Schumann, *Early Letters*, p. 228).

40 Schumann, *Werkverzeichnis* pp. 653–6; letter to Töpken of 5 April 1833, in Schumann, *Briefe*, pp. 39–44 (Schumann, *Life*, Vol. I, p. 37); letter to Wieck of 10 January 1833, in Schumann, *Jugendbriefe*, pp. 199–200 (Schumann, *Early Letters*, p. 190).

4 The *Neue Zeitschrift für Musik*, Clara and new horizons: Leipzig 1835–40

1 Letter to Gustav Adolf Keferstein of 31 January 1837, in *Robert Schumann, Robert Schumanns Briefe: Neue Folge. Zweite, vermehrte und verbesserte Auflage*, ed. F. Gustav Jansen (Leipzig: Breitkopf & Härtel, 1904), pp. 83–4; trans. May Herbert, *The Life of Schumann: Told in His Letters*, 2 vols. (London: Bentley, 1890), Vol. I, p. 111. Letter of Heinrich Probst to Breitkopf & Härtel of 22 April 1837, in Heinrich Probst, *Breitkopf und Härtel in Paris: The Letters of Their Agent Heinrich Probst between 1833 and 1840*, trans. with commentary by Hans Lennenberg, Musical Life in 19th-Century France 5 (Stuyvesant, NY: Pendragon, 1989), pp. 23–4.

2 Letter to Heinrich Dorn of 14 September 1836, in Schumann, *Briefe*, pp. 77–9 (Schumann, *Life*, Vol. I, p. 100); letter to C. F. Becker of 11 February 1839, partially quoted in Schumann, *Briefe*, p. 503, n.177 (Schumann, *Life*, Vol. I, p. 202). Carl Ferdinand Becker (1804–77): Leipzig organist, composer and writer on music.

3 Letters to Ignaz Moscheles of 26 February 1835, 8 March 1836, in Schumann, *Briefe*, pp. 62–3; 69–70 (Schumann, *Life*, Vol. I, pp. 70–1, 83). Ignaz Moscheles (1794–1870): pianist and composer. Letter to Joseph Fischhof of 14 January 1838, in Hermann Erler (ed.), *Robert Schumann's Leben: Aus seinen Briefen*, 2 vols. (Berlin: Ries and Erler, 1886), Vol. I, p. 136.

4 Letter to Keferstein of 21 March 1840, in Schumann, *Briefe*, p. 188 (Schumann, *Life*, Vol. I, p. 255). Schumann identifies the numbers '2, 12, 22, 32' etc., which also accompany his anonymous reviews in a letter to Theodor Töpken of 18 August 1834, in Schumann, *Briefe*, pp. 51–3 (Schumann, *Life*, Vol. I, p. 57). Letter to Heinrich Hirschbach of 7 September 1838, in Schumann, *Briefe*, pp. 136–7 (Schumann, *Life*, Vol. I, p. 180). Georg Dietrich Otten (1806–90). Letter to Dorn of 14 September 1836, in Schumann, *Briefe*, p. 78 (Schumann, *Life*, Vol. I, p. 101).

5 Letter to Anton Wilhelm [Florentine] von Zuccalmaglio of 8 August 1838, in Schumann, *Briefe*, p. 130–1 (Schumann, *Life*, Vol. I, p. 173); letters to Clara of 23, 25 October 1838, in Robert Schumann, *Jugendbriefe*, ed. Clara Schumann (Leipzig: Breitkopf & Härtel, 1886), pp. 292–3; trans. May Herbert, *Early Letters of Robert Schumann Originally Published by His Wife* (London: Bell, 1888 [repr. 1970]), pp. 280–2.

Different aspects of Schumann's relations with Vienna are cited in Leon B. Plantinga, *Schumann as Critic* (New Haven and London: Yale Universitiy Press, 1967), p. 30 *passim*. Letters to Clara of 23, 25 October 1838, in Schumann, *Jugendbriefe*, pp. 291, 293 (Schumann, *Early Letters*, pp. 280–282).

6 Letter to C. F. Becker of 11 February 1839, in Schumann, *Briefe*, p. 131 (Schumann, *Life*, Vol. I, p. 202); letter of Clara of 3 November 1838, in Eva Weisweiller (ed.), *Clara und Robert Schumann Briefwechsel: Kritische Gesamtausgabe*, 3 vols. (Frankfurt am Main: Stroemfeld/Roter Stern, 1981–2001), Vol. I, p. 287; trans. Hidegard Fritsch and Ronald L. Crawford, *The Complete Correspondence of Clara and Robert Schumann: Critical Edition*, 3 vols. (New York: Lang, 1994), Vol. I, p. 296.

7 Letters to Hirschbach of 13 July 1838; 16 May, 30 June 1839, in Schumann, *Briefe*, pp. 125, 155, 157–8 (Schumann, *Life*, Vol. I, pp. 165–6, 220, 224); review of Hector Berlioz, *Symphonie fanstastique*, *Neue Zeitschrift für Musik* 3/9 (1835), 50; review of Franz Schubert, Symphony in C, D. 944, *Neue Zeitschrift für Musik* 12 (1840) 81–3; review of Schubert, *Grosses Duo*, op. 140 (D. 812), *Neue Zeitschrift für Musik* 8 (1838), 177–8.

8 Schumann's contrapuntal exercises and uses of Bach-like fugue subjects are reproduced in Wolfgang Boetticher, *Robert Schumann: Leben und Werk* (Wilhelmshafen: Noetzel, 2003), pp. 521–9. Letter to Keferstein of 31 January 1840, in Schumann, *Briefe*, pp. 177–9 (Schumann, *Life*, Vol. I, p. 237).

9 Georg Eismann, *Robert Schumann: Ein Quellenwerk über sein Leben und Schaffen*, 2 vols. (Leipzig: Breitkopf & Härtel, 1956), Vol. I, p. 98 (12 September 1836); Berthold Litzmann, *Clara Schumann: Ein Künstlerleben*, 3 vols. (Leipzig: Breitkopf & Härtel, 1902–8; 1925), Vol. I, p. 89; trans. and abridged by Grace Hadow, *Clara Schumann: An Artist's Life*, 2 vols. (London: Macmillan, 1913), Vol. I, p. 75. Letter to Dorn of 14 September 1836, in Schumann, *Briefe*, p. 78 (Schumann, *Life*, p. 102).

10 Letter to Therese Schumann of 1 April 1836, in Schumann, *Briefe*, p. 72 (Schumann, *Life*, Vol. I, p. 87); letter to Clara of 13 April 1838, in Schumann, *Jugendbriefe*, p. 283 (Schumann, *Early Letters*, p. 271).

11 Letter to Clara of 13 April 1838, in Schumann, *Jugendbriefe*, pp. 283–4 (Schumann, *Early Letters*, pp. 271–2).

12 Letter to Clara of 22 December 1837, in Schumann, *Jugendbriefe*, p. 272 (Schumann, *Early Letters*, p. 260).

13 Letter to Clara of 11 February 1838, in Weisweiller, *Clara und Robert Schumann Briefwechsel*, Vol. I, p. 96 (Weisweiller, *Complete Correspondence of Clara and Robert*, Vol.I, p. 97); Litzmann, *Ein Künstlerleben*, Vol. I, p. 92 (Litzmann, *An Artist's Life*, Vol. I, p. 78).

14 Carl Banck (1809–89): song composer and music critic; contributor to the *Neue Zeitschrift* from January 1835.

15 Letters to Clara of 3 January 1838; 13, 15 August 1837, in Weisweiller, *Clara und Robert Schumann Briefwechsel*, Vol. I, pp. 68, 21–2 (Weisweiller, *Complete Correspondence of Clara and Robert*, Vol. I, pp. 68, 19–20).

16 Schumann, *Tagebücher*, Vol. II [1836–54], ed. Gerd Nauhaus (Leipzig: VEB, 1987), p. 33; letter to Wieck on 13 September 1837, in Litzmann, *Ein Künstlerleben*, Vol. I, pp. 123–4 (Litzmann, *An Artist's Life*, Vol. I, p. 105–6); letter to Clara of 18 September 1837, in Weisweiller, *Clara und Robert Schumann Briefwechsel*, Vol. I, pp. 24–8 (Weisweiller, *Complete Correspondence of Clara and Robert*, Vol. I, pp. 23–6).

17 Reprinted and translated in Robert Schumann, *Music and Musicians: Essays and Criticisms by Robert Schumann*, 2 vols. (London: Reeves, 1877), Vol. I, p. 386. Clara Novello (1818–1908): singer; daughter of Vincent Novello, founder of the major English publishing house Novello and Co.; Robena Laidlaw (1819–1901): pianist. Letter of 29 November 1837, in Weisweiller, *Clara und Robert Schumann Briefwechsel*, Vol. I, p. 53 (Weisweiller, *Complete Correspondence of Clara and Robert*, Vol. I, p. 52); letters with Therese Schumann of 25 March 1838, in Schumann, *Briefe*, p. 116 (Schumann, *Life*, Vol. I, p. 149); letter to Keferstein of 8 February 1840, in Schumann, *Briefe*, pp. 179–81 (Schumann, *Life*, Vol. I, p. 242–5).

18 Franz Grillparzer (1791–1872), 'Clara Wieck und Beethoven (F-moll-sonata)', 9 January 1838, *Wiener Zeitung für Kunst, Literatur* etc., reproduced in Eugen Wendler (ed.), *Das Band der ewigen Liebe: Clara Schumann's Briefwechsel mit Emilie und Elise List* (Stuttgart and Weimar: Metzler, 1996), p. 61. Clara's travel details are given in Litzmann, *Ein Künstlerleben*, Vol. I, pp. 266–83 (Litzmann, *An Artist's Life*, Vol. I, pp. 180–93).

19 Emilie List's letters to Schumann are given in Wendler, *Das Band der ewigen Liebe*, pp. 62–70.

20 Letter to E. A. Becker of 6 July 1839, in Schumann, *Briefe*, pp. 162–3 (Schumann, *Life*, Vol. I, p. 225). Details of the legal procedures are given in Friederike Preiss, *Der Prozess, Clara und Robert Schumanns Kontroverse*

mit Friedrich Wieck, Europäische Hochschulschriften, Reihe xxxvi: Musikologie 239 (Frankfurt am Main: Lang, 2004), pp. 83–178.

21 Preiss, *Der Prozess*, pp. 83–178.

22 Letter to Professor Bülau of 31 August 1840, in Schumann, *Briefe*, p. 193 (Schumann, *Life*, Vol. i, pp. 261–2).

23 Letter to Clara of 10 April 1839, in Weisweiller, *Clara und Robert Schumann Briefwechsel*, Vol. ii, p. 479 (Weisweiller, *Complete Correspondence of Clara and Robert*, Vol. ii, p 148); letter to Therese Schumann of 15 November 1836, in Schumann, *Briefe*, pp. 80–2 (Schumann, *Life*, Vol. i, pp. 105–9).

24 Letters to Therese Schumann of 25 March 1838, 15 December 1837, in Schumann, *Briefe*, pp. 115–16, 105 (Schumann, *Life*, Vol. i, pp. 148, 137).

25 Letter to Therese Schumann of 15 November 1836, in Schumann, *Briefe*, pp. 81–2 (Schumann, *Life*, Vol. i, p. 108); letter to Dorn of 14 September 1836, in Schumann, *Briefe*, p. 77 (Schumann, *Life*, p. 102).

26 Letter to Eduard and Carl Schumann of 19 March 1838, in Schumann, *Briefe*, pp. 114 (Schumann, *Life*, Vol.i, pp. 145–6); letter to Therese Schumann of 18 December, in Schumann, *Briefe*, pp. 143–5 (Schumann, *Life*, Vol. i, p. 198); letter to Clara of 4 January 1838, in Weisweiller, *Clara und Robert Schumann Briefwechsel*, Vol. i, p. 70 (Weisweiller, *Complete Correspondence of Clara and Robert*, Vol. i, p. 71).

27 Letter to Carl and Eduard Schumann of 19 March 1838, in Schumann, *Briefe*, pp. 114 (Schumann, *Life*, Vol. i, p. 146); letters to Clara of 13 April, 10 May 1838, in Weisweiller, *Clara und Robert Schumann Briefwechsel*, Vol. i, pp. 142, 166 (Weisweiller, *Complete Correspondence of Clara and Robert*, Vol. i, pp. 145, 171).

28 Letter of Easter Monday [1 April] 1839, in Weisweiller, *Clara und Robert Schumann Briefwechsel*, Vol. ii, p. 461 (Weisweiller, *Complete Correspondence of Clara and Robert*, Vol. ii, p. 130).

29 Letter to Clara of 4 May 1839, in Weisweiller, *Clara und Robert Schumann Briefwechsel*, Vol. ii, pp. 514–5 (*Complete Correspondence of Clara and Robert*, Vol. ii, p. 186); Hans Joachim Köhler, *Robert Schumann: Sein Leben und Werken in den Leipziger Jahren* (Leipzig: Edition Peters, 1986), p. 59.

30 Letter of Clara to Robert of 10 July 1839, in Weisweiller, *Clara und Robert Schumann Briefwechsel*, Vol. ii, pp. 631 (Weisweiller, *Complete Correspondence of Clara and Robert*, Vol. ii, p. 310). Letters to Clara of 29 November 1837, 9 January 1840, in Weisweiller, *Clara und Robert Schumann Briefwechsel*, Vol. i, pp. 50; Vol. iii, p. 857 (Weisweiller,

Complete Correspondence of Clara and Robert, Vol. I, pp. 49; Vol. III, p. 19).

31 Letters to Frau Devrient, n.d. [summer 1836], in Schumann, Briefe, pp. 73–4 (Schumann, Life, Vol. I, pp. 89–90, 91); letters to Frau Devrient of 15 September 1837, 10 March 1839, in Schumann, Briefe, pp. 99, 147–8 (Schumann, Life, Vol. I, pp. 130, 204); letter to Clara of 31 May 1840, in Weisweiller, Clara und Robert Schumann Briefwechsel, Vol. III, p. 1053 (Weisweiller, Complete Correspondence of Clara and Robert, Vol. III, pp. 211–12).

32 Letter to Clara of 11 March 1839, in Weisweiller, Clara und Robert Schumann Briefwechsel, Vol. II, p. 435 (Weisweiller, Complete Correspondence of Clara and Robert, Vol. II, p. 103); letter to Simonin de Sire of 15 March 1839, in Schumann, Briefe, pp. 150 (Schumann, Life, Vol. I, p. 211).

33 Letter to Eduard Krüger of 14 June 1839, in Schumann, Briefe, p. 157 (Schumann, Life, Vol. I, p. 223). Eduard Krüger (1807–85): music scholar and composer. Letter to Clara of [15] April 1838, in Weisweiller, Clara und Robert Schumann Briefwechsel, Vol. I, p. 146 (Weisweiller, Complete Correspondence of Clara and Robert, Vol. I, p. 150).

34 Letter to Dorn of 5 September 1839, in Schumann, Briefe, pp. 170 (Schumann, Life, Vol. I, p. 230); letter to Clara of 'Tuesday after Easter' 1838, in Weisweiller, Clara und Robert Schumann Briefwechsel, Vol. I, pp. 149–50 (Weisweiller, Complete Correspondence of Clara and Robert, Vol. I, p. 154).

35 Clara's theme is no. 4 of her Quatre pièces caractéristiques, op. 5 (1834–6); Schumann, Tagebücher, Vol. II, pp. 25, 30 (9 September 1836). Letter to Friedrich Kistner of 19 December 1836, in Erler, Robert Schumann's Leben, Vol. I, p. 101; letters to Clara of 19 March 1838; 27, 22 April, 9 June 1839, in Weisweiller, Clara und Robert Schumann Briefwechsel, Vol. I, pp. 126, 145; Vol. II, pp. 495, 562 (Weisweiller, Complete Correspondence of Clara and Robert, Vol. I, pp. 129, 166; Vol. II, pp. 166, 237).

36 Letter to Clara of 13 April 1838, in Weisweiller, Clara und Robert Schumann Briefwechsel, Vol. I, pp. 137–8 (Weisweiller, Complete Correspondence of Clara and Robert, Vol. I, p. 141).

37 Letters to Clara of 5 January, 6/7 February 1838, in Weisweiller, Clara und Robert Schumann Briefwechsel, Vol. I, pp. 75, 93, 90 (Weisweiller, Complete Correspondence of Clara and Robert, Vol. I, pp. 76, 94–5, 91–2).

38 Letter to Clara of 17 March 1838, in Schumann, *Jugendbriefe*, pp. 276–7 (Schumann, *Early Letters*, p. 264); letter to Carl Reinecke of 6 October 1848, in Schumann, *Briefe*, pp. 290 (Schumann, *Life*, Vol. II, p. 80); letters to Clara of 11 March, 12 July, 10 October 1839, in Weisweiller, *Clara und Robert Schumann Briefwechsel*, Vol. II, pp. 435, 640, 734 (Weisweiller, *Complete Correspondence of Clara and Robert*, Vol. II, pp. 103, 320, 417).

39 Letter to Clara of 29 November 1837, in Weisweiller, *Clara und Robert Schumann Briefwechsel*, Vol. I, p. 52 (Weissweiller, *Complete Correspondence of Clara and Robert*, Vol. I, p. 51); letter of Clara of 18 January 1838, in Weisweiller, *Clara und Robert Schumann Briefwechsel*, Vol. I, p. 77 (Weisweiller, *Complete Correspondence of Clara and Robert*, Vol. I, p. 78).

40 Letters of Robert to Clara of [26] January 1839, in Weisweiller, *Clara und Robert Schumann Briefwechsel*, Vol. II, p. 469 (Weisweiller, *Complete Correspondence of Clara and Robert*, Vol. II, p. 138); letter to Clara of [18] March 1838, in Schumann, *Jugendbriefe*, pp. 279–80 (Schumann, *Early Letters*, p. 267), not included in Weisweiller, *Clara und Robert Schumann Briefwechsel*; Litzmann, *Ein Künstlerleben*, Vol. I, p. 311 (Litzmann, *An Artist's Life*, Vol. I, p. 215).

41 Letters to Raimund and Hermann Härtel of 22 December 1835 and 22 May 1837 respectively, in Schumann, *Briefe*, pp. 417, 421 (Schumann, *Life*, Vol. II, p. 221–3).

42 Letter to Breitkopf & Härtel of 7 August 1837, in Schumann, *Briefe*, p. 421; letter to Raimund Härtel of 2 March 1839, in Schumann, *Briefe*, pp. 425–6 (Schumann, *Life*, Vol. II, p. 224).

43 Letter to Keferstein of 24 August 1840, in Schumann, *Briefe*, pp. 191–2 (Schumann, *Life*, Vol. I, p. 260); letter to Keferstein of 31 January 1837, in Schumann, *Briefe*, pp. 84 (Schumann, *Life*, Vol. I, p. 112); *Revue et gazette de Paris* 4/46 [12 November 1837], 488ff.

44 Letters to Clara of 11 February 1838, 27 October 1839, in Weisweiller, *Clara und Robert Schumann Briefwechsel*, Vol. I, p. 100; Vol. II, p. 768 (Weisweiller, *Complete Correspondence of Clara and Robert*, Vol. I, p. 101; Vol. 2, p. 452); Letter to W. H. Rieffel of 11 June 1840, in Schumann, *Briefe*, p. 189 (Schumann, *Life*, Vol. I, p. 257).

45 Letter to Clara of 17 March 1838, in Schumann, *Jugendbriefe*, p. 280 (Schumann, *Early Letters*, pp. 267–8); letter to Fischhof of 3 April 1838, in Schumann, *Briefe*, p. 118 (Schumann, *Life*, p. 153); letters to Clara following 19 March 1838, [26] January 1839, 13 March

1840, in Weisweiller, *Clara und Robert Schumann Briefwechsel*, Vol. I, p. 121; Vol. II, p. 367; Vol. III, pp. 980–1 (Weisweiller, *Complete Correspondence of Clara and Robert*, Vol. I, p. 124; Vol. II, p. 31; Vol. III, pp. 139–40). *Konzertsatz*: Robert Schumann, *Thematisch-bibliographisches Werkverzeichnis, Robert Schumann: Sämtliche Werke*, Series 8, *Supplemente* 6, ed. Margit McCorkle (Mainz: Schott, 2003), [B5].

5 Married life: Leipzig 1840–4

1 Berthold Litzmann, *Clara Schumann: Ein Künstlerleben*, 3 vols. (Leipzig: Breitkopf & Härtel 1902–8; 1925), Vol. I, pp. 430–1; trans. and abridged by Grace Hadow, *Clara Schumann: An Artist's Life*, 2 vols. (London: Macmillan, 1913), Vol. I, p. 299.

2 Undated letter to Mendelssohn, editorially placed between 24 September and 22 October 1845, in Robert Schumann, *Robert Schumanns Briefe: Neue Folge. Zweite, vermehrte und verbesserte Auflage*, ed. F. Gustav Jansen (Leipzig: Breitkopf & Härtel, 1904), p. 250; trans. May Herbert, *The Life of Schumann: Told in His Letters*, 2 vols. (London: Bentley, 1890), Vol. II, p. 34 (Robert Schumann, *Schumann Briefedition*, 40 vols. (Cologne: Christoph Dohr, 1998–2009), Series 2, Vol. I, p. 233, dated 27 September 1845). Robert and Clara's first two children were Marie, born 1 September 1841, and Elise, born 25 April 1843. Letter to Friedrich Wieck of 16 December 1843, in Georg Eismann, *Robert Schumann: Ein Quellenwerk über sein Leben und Schaffen*, 2 vols. (Leipzig: Breitkopf & Härtel, 1956), Vol. I, p. 136; letter to Joseph Verhulst of 19 June 1843, in Schumann, *Briefe*, pp. 228–30 (Schumann, *Life*, Vol. II, p. 302). Joseph Johann Verhulst (1816–91): Dutch composer and conductor.

3 Gerd Nauhaus (ed.), *The Marriage Diaries of Robert and Clara Schumann: From Their Wedding Day through the Russian Trip*, trans. with a preface by Peter Ostwald (1993), in Robert Schumann, *Tagebücher*, 3 vols., Vol. II [1839–54], ed. Gerd Nauhaus (Leipzig: VEB, 1987), pp. 5, 63.

4 *Ibid.*, pp. 64, 112.

5 The Inselstrasse house has recently been restored and houses a museum about Schumann. See further the detailed description of the accommodation in the exhibition catalogue: Kulturstiftung der Länder, *Das Robert-und-Clara-Schumann-Haus in Leipzig* (Berlin: Kulturstiftung der Länder, n.d. [c. 2000]); Nauhaus, *Marriage Diaries*, p. 120.

6 Kulturstiftung der Länder, *Das Schumann-Haus in Leipzig*, pp. 26–9.

7 Nauhaus, *Marriage Diaries*, pp. 183, 189.

8 Ibid., pp. 56, 194.

9 Ibid., p. 180.

10 Nancy Reich, *Clara Schumann: The Artist and the Woman*, rev. edition (Ithaca, NY and London: Cornell University Press, 2001), p. 90; Nauhaus, *Marriage Diaries*, pp. 36–7, 59, 133.

11 Nauhaus, *Marriage Diaries*, p. 185; Reich, *Clara Schumann*, p. 117.

12 Litzmann, *Ein Künstlerleben*, Vol. II, p. 41 (Litzmann, *An Artist's Life*, Vol. II, p. 335); Nauhaus, *Marriage Diaries*, p. 134.

13 Nauhaus, *Marriage Diaries*, p. 68; letter to Carl Kossmaly of 9 May 1841, in Schumann, *Briefe*, p. 206 (Schumann, *Life*, Vol. I, pp. 273–4). Carl Kossmaly (1812–93): writer on music, composer and conductor.

14 Letter to Joseph Fischhof of 28 August 1842; letter to Kossmaly of 8 January 1842, in Schumann, *Briefe*, pp. 219, 212–13 (Schumann, *Life*, Vol. I, pp. 289–90, 281); Nauhaus, *Marriage Diaries*, p. 86.

15 Nauhaus, *Marriage Diaries* (21 November 1843), p. 202; letter to Verhulst of 5 June 1844, in Schumann, *Briefe*, pp. 241–2 (Schumann, *Life*, Vol. 2, p. 20); Schumann, *Tagebücher*, Vol. III.1: *Haushaltbücher: Teil 1* [1837–47], ed. Gerg Nauhaus (Leipzig: VEB, 1982), p. 669; Nauhaus, *Marriage Diaries*, p. 197.

16 Letter to Verhulst of 19 June 1843, in Schumann, *Briefe*, pp. 228–30 (Schumann, *Life*, Vol. I, p. 303); Nauhaus, *Marriage Diaries*, p. 162; ibid., p. 204.

17 Letter to Kossmaly of 9 May 1841, in Schumann, *Briefe*, pp. 205–6 (Schumann, *Life*, Vol. I, p. 274); Gade held the position from 1844 until 1848.

18 Letter to J. G. Herzog of 4 August 1842, in Schumann, *Briefe*, p. 217 (Schumann, *Life*, Vol. I, p. 287).

19 Nauhaus, *Marriage Diaries*, p. 115.

20 The first song of February 1840 was Feste's closing song from Shakespeare's *Twelfth Night* (later published as op. 127, no. 5 in 1851); letter of Clara of 22 May 1840, in Eva Weissweiler (ed.), *Clara und Robert Schumann Briefwechsel: Kritische Gesamtausgabe*, 3 vols. (Frankfurt am Main: Stroemfeld/Roter Stern, 1981–2001), Vol. III, p. 1043; trans. Hildegard Fritsch and Ronald L. Crawford, *The Complete Correspondence of Clara and Robert Schumann: Critical Edition*, 3 vols. (New York: Lang, 1994), Vol. III, p. 201.

21 Clara Schumann and Robert Schumann, *Zwölf Gedichte aus Rückerts Liebesfrühling für Gesang und Pianoforte von Robert and Clara Schumann* (Leipzig: Breitkopf & Härtel, 1841): Robert wrote nos. 1, 3, 5–10, 12; Clara's songs comprise her own op. 12; Rückert is cited in Schumann's letter to Eduard Krüger of 25 June 1842, in Schumann, *Briefe*, p. 216 (Schumann, *Life*, Vol. I, p. 286); letter to Julius Mosen of 7 August 1833, in Schumann, *Briefe*, p. 44–5.

22 Andersen is quoted in Kulturstiftung der Länder, *Das Schumann-Haus in Leipzig*, p. 29.

23 '[E]in Oratorium, aber nicht für die Betsaal – sondern für heitre Menschen': letter to Krüger of 3 June 1843, in Schumann, *Briefe*, p. 228 (Schumann, *Life*, Vol. I, p. 298).

24 Sketches for other symphonies also exist in this period: see Robert Schumann, *Thematisch-bibliographisches Werkverzeichnis*, *Robert Schumann: Sämtliche Werke*, Series 8, Supplemente 6, ed. Margit McCorkle (Mainz: Schott, 2003) [A5–7], pp. 656–60.

25 Nauhaus, *Marriage Diaries*, pp. 30, 37, 39.

26 Letter to Härtel of 14 December 1843, in Schumann, *Briefe*, p. 438 (Schumann, *Life*, Vol. II, pp. 239–40); letter to Friedrich Hofmeister of 5 November 1842, in Schumann, *Briefe*, p. 434 (Schumann, *Life*, Vol. II, p. 231–2): Schumann, *Briefedition*, p. 262.

27 Letter to Hofmeister of 5 November 1842, in Schumann, *Briefe*, p. 434 (Schumann, *Life*, Vol. II, p. 232): Schumann, *Briefedition*, p. 262.

28 Letter to Kossmaly of 8 January 1842, in Schumann, *Briefe*, pp. 212–13 (Schumann, *Life*, Vol. I, p. 282); letter to F. C. Griepenkerl of 31 October 1841, in Schumann, *Briefe*, p. 209 (Schumann, *Life*, Vol. I, p. 279–80). Friedrich Conrad Griepenkerl (1782–1849): professor of philosophy and editor of J. S. Bach's keyboard/organ works. Letter to August Kahlert of 10 May 1842, in Schumann, *Briefe*, p. 216 (Schumann, *Life*, Vol. I, pp. 284–5).

29 Letters to Kossmaly of 1 September 1842, 5 May 1843, in Schumann, *Briefe*, pp. 220, 226–8 (Schumann, *Life*, Vol. I, pp. 291, 296).

30 Letters to Kossmaly of 9 May, 28 October 1841 and 25 January 1844, in Schumann, *Briefe*, pp. 205–6, 208, 230 (Schumann, *Life*, Vol. I, pp. 273, 278; Vol. II, p. 6).

31 Nauhaus, *Marriage Diaries*, pp. 126–7.

32 See Nauhaus, *Marriage Diaries*, pp. 229–309 for the diary of the Russian trip and letters; joint letter of Robert and Clara to Wieck, editorially

dated as mid May 1844, in Schumann, *Briefe*, p. 240 (Schumann, *Life*, Vol. II, p. 15).

33 Letter to Krüger, editorially dated 'probably October 1844', in Schumann, *Briefe*, p. 244 (Schumann, *Life*, Vol. II, p. 22).

34 Letter to Verhulst of 5 June 1844, in Schumann, *Briefe*, p. 241 (Schumann, *Life*, Vol. II, p. 18).

6 Growing ambitions: Dresden 1844–50

1 Berthold Litzmann, *Clara Schumann: Ein Künstlerleben*, 3 vols. (Leipzig: 1902–8, 1925), Vol. II, pp. 77–8; trans. and abridged by Grace Hadow, *Clara Schumann: An Artist's Life*, 2 vols. (London: Macmillan, 1913), Vol. I, pp. 366–7. The first German major male-voice choir festival was held in Dresden, 1842–3.

2 Litzmann, *Ein Künstlerleben*, Vol. II, p. 95; letter to Ferdinand Hiller of 2 January 1846, in Robert Schumann, *Robert Schumanns Briefe: Neue Folge. Zweite, vermehrte und verbesserte Auflage*, ed. F. Gustav Jansen (Leipzig: Breitkopf & Härtel, 1904), p. 226; trans. May Herbert, *The Life of Schumann: Told in His Letters*, 2 vols. (London: Bentley, 1890), Vol. II, p. 46. Ferdinand Hiller (1811–85): composer and conductor.

3 Litzmann, *Ein Künstlerleben* (26 April 1850), Vol. II, pp. 94–5 (Litzmann, *An Artist's Life*, Vol. II, p. 377).

4 Richard Wagner, *Mein Leben*, ed. Martin Gregor-Dellin (Munich: List, 1963); trans. Andrew Gray, *My Life*, ed. Mary Whittall (Cambridge and New York: Cambridge University Press, 1983) pp. 318–9; letter to Felix Mendelssohn of 18 November 1845 in Schumann, *Briefe*, p. 252 (Schumann, *Life*, Vol. II, p. 45).

5 Letters to Mendelssohn of 22 October, 9 November, 24 September, 1845, in Schumann, *Briefe*, pp. 252, 250, 253 (Schumann, *Life*, Vol. II, pp. 38, 40, 33); letter to Heinrich Dorn of 7 January 1846, in Schumann, *Briefe*, p. 256 (Schumann, *Life*, Vol. II, p. 47).

6 Letter to Mendelssohn of 22 October 1845, in Schumann, *Briefe*, p. 252 (Schumann, *Life*, Vol. II, p. 37 and note); letter to Dorn of 7 January 1846, in Schumann, *Briefe*, p. 256 (Schumann, *Life*, Vol. II, p. 48).

7 Letter to Hiller of 1 January 1848, in Schumann, *Briefe*, p. 279 (Schumann, *Life*, Vol. II, pp. 68–9); ibid.; letter to Joseph Verhulst of 4 November 1848, in Schumann, *Briefe*, p. 294 (Schumann, *Life*, Vol. II, pp. 83–4);

memoir by Marie von Lindemann, quoted in Renate Brunner (ed.), *Alltag und Künstlertum: Clara Schumann und ihre Dresdner Freundinnen Marie von Lindemann und Emilie Steffen*, Schumann Studien 4 (Zwickau: Studio, 2005), pp. 55–6.

8 Lindemann, memoir; letter to Franz Brendel of [5] July 1848, in Schumann, *Briefe*, p. 286 (Schumann, *Life*, Vol. II, p. 76: '3 July').

9 Letter to Brendel of 3 July 1848, in Schumann, *Briefe*, pp. 285–6 (Schumann, *Life*, Vol. II, p. 76); letter to Hermann Härtel of 31 January 1845, in Schumann, *Briefe*, pp. 440–1 (Schumann, *Life*, Vol. II, p. 242–3). Franz Hauser (1794–1870): operatic baritone in Dresden, and scholar.

10 Letter to Mendelssohn of 18 November 1845, in Schumann, *Briefe*, pp. 255–6 (Schumann, *Life*, Vol. II, p. 46); letter to G. D. Otten of 2 April 1849, in Schumann, *Briefe*, pp. 300–1 (Schumann, *Life*, Vol. II, p. 91); Schumann's performing materials for the St John Passion are detailed in Robert Schumann, *Thematisch-bibliographisches Werkverzeichnis*, *Robert Schumann: Sämtliche Werke*, Series 8, *Supplemente* 6, ed. Margit McCorkle (Mainz: Schott, 2003) [01], pp. 745–6; the work has been recorded on the basis of these: J. S. Bach, arr. Robert Schumann, *Johannes-Passion*, Rheinische Kantorei/Das Kleine Konzert, cond. Hermann Max (CPO 777–091–2); letter to Härtel of 9 January 1845, in Schumann, *Briefe*, p. 440 (Schumann, *Life*, Vol. II, p. 241).

11 Letter to Emil Büchner of 9 April 1848, in Schumann, *Briefe*, pp. 280–1 (Schumann, *Life*, Vol. II, p. 70); he wrote similarly to the young composer Ludwig Meinardus on 16 September 1848: Schumann, *Briefe*, pp. 289–90 (Schumann, *Life*, Vol. II, pp. 77–8). Schumann's use of Luigi Cherubini's *Cours de contrepoint et de fugue* (translated into German as *Theorie des Kontrapunktes und der Fuge* (Leipzig, 1835)) for private teaching in the later 1840s is the subject of an entire volume: Hellmut Federhofer and Gerd Nauhaus, *Studien zur Kontrapunktlehre*, Robert Schumann Neue Ausgabe Sämtlicher Werke, Series VII, Group 3, Vol. V (Mainz: Robert-Schumann-Gesellschaft, 2003).

12 Dr Helbig is quoted in Joseph von Wasielewski, *Robert Schumann: Eine Biographie*, ed. Wilhelm W. Wasielewski (Leipzig: Breitkopf & Härtel, 1906), p. 200; trans. A. L. Alger, *Life of Schumann*, repr. with new introduction by Leon Plantinga (Detroit: Detroit Reprints in Music, 1975), p. 146. Schumann recorded on 23 December 1844 'den Faust nach Kräften beendigt' ['Faust completed with great effort']: Robert

Schumann, *Tagebücher*, 3 vols., Vol. III.I: *Haushaltbücher: Teil 1* [1837–47], ed. Gerd Nauhaus (Leipzig: VEB, 1982), p. 376.

13 Letter to Eduard Krüger of (probably) October 1844, in Schumann, *Briefe*, p. 244 (Schumann, *Life*, Vol. II, p. 22); letter to Härtel of 9 January 1845, in Schumann, *Briefe*, p. 439 (Schumann, *Life*, Vol. II, p. 241); letter to Verhulst of 28 May 1845, in Schumann, *Briefe*, p. 246 (Schumann, *Life*, Vol. II, p. 23); letter of Kahlert to Wasielewski of 6 January 1857, in Wasielewski, *Eine Biographie*, pp. 356 (Wasielewski, *Life of Schumann*, p. 148).

14 Litzmann, *Ein Künstlerleben*, Vol. II, pp. 125–6 (Litzmann, *An Artist's Life*, Vol. I, pp. 398–9); Schumann, *Tagebücher*, Vol. III.I, p. 377; ibid., Vol. III.2, p. 731 n. 397.

15 Letter to G. D. Otten of 2 April 1849, in Schumann, *Briefe*, p. 300 (Schumann, *Life*, Vol. II, p. 90); letter of 26 November 1849 to Louis Ehlert, in Schumann, *Briefe*, p. 319 (Schumann, *Life*, Vol. II, p. 117). On the BACH motive as first used in Bach's *Art of Fugue*, see Chapter 3 (p. 192 n. 36).

16 Letter to Hiller of 3 December 1849, in Schumann, *Briefe*, pp. 322–3 (Schumann, *Life*, Vol. II, pp. 120–1).

17 Letter to Härtel of 28 July 1849, in Schumann, *Briefe*, pp. 307–9 (Schumann, *Life*, Vol. II, p. 106).

18 Julie: 1 March 1845–72; Emil: 8 February 1846–7; Ludwig, named after Ludwig Schuncke: 20 January 1848–99; Ferdinand: 16 July 1849–91. Letter to Verhulst of 4 November 1848, in Schumann, *Briefe*, p. 294 (Schumann, *Life*, Vol. II, p. 83).

19 Ibid.; see letter to Mendelssohn of 9 November 1845, in Schumann, *Briefe*, p. 253 (Schumann, *Life*, Vol. II, p. 39).

20 Letter to Verhulst of 28 May 1845, in Schumann, *Briefe*, pp. 246–7 (Schumann, *Life*, Vol. II, p. 24); Schumann tried to organize a memorial service at the Dresden Frauenkirche for Chopin, but the authorities refused it.

21 Litzmann, *Ein Künstlerleben*, Vol. II, pp. 185–92 (Litzmann, *An Artist's Life*, Vol. I, pp. 449–55).

22 Letter to Carl Kossmaly of 1 September 1842, in Schumann, *Briefe*, p. 220 (Schumann, *Life*, Vol. I, p. 291); letter to Mendelssohn of 18 November 1845, in Schumann, *Briefe*, p. 255 (Schumann, *Life*, Vol. II, p. 44): Schumann's parallel projects show the preoccupations of the

time: not only *Lohengrin*, but *Tristan and Isolde* and the *Niebelunglied*. See Schumann, *Werkverzeichnis*, pp. 714, 699; see also Wagner, *My Life*, p. 326.

23 Letter to Mendelssohn of 24 September 1845, in Schumann, *Briefe*, p. 250 (Schumann, *Life*, Vol. II, p. 32).

24 Letter to Liszt of 5 November 1851, quoted in Schumann, *Werkverzeichnis*, p. 486.

25 Wagner, *My Life*, p. 320.

26 Letter to Carl Reinecke of 22 January 1846, in Schumann, *Briefe*, p. 257 (Schumann, *Life*, Vol. II, pp. 49–50).

27 Letter to Härtel of 'probably about the middle of 1849', in Schumann, *Life*, Vol. II, pp. 107: letter to Brendel of 18 September, in Schumann, *Briefe*, pp. 311–13 (Schumann, *Life*, Vol. II, pp. 109–11).

28 Letter to Krüger of 20 November 1849, in Schumann, *Briefe*, p. 321 (Schumann, *Life*, Vol. II, p. 118); letter to Brendel of 18 September 1849, in Schumann, *Briefe*, pp. 311–13 (Schumann, *Life*, Vol. II, p. 111); letter to Härtel of 2 April 1850, in Schumann, *Life*, Vol. II, p. 128.

29 Letter to Härtel of 20 March 1846, in Schumann, *Briefe*, p. 446 (Schumann, *Life*, Vol. II, p. 246); letter to Otten of 2 April 1849, in Schumann, *Briefe*, p. 300 (Schumann, *Life*, Vol. II, p. 90); letter to Härtel, editorially dated 'November' 1849, in Schumann, *Briefe*, p. 465 (Schumann, *Life*, Vol. II, p. 256); letter to Hiller of 10 April 1849, in Schumann, *Briefe*, pp. 302–3 (Schumann, *Life*, Vol. II, p. 94).

30 Letter to Härtel of 21 January 1846, in Schumann, *Briefe*, p. 445 (Schumann, *Life*, Vol. II, p. 245); letter to C. F. Becker of 8 February 1847, in Schumann, *Briefe*, p. 265 (Schumann, *Life*, Vol. II, pp. 56–7); letter to Härtel of [November] 1849, in Schumann, *Briefe*, p. 465 (Schumann, *Life*, Vol. II, p. 256).

31 Letters to Härtel of 15 February 1849 and to André, of 19 November, 1849, in Schumann, *Briefe*, pp. 457–8, 460–1 (Schumann, *Life*, Vol. II, pp. 253–75).

32 Letter to Clara of 31 May 1840, in Eva Weisweiller (ed.), *Clara und Robert Schumann Briefwechsel: Kritische Gesamtausgabe* (Frankfurt am Main: Stroemfeld/Roter Stern, 1981–2001), 3 vols., Vol. III, p. 1053; trans. Hildegard Fritsch and Ronald L. Crawford, *The Complete Correspondence of Clara and Robert Schumann: Critical Edition* (New York: Lang, 1994), Vol. III, p. 212. Letter to Gustav Nottebohm of 29 July

1847, in Schumann, *Briefe*, p. 275 (Schumann, *Life*, Vol. II, p. 66); letter from Härtel (n.d., editorially placed between 17 June and 28 July 1849), in Schumann, *Briefe*, p. 307 (Schumann, *Life*, Vol. II, pp. 103–4).

33 Letter to Hiller of 19 November 1849, in Schumann, *Briefe*, pp. 318–19 (Schumann, *Life*, Vol. II, p. 113–15).

7 Triumph and decline: Düsseldorf 1850–4

1 Berthold Litzmann, *Clara Schumann: Ein Künstlerleben*, 3 vols. (Leipzig: 1902–8, 1925), Vol. II, pp. 223–4; trans. and abridged by Grace Hadow, *Clara Schumann: An Artist's Life*, 2 vols. (London: Macmillan, 1913), Vol. II, pp. 1–2. Letter to Carl Klitzsch of 9 August 1851, in Robert Schumann, *Robert Schumanns Briefe: Neue Folge. Zweite, vermehrte und verbesserte Auflage*, ed. F. Gustav Jansen (Leipzig: Breitkopf & Härtel, 1904), p. 345; trans. May Herbert, *The Life of Schumann: Told in His Letters*, 2 vols. (London: Bentley, 1890), Vol. II, p. 144. The open, tented design of the Geißler Hall, encouraging an informal atmosphere at the concerts, is shown in Figure 14.

2 The Düsseldorf concert programmes (excluding the church concerts) are given in W. H. Fischer, *Festschrift zur hundertjährigen Jubelfeier des Städtischen Musikvereins Düsseldorf ... 1918* (n.p.), pp. 106–9; see Paul Kast, *Schumanns Rheinische Jahre*, Veröffentlichungen der Heinrich Heine Institut (Düsseldorf: Droste, 1981), pp. 178–81.

3 Julius Tausch (1827–95): a highly proficient pianist and conductor who had come to Düsseldorf by Härtel's and Hiller's recommendations in 1846.

4 Litzmann, *Ein Künstlerleben*, Vol. II, pp. 229, 238 (Litzmann, *An Artist's Life*, Vol. II, pp. 6, 12); Joseph von Wasielewski, *Robert Schumann: Eine Biographie*, ed. Wilhelm W. Wasielewski (Leipzig: Breitkopf & Härtel, 1906), p. 356; trans. A. L. Alger, *Life of Schumann*, repr. with new introduction by Leon Plantinga (Detroit: Detroit Reprints in Music, 1974), p. 171.

5 Litzmann, *Ein Künstlerleben*, Vol. II, pp. 57–8, 228 (Litzmann, *An Artist's Life*, Vol. I, p. 352; Vol. II, p. 6); Richard Wagner, *My Life*, trans. Andrew Gray, ed. Mary Whittall (Cambridge and New York: Cambridge University Press, 1983), p. 319. Robert Schumann, 'Über Dirigiert', *Neue Zeitschrift für Musik* 4.31 (15 April 1836), 129–30; trans. Carl Bamberger,

'About Conducting', in *The Conductor's Art*, ed. with introduction by Carl Bamberger (New York: McGraw-Hill, 1965), pp. 61–4.

6 The Symphony in E flat, soon known by association as the 'Rhenish', was, he claimed, inspired by the first sight of the great cathedral of Cologne (still unfinished), which they saw from Deutz on their first visit in September 1850. He appended movement titles evocative of his response to the Rhineland, suppressed on publication. Wasielewski, *Eine Biographie*, pp. 455–6 (Wasielewski, *Life of Schumann*, p. 173).

7 See Schumann's article on Hiller's oratorio *Die Zerstörung Jerusalems (The Destruction of Jerusalem)* in *Neue Zeitschrift für Musik* 12 (1840), 120 (Robert Schumann, *Music and Musicians: Essays and Criticisms by Robert Schumann*, 2 vols., ed. and annotated by Fanny Raymond Ritter (London: Reeves, 1877), Vol. II, p. 26); the plans for Luther are noted in Robert Schumann, *Thematisch-bibliographisches Werkverzeichnis, Robert Schumann: Sämtliche Werke*, Series 8, Supplemente 6, ed. Margit McCorkle (Mainz: Schott, 2003) [A3], pp. 716–17.

8 Litzmann, *Ein Künstlerleben*, Vol. II, p. 240 (Litzmann, *An Artist's Life*, Vol. II, p. 14); Robert Schumann, *Tagebücher*, 3 vols., Vol. III.2: *Haushaltbücher: Teil 2* [1847–54], ed. Gerd Nauhaus (Leipzig: VEB, 1982), p. 571; Litzmann, *Ein Künstlerleben*, Vol. II, p. 229 (Litzmann, *An Artist's Life*, Vol. II, p. 7).

9 Litzmann, *Ein Künstlerleben*, Vol. II, p. 235 (Litzmann, *An Artist's Life*, Vol. II, pp. 9–10).

10 Letter to August [Paul Friedrich] Strackerjan of 13 January 1851, in Schumann, *Briefe*, p. 335 (Schumann, *Life*, Vol. II, p. 129); letter to Bernhard Schott of 10 December 1852, quoted from manuscript source in Robert Schumann, *Bühnen- und Chorwerke mit Orchester*, 3 vols., Vol. II: *Geistliche Werke: Missa Sacra, Sämtliche Werke*, Series 4, Werkgrupp. *3*, ed. Bernhard R. Appel (Mainz: Schott, 1991), p. xxiv.

11 Johann Andreas Grabau (1808–84): cellist in the Leipzig Gewandhaus orchestra, 1828–84, and dedicatee of the *Stücke im Volkston*, op. 102. Schumann dedicated the second Sonata, in D minor, to David and inscribed his copy 'Please accept it in friendship as remembrance of the beautiful hours we spent in our youth.'

12 Ruppert Becker (1830–87): son of Schumann's friend, the lawyer Ernest Adolf Becker (1798–1847).

13 Litzmann, *Ein Künstlerleben*, Vol. II, pp. 240–3; (Litzmann, *An Artist's Life*, Vol. II, pp. 15–16); Schumann, *Tagebücher*, Vol. III.2, p. 610.

14 Litzmann, *Ein Künstlerleben*, Vol. II, pp. 244–5 (Litzmann, *An Artist's Life*, Vol. II, pp. 17–18); Friedrich Niecks, *Robert Schumann: A Supplementary and Corrective Biography*, ed. Christina Niecks (London: Dent, 1925), pp. 276–82.

15 Letters to Carl Debrois van Bruyck of 17 December 1852, 18 November 1853, and to Joachim of 9 November 1853, in Schumann, *Briefe*, pp. 363, 382–4 (Schumann, *Life*, Vol. II, pp. 166, 198–201).

16 Litzmann, *Ein Künstlerleben*, Vol. II, pp. 286–8 (Litzmann, *An Artist's Life*, Vol. II, pp. 47–9).

17 Letter to Hermann Härtel of 24 February 1852, in Schumann, *Briefe*, p. 472 (Schumann, *Life*, Vol. II, p. 258).

18 Letter to Julius Kistner of 17 November 1853, in Schumann, *Briefe*, p. 486; Litzmann, *Ein Künstlerleben*, Vol. II, pp. 280–1 (Litzman, *An Artist's Life*, Vol. II, pp. 42–3); Robert Schumann, 'Neue Bahnen', *Neue Zeitschrift für Musik* 39.18 (28 October 1853), 185–6; letter to Breitkopf & Härtel of 3 November 1853, in Schumann, *Briefe*, pp. 484–5 (Schumann, *Life*, Vol. II, pp. 272–3).

19 Letter to Breitkopf & Härtel of 3 November 1853, in Schumann, *Briefe*, p. 485 (Schumann, *Life*, Vol. II, p. 274); Whistling's catalogue of 1860 is discussed in Schumann, *Werkverzeichnis*, p. 55–6; Alfred Dörfell, *Thematisches Verzeichniss sämmtlicher in Druck erschienenen Werke Robert Schumanns* (Leipzig: Schuberth, 1860 [repr. 1966]).

20 Letter to Georg Wigand of 17 November 1852, in Schumann, *Briefe*, pp. 477–8 (Schumann, *Life*, Vol. II, p. 263).

21 Letter to Joseph von Wasielewski of 11 June 1851, in Wasielewski, *Eine Biographie*, p. 484 (Wasielewski, *Life of Schumann*, p. 179); Litzmann, *Ein Künstlerleben*, Vol. II, pp. 260–1 (Litzmann, *An Artist's Life*, Vol. II, p. 24).

22 Litzmann, *Ein Künstlerleben*, Vol. I, pp. 271–2 (Litzmann, *An Artist's Life*, Vol. II, pp. 34–35); letter to Joseph Verhulst of 8 September 1852, in Schumann, *Briefe*, p. 359 (Schumann, *Life*, Vol. II, pp. 161).

23 Wasielewski, *Eine Biographie*, p. 487 (Wasielewski, *Life of Schumann*, pp. 182–3); letter to Ferdinand Hiller of 29 April 1853, in Schumann, *Briefe*, p. 370 (Schumann, *Life*, Vol. II, p. 177); letter to Strackerjan of 24 July 1853, in Schumann, *Briefe*, p. 376 (Schumann, *Life*,

Vol. II, p. 187); Niecks, *Robert Schumann*, p. 270–1; Litzmann, *Ein Künstlerleben*, Vol. II, p. 255 (Litzmann, *An Artist's Life*, Vol. II, p. 19).

24 Litzmann, *Ein Künstlerleben*, Vol. II, pp. 227, 245 (Litzmann, *An Artist's Life*, Vol. II, pp. 4, 17).

25 Eugenie Schumann (1851–1938); Felix Schumann (1854–79); Litzmann, *Ein Künstlerleben*, Vol. II, p. 265 (Litzmann, *An Artist's Life*, Vol. II, p. 28).

26 Litzmann, *Ein Künstlerleben*, Vol. II, pp. 235, 273 (Litzmann, *An Artist's Life*, Vol. II, pp. 35–6, 39); the Düsseldorf homes are illustrated in Kast, *Schumanns Rheinische Jahre*, pp. 16, 32, 40.

27 Letter to Kuntsch of 'early July' 1852, in Schumann, *Briefe*, p. 355 (Schumann, *Life*, Vol. II, p. 158); Wasielewski, *Eine Biographie*, pp. 295–6 (Wasielewski, *Life of Schumann*, p. 189). Schumann had also danced on a social domestic occasion in 1843: see Gerd Nauhaus (ed.), *The Marriage Diaries of Robert and Clara Schumann: From Their Wedding Day through the Russian Trip*, trans. with a preface by Peter Ostwald (1993), in Schumann, *Tagebücher*, Vol. II [1839–54], ed. Gerd Nauhaus (Leipzig: VEB, 1987), p. 208.

28 Wasielewski, *Eine Biographie*, p. 500 (Wasielewski, *Life of Schumann*, p. 187).

8 The end: 1854–6

1 Clara's diary of July 1854 confirms the considerate position of the committee representative, the mayor Hammers' unwillingness to consider the post vacant, and commitment to pay the salary until the New Year: Berthold Litzmann, *Clara Schumann: Ein Künstlerleben*, 3 vols. (Leipzig: Breitkopf & Härtel, 1902–8, 1925), Vol. II, p. 319; trans. and abridged by Grace Hadow, *Clara Schumann: An Artist's Life*, 2 vols. (London: Macmillan, 1913), Vol. II, p. 76. Letter to Joseph Joachim of 6 February 1854, in Johann Joachim and A. Moser (eds.), *Briefe von und an Joseph Joachim*, 2 vols. (Berlin: Julius Bard, 1911–12), Vol. I, p. 34; ed. and trans. Nora Bickley, *Letters from and to Joseph Joachim* (London: Macmillan, 1914), p. 58.

2 Litzmann, *Ein Künstlerleben*, Vol. II, pp. 296–7 (Litzmann, *An Artist's Life*, Vol. II, pp. 55–7).

3 The familiar statement that the *Geisterthema* [F39] had been dictated by the spirit of Schubert appears in Ruppert Becker's account of events: see Bernhard R. Appel (ed.), *Robert Schumann in Endenich* (1854–1856): *Krankenakten, Briefzeugnisse und zeitgenössiche Berichte*, Schumann Forschungen 11 (Mainz: Schott, 2006), pp. 54–6. That it was dictated by Schubert and Mendelssohn is in Wasielewski's account: Joseph von Wasielewski, *Robert Schumann: Eine Biographie*, ed. Wilhelm W. Wasielewski (Leipzig: Breitkopf & Härtel, 1906), p. 493; trans. A. L. Alger, *The Life of Schumann*, repr. with new introduction by Leon Plantinga (Detroit: Detroit Reprints in Music, 1975), p. 185; see also Introduction, n. 1.

4 Litzmann, *Ein Künstlerleben*, Vol. ii, p. 300 (Litzmann, *An Artist's Life*, Vol. ii, p. 58).

5 Litzmann, *Ein Künstlerleben*, Vol. ii, pp. 300–1 (Litzmann, *An Artist's Life*, Vol. ii, p. 58–9); other reports of the events of 27 February, 1854, are detailed in Appel, *Schumann in Endenich*, pp. 54–6, which chronicles all the sources of medical treatment.

6 Letter of Clara to Wasielewski of 10 March 1854, in Appel, *Schumann in Endenich*, p. 66.

7 Richarz's sanatorium and his methods are summarized in Peter Ostwald, *Schumann: The Inner Voices of a Musical Genius* (Boston, MA: Northeastern University Press, 1985), pp. 274–7; 295–307.

8 Litzmann, *Ein Künstlerleben*, Vol. ii, p. 329, 330–1 (Litzmann, *An Artist's Life*, Vol. ii, p. 80–1); letter to Clara of 18 September, in Robert Schumann, *Robert Schumanns Briefe: Neue Folge. Zweite, vermehrte und verbesserte Auflage*, ed. F. Gustav Jansen (Leipzig: Breitkopf & Härtel, 1904), pp. 398–9.

9 Letter to Clara received on 15 September 1854, in Litzmann, *Ein Künstlerleben*, Vol. ii, p. 330, 361 (Litzmann, *An Artist's Life*, Vol. ii, pp. 81–2, 99).

10 Letter of Joachim to Schumann of 17 November 1854 and letter to Joachim of 25 November 1854 in Joachim and Moser, *Joachim Briefe*, pp. 228–9 (Bickley, *Joachim Letters*, pp. 92–5); letter of Franz Richarz to Clara of 27 December 1854, in Litzmann, *Ein Künstlerleben*, Vol. ii, p. 361 (Litzmann, *An Artist's Life*, Vol. ii, p. 98).

11 Letters to Johannes Brahms of 27 November, 15, December 1854: in Berthold Litzmann (ed.), *Clara Schumann–Johannes Brahms Briefe*

aus den Jahren 1853–1896: Im Auftrage von Marie Schumann, 2 vols.
(Leipzig: Breitkopf & Härtel, 1927 [repr. Hildesheim, 1989]), Vol. I,
pp. 36–7, 53–4.

12 Litzmann, Ein Künstlerleben, Vol. II, pp. 362–3, 370, passim (Litzmann,
An Artist's Life, Vol. II, p. 101–2); letter of Brahms to Schumann of 30
January 1855, in Litzmann, Schumann–Brahms Briefe, Vol. I, pp. 68–9.

13 Letter to Brahms of [20] March 1855, in Litzmann, Schumann–Brahms
Briefe, Vol. I, p. 101; letters to and from Karl Joseph Simrock of 11, 18,
19 March, 12, 13 April, 1855, quoted in Appel, Schumann in Endenich,
pp. 229ff.; letters of Brahms to Schumann of 2, 14, March 1855, in
Litzmann, Schumann–Brahms Briefe, Vol. I, pp. 85–6, 97–8.

14 Litzmann, Ein Künstlerleben, Vol. II, pp. 262–3, 370, 374, 375–6
(Litzmann, An Artist's Life, Vol. II, p. 100, 105–6, 109); Wasielewski,
Eine Biographie, p. 290 (Wasielewski, Life of Schumann, p. 186); Bettina
[Elisabeth] von Arnim (1785–1859): poet, composer, sculptor
and dedicatee of the Gesänge der Frühe: Appel, Schumann in Endenich,
pp. 276–7.

15 Letter to Clara of 5 May 1855, in Litzmann, Ein Künstlerleben, Vol. II,
pp. 374–5, 386–7 (Litzmann, An Artist's Life, Vol. II, pp. 109, 117); Appel,
Schumann in Endenich, p. 272; letter of Brahms to Schumann of 'May,
1855', Schumann–Brahms, Briefe, Vol. I, pp. 105–6; Ostwald, Inner Voices,
p. 278.

16 Litzmann, Ein Künstlerleben, Vol. II, pp. 411–12, 414 (Litzmann, An Artist's
Life, Vol. II, pp. 136–7, 139).

17 Litzmann, Ein Künstlerleben, Vol. II, p. 415 (Litzmann, An Artist's Life, Vol.
II, p. 140).

18 Litzmann, Ein Künstlerleben, Vol. 2, pp. 382, 335, 382 (Litzmann, An
Artist's Life, Vol. II, pp. 65–6, 83, 114).

Perspective and legacy

1 See Heinrich Miesner, Klaus Groth und die Musik: Erinnerungen an Johannes
Brahms (Heide: Westholsteiner Verlagsanstalt, 1933), pp. 18ff.; and
Joseph von Wasielewski, Robert Schumann: Eine Biographie, ed. Wilhelm
W. Wasielewski (Leipzig: Breitkopf & Härtel, 1906), p. 497; trans. A.
L. Alger, The Life of Schumann, repr. with new introduction by Leon
Plantinga (Detroit: Detroit Reprints in Music, 1975), p. 187.

2 Wasielewksi indicates, with formal tact, Clara's complete unwilling-
ness to co-operate in his biography, and implies the same of Heller,
Henselt and Liszt, in Wasielewski, *Eine Biographie*, 'Vorwort', p. ix
(Wasielewski, *Life of Schumann*, p. 10). On the Romances for cello, see
Robert Schumann, *Thematisch-bibliographisches Werkverzeichnis, Robert
Schumann: Sämtliche Werke*, Series 8, *Supplemente* 6, ed. Margit McCorkle
(Mainz: Schott, 2003) [A3], p. 667. For the first public performance of
the Violin Concerto, see the Introduction to this volume.

3 Novello vocal scores are an indicator of popularity in the English-
speaking world: *Faust* (1870), *Paradise and the Peri* (1873), *Manfred* (1876).
The Requiem did not appear as a Novello vocal score until 1899, though
issued by Rieter Biedermann with English words in 1873. The Mass was
never issued by Novello in the nineteenth century.

4 See further Linda Roesner, 'Brahms's Editions of Schumann', in
George S. Bozarth (ed.), *Brahms Studies* (Oxford: Oxford University
Press, 1990), pp. 251–82; Clara Schumann (ed.), *Klavier-Werke von
Robert Schumann, Erste mit Fingersatz und Vortragsbezeichnung versehene
Instruktive Ausgabe: Nach den Handschriften und persönliche Ueberliefung*
(Leipzig: Breitkopf & Härtel, 1887).

5 *Leipziger Signale für die musikalische Welt* 10.13 (25 March 1852), 116; Chorley
quoted by C. L. Graves in *The Life of Sir George Grove* (London: Macmillan,
1903), p. 170 n. 1; see further Nicolas Marston, ' "The most significant musical question of the day": Schumann's music in Britain in the
later nineteenth century', in *Robert und Clara Schumann und die nation-
alen Musikkulturen des 19. Jahrhunderts*, ed. Matthias Wendt, Schumann
Forschung 9 (Mainz: Schott, 2005), pp. 153–65; on Schumann performance at the Crystal Palace see Michael Musgrave, *The Musical Life of the
Crystal Palace* (Cambridge: Cambridge University Press, 1995), p. 98.

6 Letter of Yehudi Menuhin to Vladimir Golschmann of 22 July
1937, reproduced in facsimile in Michael Struck, *Die umstrittenen späten Instrumentalwerke Schumanns*, Hamburger Beiträge zur
Musikwissenshaft 29 (Hamburg: K. D. Wagner, 1984), p. 342. The
Violin Concerto was first performed by Georg Kulenkampff on 26
November 1937 in Berlin and recorded on 20 December 1937 with
the Berliner Philharmoniker, conducted by Hans Schmidt-Isserstedt
(reissued as Podium POL-1022–2): Menuhin was prevented by the Nazi
government from giving this performance as he was Jewish.

7 Robert Schumann, *Szenen aus Goethes Faust*, Dietrich Fischer-Dieskau, Elizabeth Harwood, Peter Pears, John Shirley-Quirk, English Chamber Orchestra, cond. Benjamin Britten (reissued as Decca 476–154–8); Nikolaus Harnoncourt, notes to Robert Schumann, *Genoveva*, DVD (Arthaus Musik 101 327), p. 11; Gerd Nauhaus and Ingrid Bodsch (eds.), *Robert Schumann: Dichtergarten für Musik. Eine Anthologie für Freunde der Literatur und Musik* (Bonn: Stroemfeld Verlag and Stadtmuseum Bonn, 2007); A. Mayeda, K. W. Niemoller *et al.*, *Robert Schumann Neue Ausgabe Sämtliche Werke* (Mainz: Schott, 1991–).

The first biographies of Schumann were based on personal reminiscences and the limited though growing availability of letters and other material. Wasielewski's *Life of Schumann* was the most important, through four editions of increasing scope between 1858 and 1906. The biography by Niecks, which adds much independent material, was also based on personal contact, though edited posthumously in his name. Clara released relatively few letters in her lifetime, but her volume of *Jugendbriefe* went through four editions (1885–1910). Jansen's *Briefe* also went through four editions from 1871 to 1904, the second edition of the *Neue Folge* (1888) almost doubling the 1904 edition. The appearance of Litzmann's extensive biographical presentation of Clara's diary and letter extracts, based on still very selective access to Schumann's own source materials, moved the subject forward rapidly after her death: *An Artist's Life* went through no fewer than eight reprints (1902–25). Schumann's own *Gesammelte Schriften* went through five editions before Clara's death: the standard edition (1961) is the sixth. Modern biography took a huge step forward in the 1950s on the basis of the beginnings of systematic and (apparently) complete publication and critical emendation of the source documents. The centenary year of 1956 saw the publication of Eismann's two volumes of source documents, followed by the diaries (see Chapter 1, p. 181 n. 4). A systematic complete edition of the letters published by Dohr Verlag has only begun to appear since 2008 (the *Schumann Briefedition*), referenced in the present text where the volumes have so far been published.

Recently biographies have drawn richly on these materials, not least those in English. As indicated, the two extremes in the interpretation of Schumann's health and its influence on his work are represented by the biographies of Ostwald (1985) and Worthen (2008). Both are rich in biographical detail – Worthen's particularly distinguished in accuracy and discrimination of references – and are essential further reading, though neither deals with the music in any detail. Prior to Ostwald, Ronald Taylor's *Robert Schumann* (London: Granada, 1982) gave a highly readable presentation with strong reference to the German literary and educational background, though it lacks detailed reference. The major modern life and works is the late John Daverio's *Robert Schumann: Herald of a 'New Poetic Age'* (New York and Oxford: Oxford University Press, 1997): an extensive and scholarly chronological discussion with constant perspective on the music through many examples. In the Master Musicians series of life and works, Eric Frederick Jensen's *Schumann* (New York: Oxford University Press, 2001) is essential reading for its independent line on various important issues. Of short studies, Barbara Meier's *Robert Schumann* (London: Haus, 2004), translated from the German original, is well referenced and very readable, though not fully edited in the transcription.

Following Alan Walker's *Schumann: The Man and His Music* (London: Barrie and Rockliffe, 1976), more recent essay collections in English on Schumann's life and works reflect the huge broadening of critical approaches to Schumann: the Schumann volume of the Bard Festival, *Schumann and His World*, ed. R. Larry Todd (Princeton: Princeton University Press, 1994), and recently *The Cambridge Companion to Schumann*, ed. Beate Perrey (Cambridge: Cambridge University Press, 2008) cover wide biographical and musical territory, whilst Laura Tunbridge's essays in

Schumann's Late Style (Cambridge: Cambridge University Press, 2007) add timely focus to this neglected period.

Finally, Clara's perspective is essential. Of an increasing number of recent publications (which include reissues and new editions of her music as well as many recordings), Nancy Reich's biography of the artist, now in a revised second edition of 2001, remains central: *Clara Schumann: The Artist and the Woman* (Ithaca, NY and London: Cornell University Press, 2001). Monica Steegmann's *Clara Schumann* (London: Haus, 2004), the parallel volume to Meier's *Robert Schumann*, is comparable to it as a reliable brief study.

Of iconography, the magnificent documentary volume by Ernst Burger, *Robert Schumann: Eine Lebenschronik in Bildern und Dokumenten* (Mainz: Schott, 1999) brings the subject vividly to life in its lavish illustrations of source material. And Kurt Hofmann's *Die Erstdrucke der Werke von Robert Schumann* (Tutzing: Schneider, 1979) provides illustrations of all first edition title pages as well as publication details.